Developing Cisco IP Phone Services

Darrick Deel
Mark Nelson
Anne Smith

Cisco Press
800 East 96th Street
Indianapolis, IN 46240 USA

D1410091

Developing Cisco IP Phone Services

Darrick Deel, Mark Nelson, and Anne Smith

Copyright© 2002 Cisco Systems, Inc.

Published by:
Cisco Press
800 East 96th Street
Indianapolis, IN 46240 USA

Printed in the United States of America

4 5 6 7 8 9 0

Fourth printing January 2007

Library of Congress Cataloging-in-Publication Number: 00-105177

ISBN: 1-58705-060-9

Warning and Disclaimer

This book is designed to provide information about selected topics for Cisco IP Phones. Every effort has been made to make this book as complete and as accurate as possible, but no warranty or fitness is implied.

The information is provided on an "as is" basis. The authors, Cisco Press, and Cisco Systems, Inc., shall have neither liability nor responsibility to any person or entity with respect to any loss or damages arising from the information contained in this book or from the use of the discs or programs that may accompany it.

The opinions expressed in this book belong to the author and are not necessarily those of Cisco Systems, Inc.

Trademark Acknowledgments

All terms mentioned in this book that are known to be trademarks or service marks have been appropriately capitalized. Cisco Press or Cisco Systems, Inc., cannot attest to the accuracy of this information. Use of a term in this book should not be regarded as affecting the validity of any trademark or service mark.

Feedback Information

At Cisco Press, our goal is to create in-depth technical books of the highest quality and value. Each book is crafted with care and precision, undergoing rigorous development that involves the unique expertise of members from the professional technical community.

Readers' feedback is a natural continuation of this process. If you have any comments regarding how we could improve the quality of this book, or otherwise alter it to better suit your needs, you can contact us through e-mail at feedback@ciscopress.com. Please make sure to include the book title and ISBN in your message.

We greatly appreciate your assistance.

Publisher	John Wait
Editor-in-Chief	John Kane
Cisco Systems Management	Michael Hakkert
	Tom Geitner
	William Warren
Executive Editor	John Kane
Production Manager	Patrick Kanouse
Acquisitions Editor	Amy Lewis
Development Editor	Melissa Thornton
	Megan Couch
Project Editor	Marc Fowler
Copy Editor	Chuck Gose
Technical Editors	Gerardo Chaves
	Paul Clark
	Zebadiah Kimmel
	May Konfong
Team Coordinator	Tammi Barnett
Book Designer	Gina Rexrode
Cover Designer	Louisa Adair
Composition	Argosy
Indexer	Tim Wright

CISCO SYSTEMS

Corporate Headquarters
Cisco Systems, Inc.
170 West Tasman Drive
San Jose, CA 95134-1706
USA
www.cisco.com
Tel: 408 526-4000
    800 553-NETS (6387)
Fax: 408 526-4100

European Headquarters
Cisco Systems International BV
Haarlerbergpark
Haarlerbergweg 13-19
1101 CH Amsterdam
The Netherlands
www-europe.cisco.com
Tel: 31 0 20 357 1000
Fax: 31 0 20 357 1100

Americas Headquarters
Cisco Systems, Inc.
170 West Tasman Drive
San Jose, CA 95134-1706
USA
www.cisco.com
Tel: 408 526-7660
Fax: 408 527-0883

Asia Pacific Headquarters
Cisco Systems, Inc.
Capital Tower
168 Robinson Road
#22-01 to #29-01
Singapore 068912
www.cisco.com
Tel: +65 6317 7777
Fax: +65 6317 7799

Cisco Systems has more than 200 offices in the following countries and regions. Addresses, phone numbers, and fax numbers are listed on the
Cisco.com Web site at www.cisco.com/go/offices.

Argentina • Australia • Austria • Belgium • Brazil • Bulgaria • Canada • Chile • China PRC • Colombia • Costa Rica • Croatia • Czech Republic
Denmark • Dubai, UAE • Finland • France • Germany • Greece • Hong Kong SAR • Hungary • India • Indonesia • Ireland • Israel • Italy
Japan • Korea • Luxembourg • Malaysia • Mexico • The Netherlands • New Zealand • Norway • Peru • Philippines • Poland • Portugal
Puerto Rico • Romania • Russia • Saudi Arabia • Scotland • Singapore • Slovakia • Slovenia • South Africa • Spain • Sweden
Switzerland • Taiwan • Thailand • Turkey • Ukraine • United Kingdom • United States • Venezuela • Vietnam • Zimbabwe

Printed in the USA

About the Authors

Darrick Deel is a Software Engineer for Cisco Systems' Enterprise Voice, Video Business Unit. He is the primary designer of the services and directory infrastructure for Cisco IP Phones. Darrick has expertise in Web application development, HTML, HTTP, JavaScript, VBScript, Windows programming with Visual Basic, Windows Scripting Host, ActiveX component development, Windows NT administration, SQL Server, and SQL92 programming.

Mark Nelson is a programmer in the Cisco Systems Enterprise Voice, Video Business Unit and has authored a number of books including *The Data Compression Book*, Second Edition, *Serial Communications: A C++ Developers Guide*, Second Edition, and *C++ Programmers Guide to the Standard Template Library*. Mark has written numerous magazine articles and is an online columnist for Dr. Dobb's Journal.

Anne Smith is a technical writer in the CallManager engineering group at Cisco Systems. She has written comprehensive technical documentation for Cisco Systems since the Selsius Systems acquisition in 1998. Anne was a member of the team that developed the original IP Phone documentation for Selsius and wrote the original **i** button help for the first Cisco IP Phone models 7960 and 7940. She is the co-author of *Cisco CallManager Fundamentals: A Cisco AVVID Solution*.

About the Technical Reviewers

Gerardo Chaves is the Marketing Product Manager for the XML Services applications on the 7960 and 7940 Cisco IP Phones. Prior to his current position, he was a software engineer in EVVBU developing voice applications. Gerardo holds a BS in Computer Science.

Paul Clark is a senior software engineer with Cisco Systems in the Enterprise Voice, Video Business Unit. Paul was one of the original Selsius Systems engineers, and has been developing support applications for CallManager since 1995. Paul is currently working on new development projects for Cisco IP SoftPhone. Paul served four years in the United States Air Force after which he attended Texas A&M University where he received his Bachelor's degree. He and his wife are attempting to raise seven beautiful daughters from their home in Frisco, TX.

Zebadiah Kimmel is an independent software consultant and developer. He has built highly innovative technologies in areas ranging from Internet collaboration to cardiac imaging, and worked on products for some of the world's most prominent universities and companies. He is the author of award-winning software for the Cisco series of IP phones. An Adjunct Lecturer in Computer Science at New York University, Mr. Kimmel holds the BA in Physics from Brown University and the MS in Computer Science from the University of Illinois at Urbana-Champaign.

May Konfong is a Technical Marketing Engineer for Cisco Systems' Enterprise Solutions Engineering group, focusing on Cisco AVVID IP Telephony applications systems design. With over six years experience in design and development of CTI applications, May works with customers on how to integrate their existing software applications with the Cisco AVVID architecture to provide a business solution.

Dedications

Darrick Deel—I would like to dedicate this book to my mother, Pam, for making me a dreamer and to my father, Tom, for giving me the discipline to achieve my dreams. I would also like to mention family, friends, co-workers, and mentors who have helped me get to where I am: David Deel, Dave Silva, Donna Deel, Tim Carleton, Julie Bielsik, Dennis Szoke, T. Rose, Jeff Sanders, Anton Wenter, and Duane Guthrie.

Mark Nelson—H.L. Mencken said "Love is the delusion that one woman differs from another." My piece of this book is dedicated Denise, the one who truly does differ. Without her I would not even cast a shadow.

Anne Smith—My father once told me that conviction is the birthright of truth, strength, and character. I dedicate my work on this book to the many people who have believed in me.

Acknowledgments

The authors would like to acknowledge the contribution of the following people for their assistance on this book: Lisa Beasley, Doug Bowlds, Ken Bywaters, Matt Campisi, Cari C'deBaca, Gerardo Chaves, Paul Clark, George Engelbeck, Doug Fink, Zeba Kimmel, May Konfong, Amy Lewis, Huifang Wang, and Frank Zerangue.

Many thanks to Rowan McFarland for his fine work on CallManager Simulator. His test program written for internal use at Cisco provided nearly all of the code used in our Simulator.

Darrick Deel—I would like to thank the following people for their patience, support, and contributions: Rick Dunlap, Laura Cooney (The Enchantress of Flash), Susan Sauter, Rowan McFarland, Alvin Lee, and Rod Salsbury.

Mark Nelson—First and foremost, I have to thank Richard Platt and Jeff Sanders, who were kind enough to ask me to join what has turned out to be the best workplace imaginable. Second, I thank all the members of the phone firmware team who created the incredible products that we wrote about in this book.

Most importantly I have to acknowledge the hard work and dedication of my two coauthors, Darrick and Anne. Darrick deserves credit for having the courage to take on this project with little or no background in technical writing. Anne deserves even more credit - she knew what she was getting into and willingly took the plunge. Her professionalism, hard work, and dedication were invaluable, and we could not have completed this book without her.

Thanks again to the people we have mentioned here, and to dozens of others at Cisco Systems and Cisco Press who contributed in one way or another to this book.

Anne Smith—I'd like to thank Richard Platt and Scott Veibell for their continued support and encouragement. Scott is hands down the best manager I've ever had the privilege of working with. Thanks to all the folks at Cisco Press, in particular, Amy Lewis, Chris Cleveland, and John Kane. And finally, I especially want to thank Mark and Darrick for making this book possible and providing a unique and gratifying authoring experience.

Contents at a Glance

Contents

Foreword

In September of 1997, David Tucker and I (the two co-founders of Selsius Systems, Inc.) strung cable from the kitchen to the living room of Voice On the Net (VON) pioneer Jeff Pulver. At the end of two of the cables we connected two of the first production units of the Selsius-Phone, the world's first production-ready Ethernet phones that utilized the Internet Protocol (IP). Jeff had graciously allowed us twenty minutes to demonstrate this "crazy but interesting" technology before his wife returned home and ran us out of his house. We connected a third cable to our laptop, which was running the Selsius-CallManager software. We asked Jeff to proceed to the living room and await "a phone call." From the kitchen we made a very ordinary phone call utilizing a very extraordinary phone. Thus began a remarkable series of events.

Jeff was amazed enough to invite us to participate in his keynote at the VON Fall conference where the pioneers of the nascent VoIP (Voice over IP) industry gathered. We were deluged by interested companies and within one month Selsius Systems began shipping and deploying the very first VoIP systems that included IP phones. Almost exactly twelve months later, Cisco Systems, Inc. acquired Selsius and work on the second-generation IP phones began.

In June of 2000, Cisco released this second generation of phones. Several notable changes were introduced. Gone was the two-port 10 Mbps Ethernet hub—replaced by a two-port 10/100 Mbps Ethernet switch with full QoS capability. Performance was quadrupled, but perhaps most dramatic was the addition of a large screen and HTTP/XML capability to drive it. This was just what the market needed. Within about twelve months, Cisco sold over half a million IP phones in spite of a slowing economy.

A fundamental change was occurring in the traditional enterprise phone system. No longer would the phone function merely as an instrument of legacy voice communication. The day had arrived that married the Internet and the Web to the Plain Old Telephone Set (POTS). The transition from an instrument of control by backroom telecom departments to the "Personal Telephone" (PT) had been achieved.

The HTTP/XML capability of Cisco IP Phones has not only helped the movement toward the Personal Telephone, but it has provided new and interesting methods to accomplish both traditional and novel telephony features. For example, the traditional method for integrating voice mail typically consisted of a set of voice prompts. With the HTTP/XML capability of Cisco IP Phones, messages and navigation can additionally invoke the senses of sight and touch. Additionally, conferencing becomes much more interesting when participants can be identified by names and icons that highlight when the participant's voice is heard. New applications such as event banners on dormitory phones, localized advertising on hotel phones, and directory lookup/dial on enterprise phones are easily accomplished through simple Web server development.

The contents of this book provide insight into the HTTP and XML capability of Cisco IP Phones. Additionally, information on application development is provided with many examples. This is the secret behind the success of Cisco IP Phones—they are open for third-party development.

The authors of this book have been associated with the development of the IP phones either since the inception of the original phone or since the initial design of the second generation. Mark Nelson, an author of several other books, leads the team in charge of the phone application infrastructure. Darrick Deel is one of the original designers of the HTTP/XML capability of the phone. Anne Smith provided much of the technical documentation of the IP phones since the very first design. And although not an author of this book, special mention must be made of Rick Dunlap, the mastermind behind the original architecture.

Death to archaic, closed phone sets! Long live the Personal Telephone!

Richard B. Platt

VP of Engineering

Cisco Systems, Inc.

Introduction

Developing Cisco IP Phone Services provides detailed information about how to write phone services that are deployed on select Cisco IP Phone models. At the time of this writing, Cisco IP Phone models 7960 and 7940 support phone services; however, Cisco may introduce additional models that also support phone services. To learn more about Cisco phones, review the following illustration of the 7960 phone. Note that there is also a global version of Cisco IP Phones that have icons on the buttons instead of English words. On the global phones, the **i** button is replaced with a **?** button.

Figure I-1   *Cisco IP Phone 7960 with One Expansion Module*

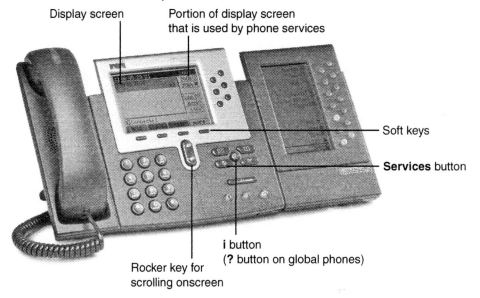

Display screen

Portion of display screen that is used by phone services

Soft keys

Services button

i button
(**?** button on global phones)

Rocker key for scrolling onscreen

Unless otherwise specified, when we refer to phones in this book, we are referring specifically to Cisco IP Phones that support phone services, such as Cisco IP Phone models 7960 or 7940.

Similarly, when we refer to objects or XML objects, we are referring specifically to Cisco IP Phone objects, unless otherwise specified.

Cisco Systems provides the Cisco IP Phone Services Software Developer's Kit (Cisco IP Phone Services SDK) for use in developing phone services. This book complements and expands on the documentation and tools provided with the SDK. On the CD-ROM accompanying this book, you will find additional tools and code not provided on the SDK that can help you write phone services.

You can download the latest Cisco IP Phone Services SDK free of charge and learn about technical support options at the following location:

```
http://www.cisco.com/go/developersupport
```

Objectives

XML transported over HTTP is used to provide services to Cisco IP Phones. Use the information in this book to develop services that integrate with Cisco IP Phones using XML. This information is not just useful but necessary to successfully integrate with CallManager or Cisco IP Phones. This book aims to:

- Teach you how to successfully build a service for use with Cisco IP Phones.
- Provide source code that you can use to provide some basic services.
- Provide tools that can be used to create advanced services.
- Provide a CallManager Simulator (CM-Sim) that can support a phone for development purposes. Neither Cisco Systems nor the Cisco Technical Assistance Center provides support for CM-Sim.

Audience

This book is most relevant to anyone interested in developing a service that will work with Cisco IP Phones. This group includes company personnel at any level (technical or non-technical).

We have assumed a readership with a modest technical ability. We address the minimum requirements to successfully build a service. We recognize that experience varies greatly from one person to the next. We have written this book to require only a general understanding of Web programming, and we provide a basic understanding of CallManager.

Organization/Chapter Organization

This book is meant to complement and expand on the information provided with the Cisco IP Phone Services SDK. The chapters provide the following information:

Chapter 1: How This Book Can Help You Achieve Business Goals shows you how other companies and organizations have solved complex business problems using phone services. The problems addressed include increasing productivity, gaining the competitive advantage, and generating revenue. General information about developing phone services is also provided, along with tips for creating successful services, information about the phone services forum on HotDispatch, and an explanation of the contents on the accompanying CD-ROM.

Chapter 2: The Basics provides information about CallManager, Cisco IP Phones, developing phone services, and the XML message format used by the phones.

Chapter 3: Phone Services Primer discusses the various aspects of the phone and some of the basic elements of developing a phone service, including the history behind why Cisco chose XML to deploy phone services and information about the HTTP client and server.

Chapter 4: Using Cisco IP Phone XML Objects and Tags provides detailed information about the XML objects and tags that you use to build phone services. A discussion of soft keys and URIs is also provided, along with quick reference tables for each object. You can also find a PDF containing the quick reference tables in the Chapter 4 directory on the accompanying CD-ROM.

Chapter 5: Using HTTP discusses the Web client and the Web server capabilities of the phone. Key HTTP Headers that the phones support are examined, including Refresh, Expiration, Set-Cookie, and more.

Chapter 6: XML Conventions provides detailed information about XML, XML tags and attributes, escape sequences, and the CiscoIPPhone schema. If it's about XML, it's in this chapter. Pointers to additional sources of information are also included.

Chapter 7: Building a Service uses an example service, Voice Anomaly Tracking (VAT), to show how to build a user-friendly service. The code used to build the VAT service is dissected and explained in detail. The VAT service is provided for your use in the Chapter 7 directory on the accompanying CD-ROM.

Chapter 8: Building a Directory shows you, using detailed source code examples and diagrams, how to build a custom directory. You are also shown how to leverage your existing LDAP directories as integrated custom directories on the phone.

Chapter 9: Integrating a Service with Cisco IP Phones describes the steps that must be taken in Cisco CallManager Administration to make your service available to users.

Chapter 10: Techniques for Advanced Services provides insight to some advanced techniques for runtime generation of content, including generating Cisco IP Phone images. An in-depth discussion including sample code is provided about graphics and soft key customization.

Chapter 11: XML Development Tools details the tools provided on the Cisco IP Phone Services SDK and the CD-ROM accompanying this book. The discussion includes the following tools:

- Graphics Conversion control
- URL Proxy control
- LDAP Search control
- Photoshop Graphics filter
- Validator

Chapter 12: Cisco CallManager Simulator discusses CM-Sim, a debugging and prototyping software application that simulates a CallManager. This chapter provides instructions about how to install and use the CM-Sim software provided on the CD-ROM accompanying this book.

Appendix A: Glossary provides a list of terms used in the book. If you are unfamiliar with an acronym, check the glossary.

Book Features and Text Conventions

This book uses the following formatting conventions to convey additional meaning:

Key terms are *italicized* the first time they are used and defined.

Notes and sidebars emphasize information of a noteworthy or unusual nature.

Tips and hints are handy information bits about the subject.

Commands or actions and names of buttons or soft keys are presented in **boldface**.

Code is presented in a `courier` font.

Target Release—Cisco CallManager 3.1 Through 3.2(2)

This book targets Cisco CallManager release 3.1 through 3.2(2). Use the latest firmware release to ensure access to bug fixes and new features.

Updates for This Book

Check the *Developing Cisco IP Phone Services* book listing on www.ciscopress.com for updates to the book. You can find updates by clicking the link to **Errata**.

Comments for the Authors?

The authors are interested in your comments and suggestions about this book. Please send feeback to the following address:

phoneservices@cisco.com

Icons Used in This Book

LAN/WAN Device Icons

PC

Laptop

Server

PC w/software

Modem

POTS Phone

Relational
Database

Fax machine

Media/Building Icons

Network Cloud

Ethernet connection

Serial connection

Telecommuter

Building

Branch Office

Network Device Icons

Cisco CallManager

Cisco
IP Phone 7960
or Generic
Cisco IP Phone

Cisco
IP Phone 7940

Cisco
IP Phone 7910

Cisco
IP SoftPhone

Stations

Layer 3 switch

Cisco
Directory
Server

Router

Switch

Access Server

PIX Firewall

Gateway or
3rd-party
H.323
server

Voice-enabled
switch

Tower
Used for:
Voice mail server
MOH server
SW conference bridge
MTP

Used for:
Voice-enabled router
Gateway
Gatekeeper
HW Conference bridge
Transcoder
Analog gateway
H.323 gateway
DHCP
DNS

PBX Switch

PBX (small)

CHAPTER 1

How This Book Can Help You Achieve Business Goals

This chapter gives you a view into the services that some organizations and businesses have developed to help them solve three important business goals:

- Increase productivity
- Gain the competitive advantage
- Generate revenue

As you will see in the following sections, phone services can help you accomplish these three goals. Cisco Systems provides the Cisco IP Phone Services Software Developer's Kit (Cisco IP Phone Services SDK) for use in developing phone services. This book complements and expands on the documentation and tools provided with the SDK. On the CD-ROM accompanying this book, you will find additional tools and code not provided on the SDK that can help you write phone services. See the section, "Training and Support for the XML SDK" in Chapter 2, "The Basics," for more information about the SDK and Cisco-provided support for the SDK.

Increase Productivity

"If you pick up the phone and have to rest the handset on your shoulder to type something at your computer, then you need an application that interfaces with a phone service."

—Ken Bywaters, Berbee

Consider that statement . . . instead of working on your computer for the various tasks you may need to perform while speaking with a client, customer, parent, student, partner, or other individual, you can use the phone to accomplish those tasks instead. With Cisco IP Phones, the telephone is not just a phone anymore. By using phone services or interfacing a phone service with an external application, you can use Cisco phones to solve business problems. The problems the phones and services can solve are as widespread as the companies and individuals that put them to use.

Take Berbee, for example. Founded in 1993, Berbee is a small, independent company that helps customers profit from computer networking and the Internet. Berbee was at the forefront of resellers implementing the Cisco AVVID IP Telephony solution and quickly realized the potential that phone services offered. For customers working in professions that bill by the hour or minute, such as lawyers, Berbee developed a service that allows the phone user to select an account code to which the call should be billed. Figure 1-1 shows the main screen for the Berbee Account Code Biller service.

Figure 1-1   *Billing Options Menu*

By interfacing with a database (via Web input or tab-delimited text file), phone users or the company's accounting department set up the account information in the database. Once added to the database and to the service, the codes for each account are available when the phone user selects the Account Code Biller from the list of services. The Account Code service goes a step further, using the called/caller ID information provided by CallManager to automatically match accounts based on the phone number, saving the phone user a step each time a call is placed or received. The phone user selects the account that matches the called/caller ID number (in Figure 1-1, the first option is to bill to the account recognized by caller ID), enters an account code, or searches for an account.

What about calls for a specific account placed from an unknown number? The service allows the phone user to add the new number to the database with the touch of a soft key, as shown in Figure 1-2.

Now the phone user has billed the call to the proper account and updated the database of contact information for the specified account without ever typing a key on the computer.

Figure 1-2   *Adding a New Phone Number to the Database Using the Cisco IP Phone*

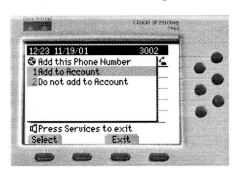

By teaming a service with an application, you can accomplish a multitude of tasks. Consider the following true story:

Frederick County, occupying the northern-most tip of Virginia, is home to just under 11,000 school-age children. In December 2000, a severe snowstorm brought the public switched telephone network (PSTN) down during the start of the school day. Phone service was out all over the county. Buses were already in route when the storm hit and one bus containing dozens of grade school children was stuck in the snow. Because phone service was down, the bus driver could not call the school district to ask for help and the school district headquarters could not contact the schools to tell them to close for the day. In March 2001, the school district conducted a security audit of their 17 schools. Four of the schools were found to have no means of communication from the school office to the classroom. Frederick County Public Schools had two problems to solve: one, establish communication in four schools that were not wired for intercoms or phones in the classroom; and two, find a backup means of communication when the PSTN fails.

Enter AAC Associates, Inc., a company focused on designing and implementing converged networks. AAC worked with the school district to install a CallManager solution at district headquarters, with each school connected via the metropolitan area network (MAN). Because the classrooms had already been wired for Ethernet when the district outfitted schools with computers, the Cisco phones were a simple addition to classrooms. By deploying Cisco AVVID IP Telephony, the school district accomplished their two primary objectives. But AAC and Frederick County Public Schools were not through brainstorming. Working together, they determined a number of other areas where they could improve on the old way of doing business. AAC built a service that allows the teacher to take attendance on the Cisco phone. By integrating the attendance phone service with a Lotus Notes database, attendance data is automatically saved to the main database. Frederick County Public Schools and AAC are working on taking this a step further by displaying the student attendance data on a Web site that parents can access to determine if their children have skipped one class or all of their classes, real-time or historically.

Because each phone is installed in a classroom, schedules for the classes to be held in that room are programmed for each phone, as shown in Figure 1-3.

Figure 1-3   *Class Schedule for Classroom*

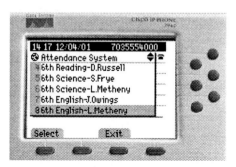

Teachers retrieve the attendance list for their class shown in Figure 1-4. The system alerts teachers to pre-approved absences by a (*) flag and upcoming birthday students by a (:-) flag. Teachers — particularly substitutes and hall monitors — also benefit from the ability to call up a student profile (no pun intended) on any Cisco phone and view their photograph.

Figure 1-4   *Student Attendance List on the Phone*

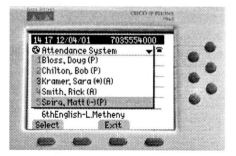

Figure 1-5 shows the ability to view the student's photograph and press a soft key to mark the student present or absent.

Having brought attendance-taking into the 21st century, AAC next attacked the antiquated method of permitting students access to and from the principal's office, nurse's station, or bathroom. For decades, students have traversed school hallways during class time with small slips of colored paper bearing their name, the time, destination, and the approving teacher's name as their only right of passage. With hall monitors placed strategically throughout school, imagine the fear that courses through a young student's body if some terrible tragedy should befall that slip of paper while in the bathroom. Imagine, too, the spirited freedom that results from an illegal journey through those quiet halls carrying a forged hall pass. School children no longer have to carry those slips of paper; they can use electronic hall passes that hall monitors access using Cisco IP Phones installed in the school hallways. The hall pass service also provides greater security because a teacher can verify the identity of the student by viewing the student's picture.

Figure 1-5   *Viewing Photograph While Taking Attendance*

The hall pass services works like this: when a student must leave during class time, whether to the bathroom or principal's office, the teacher simply calls up the student's name on the phone as shown in Figure 1-6. (The attendance and hall pass applications are password protected.)

Figure 1-6   *Identifying Who Needs a Hall Pass*

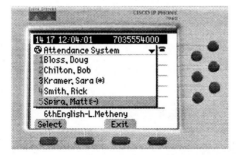

Next, the teacher identifies the destination for the hall pass (Figure 1-7).

Figure 1-7   *Identifying the Destination for a Hall Pass*

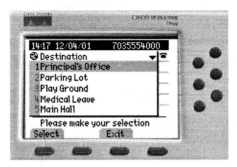

The hall pass is then generated by the system (Figure 1-8) and the data recorded to a database accessible from any phone in the network.

Figure 1-8   *Issued Hall Pass*

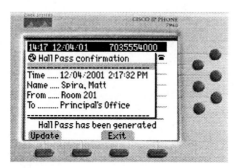

When the student is stopped in the hallway by a hall monitor, the monitor can retrieve the student's hall pass by searching for the student's name or the destination (Figure 1-9). This function allows school administrators and security personnel to see how many hall passes are active at a given time, or how many students are visiting the library at a given time, and so on.

Figure 1-9   *Search for Current Hall Passes*

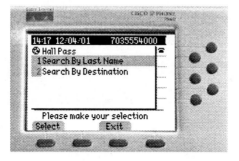

Figure 1-10 shows the hall pass that the system displays on the phone when retrieved by the student's last name.

Figure 1-10 *Hall Pass Verification*

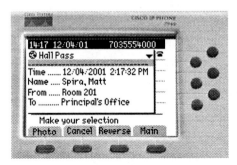

The monitor can use the soft keys on the phone to view the student's photo as shown in Figure 1-11, cancel the hall pass (normally done once the student returns from his or her trip), or reverse the hall pass. For example, the principal can reverse the pass to allow the student passage back to the original classroom once the student has reached the principal's office.

Figure 1-11 *Identity Verification*

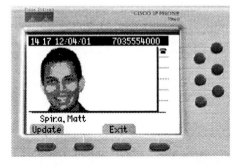

The next step is to merge the school's visitor passes with the hall pass application, coupled with photos of visitors taken at the reception desk. This provides hall monitors with the ability to verify the identity of school visitors for even greater security purposes.

By deploying phone services on their converged network, Frederick County Public Schools resolved the two problems they had and leveraged the Cisco AVVID IP Telephony solution to achieve the following additional benefits:

- More efficient management of their student rolls.
- A method to keep parents informed about their child's attendance.
- Access to student pictures.
- Reduced paper waste by eliminating the need to print daily class sheets for attendance.
- No more hall passes.

- Greater hallway security.
- Accountability of students in the school.

Keeping track of children while they are in school is a complex problem, but so is managing a large sales organization with many leads. Precious time is wasted searching through contacts on the computer, setting reminders to call customers, and jotting down phone numbers when talking with customers. Berbee attacked this business problem using the technology already provided by the Cisco phones in their office. Berbee's desires were two-fold: first, eliminate wasted time; and second, ensure consistent customer contact. Berbee considered several systems for customer relationship management (CRM) and chose salesforce.com because they proved easier to integrate with than other similar companies and provided the ability to track leads and opportunities, manage task lists, and store contact information. Berbee developed an application that interfaces with salesforce.com so that when a customer visits the Berbee Web site and downloads a free evaluation copy of their software (including certain Cisco phone services), a task is created at salesforce.com, including the contact information and the date of the download. Account managers (AMs) can use their Cisco phone to retrieve contact or task information, as shown in Figure 1-12.

Figure 1-12 *Main Menu for CRM Application*

When an incoming call is received by an AM, pressing 1 retrieves the contact details. Contact details are returned, as shown in Figure 1-13, when the caller ID matches a number defined in the customer profile.

By demand or on a daily basis, Berbee's Cisco phones poll the salesforce.com Web site to gather task lists for the account managers. The AM can either call up the task list as shown in Figure 1-14, or, when the free trial expires, the AM is flagged to call the customer as shown in Figure 1-15.

Figure 1-13 *Contact Details Based on Caller ID*

Figure 1-14 *Viewing Tasks for an Account Manager*

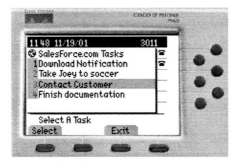

Figure 1-15 *Task Details*

The service allows the account manager to mark the task as complete, as shown in Figure 1-16. Completed tasks are removed from the task list.

Figure 1-16 *Completing a Task*

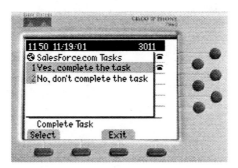

Helping new employees determine who to call when they need help represents another common problem easily solved using a phone service. The Functional Directory developed by AAC Associates integrates with the company's email system and provides phone extension information based on job function or title rather than an individual's name. The main menu is shown in Figure 1-17.

Figure 1-17 *Directory Listing by Job Function*

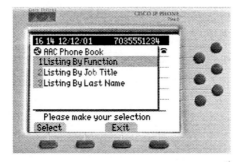

Listed in alphabetical order, new employees (or students because this application could easily be adapted to the university environment) scroll through a list of functions such as Payroll, Human Resources, and Computer Support as shown in Figure 1-18. When the desired function is located, the user selects it from the menu and is provided with the contact name and number, which can be conveniently dialed with the press of a soft key. Figure 1-19 shows the person to contact to report computer problems.

Figure 1-18 *Locating a Contact by Function*

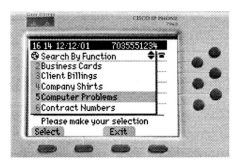

Figure 1-19 *Functional Directory Results*

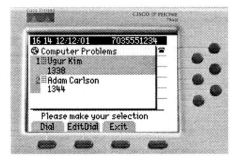

So far, we've examined services created to increase productivity by making routine tasks more integrated and more efficient. But phone services can also help you position your company or organization ahead of competitors by enhancing user experience or increasing convenience.

Gain the Competitive Advantage

"By leveraging the power of XML applications on Cisco phones, organizations enhance the user experience by providing convenience and customization. This ability represents a tremendous advantage over the competition."

—Doug Bowlds, AAC Associates

Continental Airlines gained a competitive edge by deploying Cisco AVVID IP Telephony as part of their "airport of the future." Cisco phones provide a high tech voice solution for business travelers with the added bonus offered by the customer-oriented phone services created by Continental engineers. Available today in the Houston, Texas President's Club, Continental plans to deploy phone services in President's Clubs worldwide. The services include checking flight status, viewing weather information at Continental hubs, and completing customer satisfaction surveys.

Calence, an internetworking consulting company specializing in IP telephony, has developed a suite of hospitality services. Geared toward cruise ships in this example, the services can be redesigned for other hospitality industries as well. The services enhance the passenger's experience and provide a competitive advantage. Figure 1-20 shows the main screen that displays when a passenger presses the **services** button.

Figure 1-20   *Hospitality Services*

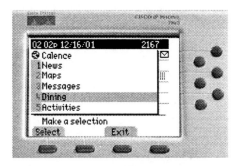

The suite of hospitality services includes a service that provides the passenger the ability to track the ship's location using global positioning satellite (GPS) coordinates. With Cisco phones installed in each stateroom and cabin on a given cruise ship, the passenger can select **Maps** and watch images that use GPS to depict the ship's current location and refresh automatically every few seconds, as shown in the series of screen captures in Figure 1-21.

Passengers can use the hospitality services to enhance their cruise ship experience. By integrating the service with a database application based on the Web, passengers can specify favorite types of restaurants or entertainment prior to departing. Then when they embark on their journey, the phone in their cabin displays only those restaurants or activities that match their interests. Figure 1-22 shows the restaurant menu for a passenger who has specified preferences for French and Chinese food.

Figure 1-21 *GPS Cruise Ship Service*

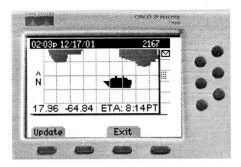

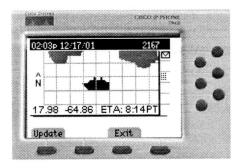

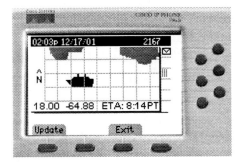

Figure 1-22 *Restaurant Selection*

The competitive advantage can also be earned by deploying services designed for the convenience of visitors to your campus. Many organizations have operations that are spread out over a large campus environment, sometimes making it difficult to locate an individual. To solve this problem, AAC developed a Cube/Office Locator service that provides directions from the you-are-here location to the specified cube or office. Used in conjunction with extension mobility (a CallManager release 3.1 feature), the cube locator service enables someone to locate an individual by finding the phone assigned to that person or to which he or she has logged into. Users can search by name or location, as shown in Figures 1-23 and 1-24.

Figure 1-23 *Using the Office/Cube Locator Service*

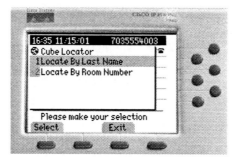

When the desired user or location has been identified, the service displays directions to the cube from the present location. Figure 1-25 shows the directions in text format, but future releases of the service will provide graphical displays and direction printouts (for a printer that plugs into the RS-232 port on the back of Cisco IP Phone models 7960 and 7940 or Web-enabled network printers).

Figure 1-24 *Specifying the Destination*

Figure 1-25 *Directions for a Search by Last Name*

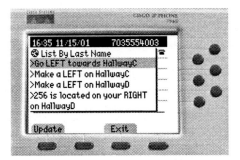

If the person looking for an office loses his or her way or needs to check the directions, he or she can perform the same search on a nearby Cisco phone. The directions to the office or cube will be provided using the current location as the new starting point.

In addition to enhancing productivity and user satisfaction, phone services can also be used to generate revenue for businesses and organizations.

Generate Revenue

"Cisco IP Phone service technology creates a unique ability to drive revenue using the Cisco AVVID IP Telephony solution customers and organizations have already purchased to solve their telephony needs."

—Doug Fink, Calence

Profit-thinking organizations and enterprises can develop phone services that, when invoked by the user, generate revenue. The large display on the Cisco phone can also be utilized to display advertisements; revenue is generated by businesses paying a fee to be featured on the phone. Consider what Calence plans to do for the hotel industry, or what some universities around the country have already done in dorm rooms. By deploying a menu-driven service that displays local restaurants such as pizza joints, or activities such as bowling alleys, movie theaters, or pool halls (complete with hours of operation and phone numbers to call for directions), the hotel or university can charge local businesses to be included in the listings. Doing so provides a much-needed service for visitors and students alike, while providing the option of revenue generation. You can use the `IdleURL` command to display a banner on the phone when it is idle for more than ten seconds. The banner can be any form of message or advertising, from a listing of important numbers such as reception, wake-up call, and hotel restaurant, to a logo for the Pizza Hut located just down the street from the dorm room.

Hotels in Reno and Las Vegas can add to their bottom line and continue on the gambling theme by providing games on the phone. Users can access a selection of games for a small fee assessed by the hotel. This concept can be implemented with success anywhere gamers can be found, and a wide range of games can be developed using services. At the Cisco office in Dallas, one of this book's co-authors developed (and deployed on our internal system) a version of Black Jack that provides a nice diversion for the lunch hour.

If You Want Something Done Right . . .

After reading the success stories of other businesses or organizations, you may find yourself questioning how to go about developing services for your enterprise. Do you build it yourself? Do you contract someone to build it for you? Do you consult with a company that specializes in service development to create a custom service or suite of services for you? Are you an individual application developer considering the likelihood of making a living developing phone services? For those matching the latter description, be sure to read the section, "Can I Get Rich Developing Services?" later in this chapter. For everyone else, consider the following.

Many companies are perfectly capable of developing services in-house using the information and tools provided by the Cisco IP Phone Services SDK and this book. The development itself is not overly difficult. Often times you will be best positioned to create a service that fulfills your needs because you are in a unique position to evaluate those needs. Best of all, using application developers already on staff means no additional cost associated with creating the service. If you do not have application developers on staff, you can always contract someone to build the service to your specifications.

However, the old adage, "If you want something done right, do it yourself," does not necessarily hold true in this case. Consulting companies with experience evaluating business needs and developing services targeting those needs can often take a basic problem and expand on it to create a robust suite of services that solves multiple productivity or user satisfaction issues. The value provided by a consulting company is experience, expertise, and support. You can learn more about the consulting companies discussed in this chapter in the section, "The Horse's Mouth," later in this chapter. You can learn more about locating development resources in the section, "Forum on HotDispatch."

Can I Get Rich Developing Services?

Well that's a good question. Like any innovator who creates a product people really need, you could stand to earn a satisfactory income by developing a much-needed service or suite of services. How successful you are at earning money by developing services depends on the effort, planning, and marketing you put into it. Like the other professional companies out there already doing it, you must provide reliable code, documentation that effectively describes how to use the service, and customer support. Alternatively, you can develop the service and sell it to another company to market, thereby passing the administration headache onto someone else.

Deploying Services on Cisco IP Phones

Cisco IP Phone models 7960 and 7940 provide a display plane that can be used by services. Because the phone can be used to answer or place calls while a service is displayed, portions of the display are considered hands-off for services. The first line (showing the date, time, and extension) cannot be overwritten by a service. This information will always display along the top. Also, the message and status area flashes to the caller ID information (if available) during an incoming call. The area along the right side is also reserved so that users can press the appropriate line button or speed dial even while a service is displayed.

The area used by services (133 x 65 pixels) is defined in Figure 1-26.

Figure 1-26 *Services Panel and Number of Pixels*

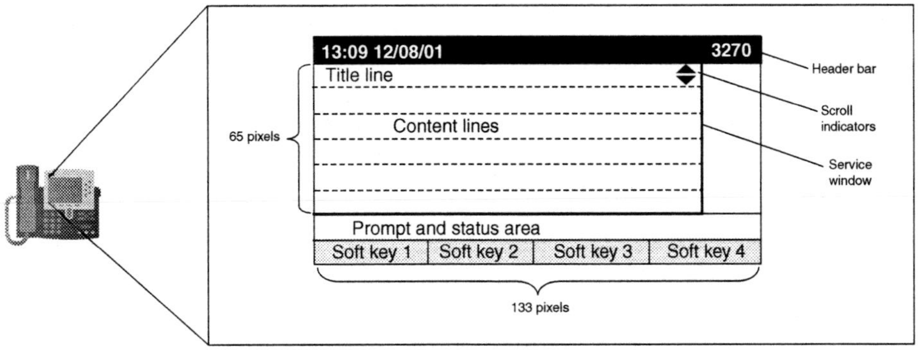

Tips for Building Successful Services

The following tips and tidbits of information have been passed on from experienced service developers and usability studies performed by Cisco.

- Try to build a service that does not require a lot of scrolling or use the status area to display a line of text that prompts users to scroll for more options. Inexperienced users often do not realize they need to scroll on a menu or do not recognize the arrows that indicate scrolling is possible.

- Use consistent wording. Because users may already be familiar with services provided by Cisco, use consistent terminology where applicable. For example, Cisco uses the term "Exit" on soft keys. Increase ease of use by sticking with known terms such as "Exit" (over another term such as "Close" or "GoodBye") and use the same terms consistently.

- Use the same soft keys Cisco provides where applicable. For example, if you have a service that allows data entry or dialing of a number, it is wise to include the soft keys users are familiar with and have come to expect, such as **EditDial** and **<<** (backspace).

- Test your service on people around you before subjecting the innocent masses to it. A lot of good usability feedback can be gained by letting your co-workers tear your hard work apart with their constructive criticism.

- Consider whether your service needs a main menu or a home page. Some services are simple enough to let the user jump right in, rather than forcing the user to wade through an opening screen to get to the functionality.

- Support type-ahead menu selection. A good menu provides numeric identifiers for each line item. By supporting type-ahead, you allow users familiar with the service to get deep into the service by entering a string of menu selections without waiting to see the associated menus. Figure 1-27 shows an example of the settings menu. To quickly find the phone's MAC address, users can press the **settings** button, then press **3** for Network Configuration (A), and then press **3** again for the phone's MAC address (B).

Figure 1-27 *Type-Ahead Menu Selection*

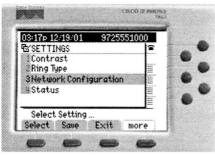

A

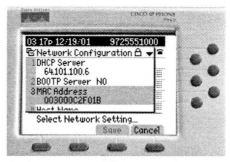

B

- Write useful prompts. If your menu lists several items, be sure your prompt is generic enough to apply to all line items equally. "Make a selection . . ." is an example of a good prompt because it is a complete sentence yet is succinct, starts with an action (verb) and applies generically to all menu items when a **Select** soft key is also provided.

- Order tasks in a menu or list by anticipated popularity, listing those tasks that will be the most heavily used first. When popularity is not a concern, use such natural ordering as listing items alphabetically.

- Use common abbreviations. Because of the limited number of characters allowable on soft keys, you may feel compelled to get creative with your abbreviations. Determining understandable abbreviations is another time when bouncing ideas off your co-workers would be beneficial.

About the CD-ROM

The CD-ROM included with this book supplements the information you will find in these pages. Refer to the CD-ROM interface for descriptions of the CD-ROM contents. The following items are included:

- **CallManager Simulator (CM-Sim)**—An application that provides a small subset of CallManager features, named CM-Sim, is provided for debugging purposes. CM-Sim supports phone-to-phone test calls, but not much else. You can develop services and then test them using CM-Sim. Of course to do this, you must purchase Cisco I P Phones if you do not already have any. No more than two would be required to effectively test your service. Read more about CM-Sim in Chapter 12, "Cisco CallManager Simulator."

- **XML Validator**—The Validator is a command line tool that parses the XML content of a file or Web page and authenticates it against the schema for Cisco IP Phone XML objects. The Validator program discussed in Chapter 11, "XML Development Tools," requires that you install Microsoft's MSXML 4.0 parser component. Details on how to accomplish this and more information about the Validator are provided in Chapter 11.

- **Code samples, applications, services, and routines**—The previously listed advanced techniques are described in the book. A screen capture application is provided that captures the phone's display in a Web browser. You can then use any screen capture utility to save the screen in the desired format for use in documentation or other explanatory text.

- **JavaScript routine that runs on IIS**—A JavaScript routine that runs on IIS is provided that uses the CiscoIPPhoneImage component for resizing images. You can use the routine to resize an image that is too large to display on the phone's LCD. With this routine, an image's height is resized to match the displayable area on the phone, and then the width is resized to match the ratio, maintaining aspect ratio on the display and allowing a larger image to display properly on the phone. This routine is useful because the CiscoIPPhoneImage object does not maintain aspect ratio. Read more about the applications and routines in Chapter 10, "Techniques for Advanced Services."

- **Voice Anomaly Tracking service**—A Voice Anomaly Tracking service, which is used as the example service in Chapter 7, "Building a Service," is provided for your use. When users encounter audio problems, they can use the VAT service to pull call statistics off their phone's Web server. VAT logs the statistics to a CSV file that administrators can access to assist with troubleshooting.

- **Code samples for various graphical uses**—Code samples for various graphical uses are provided. Among the samples are an explanation for using an Adobe Photoshop plug-in to draw graphics on the phone (such as a calendar) and an image navigation component that when integrated as part of a service allows a user to zoom in, zoom out, and navigate around an image (such as a map or weather picture). Read more about the applications and routines in Chapter 10.

Forum on HotDispatch

Cisco worked with HotDispatch to provide a community forum for exchange of ideas and services about Cisco IP Phone services. Figure 1-28 shows the Cisco home page on HotDispatch.

HotDispatch provides an infrastructure on the Web that companies such as Cisco can use to build a forum for discussion and exchange of ideas about products or services. HotDispatch has proven that users can save money using HotDispatch over purchasing technical support, receive speedy resolution to problem issues, and increase project savings over traditional out-sourcing methods. While Cisco offers reasonably priced support for your service development, you may also find the services of the Cisco site on HotDispatch to be of considerable value.

Figure 1-28   www.hotdispatch.com/cisco-ip-telephony

The Cisco site on HotDispatch provides the following options:

- End Users—The End Users area gives you several ways to access development resources for phone services. You can post a question and the amount of money you are willing to pay an expert for the answer. Experts in Cisco IP Phone services register with HotDispatch, and if an expert provides a solution or answers a question and the resolution is satisfactory to you, funds are transferred from your online account to the registered expert's account. You can also browse service solutions for sale or post a request for project outsourcing. For example, you have identified the service you need to solve your organization's goal, but do not have the resources to develop the service. You can post a project request and registered experts can bid on the job.

- Developers—The Developers area lets registered experts browse the list of questions posed by end users, along with the price to be paid for a satisfactory resolution. You can also browse service solutions offered for sale or bid on a request for project outsourcing.

- OfficeFronts—The OfficeFronts area lets third-party individuals and companies who develop Cisco IP Phone services market their products to the audience of HotDispatch users. Users can browse the OfficeFront to learn about services that are available for purchase. This service helps developers earn a living from their innovation and expertise and fulfills the business needs of various users.

- Discussion Forum—The Discussion Forum (a chat room) is a free-for-all discussion about Cisco IP Phone services. Users describe success stories, ask questions of other users to help in troubleshooting service development, lodge complaints, and more. The Discussion Forum is available in the End Users and Developers areas.

The Horse's Mouth

To get more information about the services profiled in this chapter, speak to the best authorities on the subject: the people who developed those services. You can research additional phone service developers in the OfficeFronts area on HotDispatch (www.hotdispatch.com/cisco-ip-telephony).

AAC Associates

AAC Associates (www.aac.com) is a Cisco Premier Certified Partner and recognized by Cisco as a certified sales expert for Cisco AVVID IP Telephony.

Berbee

Berbee (www.berbee.com) is a Cisco Gold Certified Partner and has been awarded Advanced IP Telephony Partner status by Cisco Systems.

Calence

Calence (www.calence.com) is a Cisco Gold Reseller and Cisco AVVID IP Telephony specialist.

Conclusion

Cisco IP Phones expand the capabilities of the traditional phone. While the expected phone functions are provided (call connection, transfer, conference, hold, and so on), the addition of phone services enables you to use Cisco phones to solve complex business problems. In this chapter, you learned the value IP phone services can provide and read about services that other companies have developed to solve their own business needs or the needs of their customers. More than just a communication device, the Cisco IP Phone can be leveraged for standard business functions including generating revenue, convenience, increasing productivity, entertainment, gaining a competitive advantage, and more. All it takes from you is a little imagination and some code. In this book, we provide the education for using the code to create services—you provide the ingenuity.

You also learned about the open community forum hosted by Cisco on HotDispatch. Using the information provided in this book, you should be able to develop services that solve business problems or your organization's goals.

In the next chapter, you will learn about the basics of Web development, the overall architecture of Cisco CallManager and the role the Cisco IP Phones play in that environment, as well as basic information about Web servers, Web hosting, and the XML message format.

CHAPTER 2

The Basics

The goal of this book is to teach you how to develop applications (also known as services) for Cisco's series of Internet Protocol (IP) phones. This chapter covers the following basic topics:

- An overview of the network architecture the Cisco CallManager uses
- How Cisco IP Phones operate as part of that network architecture
- How a Web server sends XML objects to the Cisco IP Phone
- The basics of developing Web-based services for the IP Phone
- The XML message format used by Cisco IP Phones
- Resources for further study

Master these sections and you can write Cisco IP Phone services.

CallManager Architecture

A typical installation of CallManager in a corporate network can be a complicated piece of work. Such a system can have hundreds or thousands of phones, dozens of gateways, and five or six CallManager servers, not to mention all the hubs, routers, and switches that make up the basic plumbing of the network. Designing or even just understanding such a system can require quite a bit of training and knowledge.

Fortunately, building IP Phone services can be created with a limited knowledge of the overall architecture.

Key Components of the Network Architecture

Figure 2-1 displays the portions of typical corporate network architecture that are important to developing services for the Cisco IP Phone.

Figure 2-1   *Network Components Important for Cisco IP Phone Services*

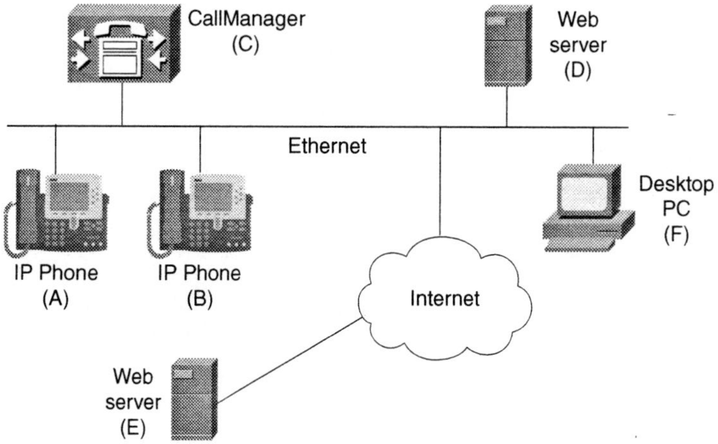

For the purposes of developing IP Phone services, we can simplify the network to that shown in Figure 2-1. Figure 2-1 shows a few elements that you find in a typical corporate IP phone system. The pieces we are concerned with are

- **Phone**—This is an IP Phone. The Cisco IP Phones used by CallManager at this writing include the 7960, 7940, and 7910 models. A typical system has hundreds or thousands of phones.

- **CallManager**—CallManager is a Windows 2000 server running Cisco's CallManager software packages. Although only one CallManager is shown in the figure, a standard corporate installation has at least two and as many as five CallManagers in a cluster.

- **Web server**—This designation is for a Web server on the same corporate network as the IP phones and CallManager.

- **Web server**—This Web server is outside the corporate network and supplies content developed by a third party.

- **Desktop PC**—This is a normal desktop PC, much like you probably have on your desk.

I have left out major components of the typical corporate network here, including firewalls, switches, routers, and gateways. While they are all important parts of the phone system, they are not important for understanding IP Phone services.

Low-level Networking

What makes Cisco's phone system revolutionary is the most important thing to note about Figure 2-1—all the devices shown in the figure are connected via an IP network. The portions inside the enterprise are connected via an Ethernet, which happily routes IP packets. The portions outside the enterprise are routing through the Internet, which uses various types of hardware but is all IP.

The acronym IP refers to Internet Protocol, which is simply a low-level convention for routing packets on a network. The Cisco IP Phone does virtually all its communications using IP in one of two modes: TCP (a guaranteed packet delivery system) and UDP (a more streamlined but less reliable method of delivering packets).

IP, TCP, and UDP are all protocols defined as part of the TCP/IP stack, an interface used by the low-level firmware in the phone for communications.

But you really do not need to know anything in particular about TCP, IP, or UDP to work with Cisco phones. Those low-level protocols are important to people working on network plumbing, but application developers are free to treat them with casual hand waving.

Higher-level Communication Protocols

Higher-level communication protocols describe the exchange of large amounts of data between devices (e.g. database queries and Web pages). The following high-level protocols are important for Cisco phone services:

- Phones (A) and (B) in Figure 2-1 communicate with CallManager using Cisco's proprietary Skinny Client Control Protocol (SCCP or Skinny). This simple protocol rides on top of TCP and is used to send events and commands back and forth between phones and CallManager. You won't use this protocol directly as a service writer, but you should be aware of it.

- When a call is set up between IP Phones (A) and (B), they send voice packets back and forth between one another using the Real-Time Transport Protocol (RTP). This UDP-based protocol is specially tuned for sending voice, video, and other time-sensitive data across networks. Applications you write might well route RTP data streams to or from IP Phones.

- When a phone is executing a Web-based service, it communicates with a Web server using Hypertext Transfer Protocol (HTTP). This is the same protocol used by Web browsers such as Internet Explorer to pull data from a Web server. In this case, Phone (A) might pull data from Web server (D) or (E) to display on the phone's screen.

- The IP Phone can also use the HTTP protocol as a Web server. For example, the Desktop PC (F) can use Internet Explorer to browse into the phone itself. The HTTP server in the phone not only allows the phone to provide information to other devices on the network it also serves as a way to send asynchronous commands to the phone.

The phone uses protocols HTTP, RTP, and Skinny. While you do not have to go so far as to implement these protocols, you need to know how to make use of them and how to use them indirectly such as through a Web server.

Figure 2-2   *High-level Communication Protocols Used by the Cisco Phone System*

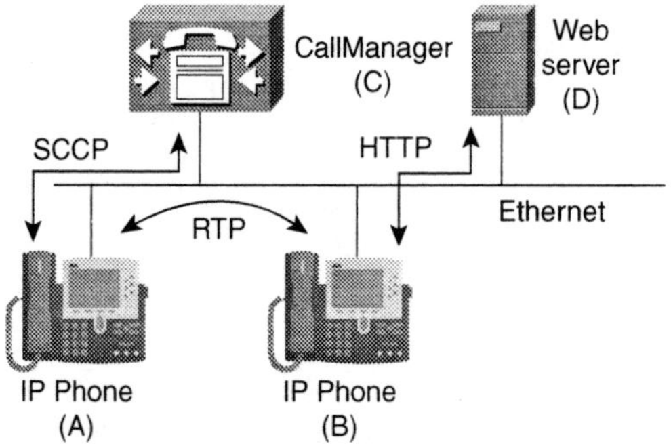

Figure 2-2 shows these high-level protocols in action on a typical network. Phone A sets up a call to Phone B by communicating with CallManager using Skinny messages. CallManager used Skinny to instruct the two phones to start sending voice streams to one another using RTP. At that point a voice call is in progress, and the phones do not need any additional communication with CallManager until it is time to hang up, transfer, or perform some other call control function.

While the call is in progress, the phones may be using additional protocols for functions totally unrelated to voice. For example, Phone B might access email via the Web Server D while RTP voice packets are streaming between Phone A and Phone B. This would be done using HTTP.

The Cisco IP Phone

Cisco makes and sells a variety of IP Phones, and as you read this book there might be new models that did not exist as of this writing. This book discusses only IP Phones that support Cisco XML services; these include the Cisco 7940 and 7960 IP Phones. Figure 2-3 shows the 7960 model. The 7940 is nearly identical, but lacks four of the line buttons shown to the immediate right of the display.

As discussed earlier in this chapter, the phone communicates with CallManager using the Skinny protocol. All the operations needed to place phone calls, retrieve voice mail, put calls on hold, and so forth are initiated and/or modulated by the exchange of Skinny messages between the phone and CallManager.

Likewise, all the voice data that goes in or out of the phone is sent via RTP streams. The phone has the ability to listen to multiple streams, issue multiple streams, and mix streams in the phone. The phone supports G.711 and G.729 streams. G.711 is the primary format for voice data on the Public Switched Telephone Network (PSTN), while G.729 is a low-bandwidth format typically used over a corporate network during toll bypass.

Figure 2-3   *Cisco 7960 IP Phone*

The IP Phone can be reprogrammed on the fly, which means new features and capabilities might be supplied in each firmware release. In addition, the same phone can be loaded with firmware that isn't even compatible with CallManager. For example, there are firmware loads for the 7960 that manage call control through MGCP or SIP protocols. While these are certainly interesting developments, we are not looking at them from the phone's perspective.

IP Phone Services Capability

Since using the IP Phone to make telephone calls is not unlike making calls from any modern PBX, this book will not go into any details regarding that aspect of Cisco phones.

Where these Cisco IP Phones differ from modern PBX phones is in their ability to deploy services completely independently of CallManager. Traditional PBX phones would have a difficult time implementing the services, as they are physically limited to a connection to a proprietary PBX. On the other hand, Cisco's phones are on a network and can communicate with any other compatible device on the network. These devices include Web servers, mail servers, and a wide variety of other IP-based devices.

When the engineers at Cisco were working on the concept of Cisco IP Phone services, they started with a blank slate. The first question to solve was how the phones would communicate with other computers in order to deploy services. The best fit seemed to be to let the phones act as browsers, with the service suppliers acting as Web sites.

Web browsers and servers operate in a client/server fashion and communicate by sending data using the HTTP protocol. The protocol is fairly simple and is successfully deployed on a variety of platforms. Initially, the phone was set up to have an HTTP client that it would use to access data on external Web servers.

Unfortunately, the phone is only able to give up a 132 by 64 pixel window for services, which completely rules out using Web pages created for conventional PCs. In addition, the limited horsepower in the phones means that rendering HTML pages is fairly difficult.

As a result, the designers chose to use HTTP to transport data back and forth to the phones, but decided to use a proprietary set of XML tags for display and command information. Chapter 4, "Using Cisco IP Phone XML Objects and Tags," describes these XML objects in detail. The phone is also capable of displaying pure ASCII text, independent of any XML.

Phone-Initiated Service

The very first services that were created for IP Phones used HTTP to retrieve simple text files. Figure 2-4 shows the sequence of events that transpire when the phone requests the service. The phone simply issues the same HTTP GET command that a browser would issue to retrieve file *Message.txt* from the Web server. The Web server responds by sending the content of the file back to the phone.

Figure 2-4 *Simplest Sequence of Events to Implement a Service*

http://CM/Message.txt

Welcome to
Cisco's IP
phone service

When the phone receives this text, it displays it without any special formatting on the phone display. The result is shown in Figure 2-5.

This is the simplest possible form of a service, but there are some really powerful things taking place here. First, this service is implemented using a standard Web server, which responds to a completely normal request. (In fact, selecting a URL of http://CM/ Message.txt in Internet Explorer would pull the same text into the browser window.)

Just as importantly, the phone does all this without any help from CallManager. In fact, the user of the telephone could have a call up and be talking to somebody while the service is invoked, and CallManager would be none the wiser.

Figure 2-5   *Display of a Simple Text File*

Finally and perhaps most importantly, a Web content developer can develop this service. It doesn't take a highly skilled programmer—anyone who can develop text files can create services.

Beyond Simple Text

Sending simple text to the phone is nice, but fairly limited in what it can accomplish. Fortunately, the addition of the XML message set gives the service developer the option to create truly interactive applications.

We won't describe all the capabilities of the XML commands here, but some of the features service developers can invoke via XML include:

- Display of menus, which allow end users to make selections from a list of options.
- Display of directory information, with soft keys that enable users to dial the displayed number after making a selection.
- Display of bitmapped graphics.
- Display of graphical menus.

Creation and use of these XML objects is a bit more complicated than creating text files, but it is still no more complex than the creation of simple Web pages and requires very little if any training.

What Is an IP Phone Service?

Up to this point, all the information in this chapter has concentrated on showing you the infrastructure that Cisco's IP Phone resides in. We've seen what the network topology looks like, what devices are attached to the network, and what protocols these devices used to communicate. We have also seen how the phone can communicate with servers providing Web services.

In this section, we take a look at the actual nuts and bolts of a service. Specifically, we see what kinds of components are actually used in a service, and how those components interact with the phone.

The Services Menu

The first detail we have to cover is how the phone actually invokes a service. The phone is drawn into a service by virtue of a URL attached to a button on the phone, called the services button. This assignment is done in one of the Cisco CallManager Administration screens. Figure 2-6 shows the Phone Configuration screen that lets you assign a URL to the **services** button.

Figure 2-6 *Phone Configuration Screen in CallManager Administration*

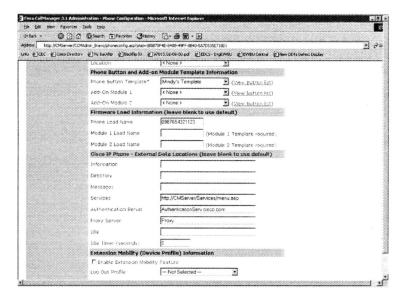

The **services** button by default is assigned a URL that points to a Web page on the CallManager server called GetServicesMenu.asp. It simply presents the user with a menu of services that have been configured for that phone. Figure 2-7 shows the normal view a user would see after pressing the **services** button.

Each of these menu items is connected to another URL. (You see how this is done when you examine the *CiscoIPPhoneMenu* object in Chapter 4.) A user executes these services by simply moving the selection bar up or down to the correct service, then pressing the soft key that executes the service.

Figure 2-7   *A Typical Services Menu on a Phone*

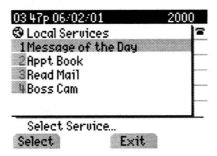

The menu in Figure 2-7 is the one that users see by default; system administrators are free to assign completely different menus to individual uses or groups of users. It is important to remember that the Services Menu you are used to seeing on your CallManager system is only one of many possible ways to invoke services.

The Cisco IP Phones can also have a URL attached to the **directories** button and the **messages** button. Most system administrators will confine the use of those buttons to specialized services.

Service Architecture

Although it looks to the user as though a Cisco IP Phone service is running on their phone, nothing could be farther from the truth. The phone is primarily an I/O device, being used to render screens of data and get input from the user. The real work usually takes place on a Web server.

Figure 2-8   *Typical Service Architecture*

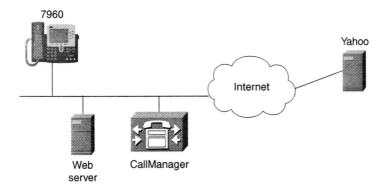

The architecture shown in Figure 2-8 is for a stock quote service that relies on real-time quotes from Yahoo!, an Internet portal. It requires the cooperation of a Web server, CallManager and its LDAP directory, the IP Phone, and Yahoo!.

Understanding how this architecture works is simply a matter of following the flow of control from the beginning to the end. The steps in order are:

- The user first presses the **services** button on her 7940 phone, which sends the URL `http://CMServer/getservicesmenu.asp` to CallManager. The corresponding script on the CallManager server dynamically builds a menu of services, which is sent to the 7940 for display.

- The user invokes the service by selecting it from the menu shown on the 7940 display. The firmware in the telephone does this by sending an HTTP request to the Web server, which in this case would be identical to typing `http://server/StockQuote.asp?stock=LU`.

- The Web server in this case is IIS running on a Windows 2000 server. It starts up page StockQuote.asp. This Active Server Page uses JavaScript to perform the program logic.

- The JavaScript first extracts the argument that was passed to the service, which indicates that the user wants to get a quote on her favorite stock, Lucent. The script then builds a query URL and sends it to Yahoo!, which has an HTTP service for retrieving real-time stock quotes.

- Yahoo! receives the URL asking for a stock quote, then packages a response as an XML object and sends it back to the Web server as an HTTP response.

- The JavaScript in the Web Server parses the incoming XML object extracting the price, which at this time is $8.00. That price is packaged into an XML object and sent to the phone.

- The phone, which has patiently been waiting for a response to its HTTP request, receives the XML object, parses it, and displays the result on the screen, as shown in Figure 2-9.

Figure 2-9   *Results of the Sample Stock Quote Service*

As this example shows, most IP Phone services are centered on a Web server, but also generally involve many distributed processes. The core Web server receives the request from the phone and often does some parsing, but it then relies on additional components, programs, and processes to do the back-end work. Only the simplest services do all their processing in one place.

Web Servers, Web Development

From the tone of this chapter, you should be starting to realize that the focal point of most of the services you develop is a Web server. As a developer, this means you need to find an environment that works for you.

There are literally billions of Web pages available in the world and millions of computers functioning as Web servers. Despite these huge numbers, there isn't a lot of diversity out there. The top three software packages account for over 90 percent of the sites on the Web.

Table 2-1   *Web Server Population Statistics*

Server Name	Supplier	Comments
Apache	The Apache Software Foundation http://www.apache.org	This free server is incredibly popular, and is closing in on owning two-thirds of the market. It runs on a variety of platforms, including various flavors of Linux and UNIX, as well as Microsoft's operating systems.
IIS	Microsoft	Microsoft's Internet Information Server ships with their server products and integrates tightly with Windows NT and 2000. IIS has clawed its way up to a strong second-place finish in the Web server popularity race, but can barely see front-runner Apache from its current position.
iPlanet	Netscape/iPlanet	Netscape's server was an early entrant in the Web server business, but was not able to turn the early start into market share.

There are many important factors that play into your choice of a Web server. Some of the most important ones are:

- **Corporate Policy**—If your company is Microsoft through and through, selecting anything other than IIS is going to be swimming against the tide. Likewise, if you work for a company that swears by Sun for all corporate infrastructures, an iPlanet server would probably be viewed with great favor by the powers-that-be.

- **Finances**—There's no doubt that the Apache server is a fine piece of work, but perhaps the biggest factor in its success is completely unrelated to technical virtue. Apache carries a price tag of exactly $0, which suits a lot of purchasing departments quite well. Combining Apache with the Linux operating system (priced identically) gives you a powerful, reliable Web serving system for the price of your hardware only. You can't beat that.

- **Development issues**—As you will see later in this chapter, there are quite a few different ways to write the code that drives your Web applications. Scripting languages like JavaScript and VBScript work well on IIS. Linux developers find Perl to be an excellent fit for their servers. Java developers might want to base their applications on servlets. And regardless of the Web server, your development teams feel more comfortable on some platforms than others.

Already a Web Developer?

Many of you reading this book might feel that your years of Web experience mean you'll be developing Cisco IP Phone services in no time flat. While that might be true, there are a couple of important points to consider.

First, all of your knowledge regarding HTML design and layout is irrelevant here. Cisco IP Phones don't understand HTML, so the specifics of that language aren't particularly useful. Additionally, much of the time one spends learning HTML is spent on some of the more complex and exotic aspects of Web pages, such as frames, complex tables, or perhaps DHTML. Cisco IP Phone services simply do not have any rendering issues that are anywhere near this complex.

If much of your Web development knowledge is concentrated on back-end issues (such as database access, scripting, security, and interfacing with scripts and CGI), however, you might find that your skills translate readily to Cisco IP Phone services.

In a nutshell, most of what you know about the layout and appearance of Web pages doesn't translate, but much of what you know about programming and data processing from a Web server is just the ticket.

Languages

The World Wide Web started as a system for sharing documents. HTML was a language that allowed Web developers to format pages in such a way so that they would be attractive, easy to read, and informative. The dynamic creation of content was not part of the picture.

It quickly became obvious that with a programmatic interface, Web servers could serve up content dynamically. For example, a Web server could ask a user for his name, then pass that name to a custom program. That program could look up the user's credit card account information from a database, then format the information into HTML, and pass it back to the server.

This code that performed this was originally referred to as a CGI program, but now we generally just refer to it as Web programming. Nearly all the services you create for Cisco IP Phones actively create XML objects using some sort of programming.

Web programming can be done with a huge variety of languages, including most popular compiled and scripted languages. The best language to use depends on quite a few different factors, including:

- The Web server you are using. Each type of server has unique, proprietary methods to integrate programs. Writing programs to work with Apache is often radically different than the same process used for IIS.

- The type of task your program is being asked to perform. C++ is really good at computationally intensive tasks, but Perl is just the ticket for many text-processing jobs.

- The complexity of your task. If you're going to be producing a big program that a dozen developers are working on, you might tend to avoid scripting languages and go with an Object Oriented Programming (OOP) language such as Java.

- What you know. Regardless of all the other factors, a so-so fit in the language you know and love might get your work done faster than having to learn a new language from scratch. Many a big project has fallen to ruins when it turned out to be an educational project for the programming team.

The most common programming languages are broken down into three different categories and discussed below. Beware that a few paragraphs can't even begin to dig into the complexities you need to take into account for your decision-making process. You should view these descriptions as a point for further study and analysis.

Traditional Compiled Languages

These languages have well-defined structure, rigid type checking, large libraries, and good methodologies for team programming. The classic example for CGI programming is traditionally C or C++. In the past few years, however, server-side Java seems to be rapidly gaining adherents, leading some to claim it either is or soon will be the leading language for Web programming.

Java can be employed on the server as a straight application invoked by a CGI interface, or as a Servlet. Servlets are used in the JSP (Java Server Pages) system, which combines much of the best of scripting with the strengths of a compiled language. Note that setting up a Web server to run Servlets is still a bit of an adventure; most servers in 2001 don't support Servlets straight out of the box.

C and C++ have well defined libraries and interfaces with all popular Web servers. The only concern you need to have is that you'll find yourself coding new interfaces for each server you use. C++ code that works with IIS has to be modified to work with Apache, and modified again to work with Netscape's server. On the plus side, you generally have a wide variety of sample code and libraries to work with.

Scripting Languages

Scripting languages are often thought of as lightweight siblings of compiled languages. JavaScript, VBScript, Perl, and Python all share a few things: lack of compilation, looser type checking, and execution via a script engine, not via compiled code.

Writing script programs is usually much faster and simpler than using compiled languages such as C++. Changes don't have to be compiled, and frequently type checking is either non-existent or lax.

IIS developers are heavy users of scripting languages. Microsoft's Active Server Pages (ASP) allow users to write scripts in VBScript or JavaScript. In addition, Microsoft supplies good management tools for working in groups on these types of projects. But code written as ASP pages is difficult to port to other platforms.

Perl is an excellent choice for developing Web pages when your target system is a Linux or UNIX system running Apache. This is a marriage made in developer heaven. Even better, there is an enormous body of knowledge and code relating to Perl applications targeted for Web developers that is easy to find and usually free.

Hybrid Systems

Some programming systems are a hybrid of a scripting system combined with new server-side capabilities. A couple of examples that come to mind are PHP and DHTML. Creating pages for both systems feels a lot like making normal HTML pages, but some special commands allow easy creation of animation, user interactions, database lookup, and so on.

Again, when using either system you are faced with making sure your development plans are compatible with your server and deployment system. Both DHTML and PHP allow you to do some very powerful things with just a tiny speck of code; in that respect they offer you some tremendous leverage.

XML

As this book is being written, XML, Extended Markup Language, has achieved prime buzzword status garnering excitement wherever it is discussed. Now in this book you're reading that Cisco IP Phones implement services by way of XML objects served up over HTTP. Should you be excited?

The short answer is no, you shouldn't be excited. However, you should be happy that Cisco is using a well-defined way to control phones during services. To see why you should be happy, you first need to know why Cisco's engineering team used HTTP and XML. The union of these two technologies gives you, the developer, a powerful toolkit that is nonetheless an example of elegant simplicity.

A History Lesson

Engineers designing complicated systems, such as phone systems, have always had to design methods for dissimilar devices to communicate with one another. An example of note here would be Cisco's IP Phones and CallManager. Other typical examples might be a desktop computer and a printer, a remote control and a television, or a communications satellite and its ground control station.

Typically systems such as these have a digital communications channel of some sort over which they can send our favorite two numbers, ones and zeros. Unfortunately, a simple stream of ones and zeros as shown in Figure 2-10 isn't very intelligible. Just for starters, the satellite doesn't even have any way to know when one command ends and the next begins in a continuous stream such as this.

Figure 2-10 *First Attempt at a Communications Protocol*

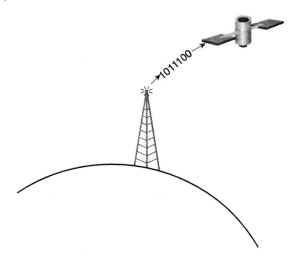

The first step in addressing a problem like this was to use a low-level hardware protocol such as RS-232 or Ethernet. This helps by organizing the bits into bytes and providing ways to determine when data streams started and stopped.

After using standard hardware components at the lowest level, engineers typically began developing customized systems for communicating with components. Usually engineers would cook up a data link layer that was used to transmit and acknowledge packets and do some error checking.

At that point the system had a fairly secure way to send data back and forth, and it was time to build up some sort of command and even packets. This was usually done in an ad hoc fashion, with data formats defined and organized according to the whim of the moment.

This might sound sort of haphazard, but in general the systems being designed never had to communicate with anything other than the components they were designed to work with. So in our satellite system, a request to start transmitting on a certain frequency might look something like that shown in Figure 2-11.

Figure 2-11 *Sample Message in a Proprietary Protocol*

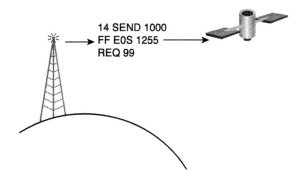

This was the state of the art until recently. Every time two devices needed to communicate, engineers would design a one-of-a-kind protocol with a one-of-a-kind set of commands, implement and debug it (often painfully), and then they would have a working system that had no hope of ever communicating with any other device in the world.

The Highly Improved Modern World

In the last decade, several events converged that changed the way devices communicated. First, the world became networked. This meant that more and more devices were able to communicate with one another. Ethernet became a de facto standard for devices of moderate complexity to talk to one another. And for devices talking on networks, TCP/IP became the protocol of choice.

Given this scenario, it was inevitable that when Cisco decided to put phones on a LAN, they would choose to have those phones communicate via IP. Much as in the olden days when it came time to choose a method for phones to communicate with CallManager, however, they developed a custom protocol, Skinny, which consumed less bandwidth than other existing protocols.

There's nothing wrong with Skinny—it works fine—and third party phone manufacturers have successfully implemented it so their devices can talk to CallManager as well. But Skinny might be the last pure proprietary protocol you ever see in a CallManager system.

There are two good reasons for this prediction of doom for the world of the proprietary:

- The HTTP protocol used by Web browsers and servers
- The invention of XML

HTTP—A Generic Envelope

Web browsers and servers use HTTP to send requests and responses across networks. It basically serves as an envelope that can be used to package up messages and conveniently send them across packet-switched networks.

HTTP stacks are readily available and have been ported to nearly every platform in existence, ranging all the way down to single chip microcomputers. Putting an HTTP client and server in the Cisco IP Phone made sense for many reasons, and it seemed to be a logical choice to use for pulling service content down to Cisco IP Phones.

By choosing HTTP as the protocol for services, Cisco was immediately able to leverage the presence of millions of Web servers across the world. Everyone with a Windows NT system was suddenly a publisher of content for Cisco IP Phones. The protocol was well defined, easy to implement, and cheap. It made perfect sense.

XML—A Generic Wrapper

Cisco IP Phone services clearly required several different kinds of messages that could be sent from a server. These included menus, text, graphics, and directory listings. As is the case with any protocol, the engineering team needed a way to package the payload for these messages. A prearranged system needed to be defined to send these objects to the phone so that they could be easily parsed and handled.

It turns out that the timely choice for doing this is XML. XML had been around for a few years before Cisco's IP Phones, but it was not until the turn of the century that it really started to acquire critical mass. By that time it became the obvious choice to use to package the objects used in IP Phone services.

XML—What Is It?

There are entire books written on XML. When viewed in detail, this powerful language has a huge variety of features and options. None of that matters in the context of Cisco IP Phone services. These services use a minimal core of XML—a small enough core that you can understand it in five minutes.

XML is known as a markup language, which is a name also applied to HTML. Like HTML, XML creates hierarchical documents using tags, which are simple text phrases enclosed in angle brackets.

By creating and defining a set of tags, you use XML to create a language for a specific application. XML tells you how to use these tags, but leaves their definition up to you, making it more of a meta-language. By using descriptive tag names and a simple structure, a well-defined XML language can be quite readable.

A simple example of an XML object fragment is almost self-explanatory:

```
<Book>
  <Title>The Data Compression Book</Title>
  <Author>Mark Nelson</Author>
  <ISBN>1558514341</ISBN>
</Book>
```

In this example, the XML vocabulary defines an object known as Book, and defines sub-objects within it for the Title, Author, and ISBN attributes.

Note that tags show up in pairs, with a beginning tag and an end. The end tag is marked with a leading slash character.

Tags can be nested, but cannot overlap one-another. For example, this is not valid XML:

```
<Book>
  <Title>Almost Heaven, West Virginia
  <Author>Mark Nelson</Title>
  </Author>
  <ISBN>1558514341</ISBN>
</Book>
```

However, appearances of a tag can be repeated within an object:

```
<Book>
  <Title>Our Years In The White House</Title>
  <Author>Hilary Clinton</Author>
  <Author>Bill Clinton</Author>
  <ISBN>31558514341Z</ISBN>
</Book>
```

Finally, an XML document can only have one top-level object. And the top-level objects defined for Cisco IP Phones are the only ones you need to know about in order to create services. So when serving up objects from your Web server to a Cisco IP Phone, you will send XML documents that define a single object, with typical objects having names such as:

- CiscoIPPhoneText
- CiscoIPPhoneMenu
- CiscoIPPhoneImage

The details on the tags within these objects are covered in Chapter 4.

XML—A Few Details

The Cisco IP Phone is somewhat limited in its code space, so it doesn't actually implement a complete XML parser. A true XML parser is smart enough to ignore material it does not understand, but this is not always true with Cisco IP Phones.

For example, in addition to tags, XML allows you to define attributes that show up within tags. A typical use of an attribute might look like this:

```
<Book genre="Science Fiction">
  <Title>Shopping For Shoes - One Man's Story</Title>
</Book>
```

The firmware in the Cisco IP Phone will fail to parse an XML object if it encounters an unexpected attribute in one of the predefined tags.

XML has a couple of powerful mechanisms that can be used to define the vocabulary used in a specific language. The first attempt to do this was with what is known as a DTD, or Document Type Definition. The DTD seems to be giving way to what is now referred to as XML Schema. Both of these are ways to define all the elements of an XML vocabulary, which is very helpful when automated tools are being used to create and parse XML objects.

Again, these advanced features are simply not used in the phone's parser. While you would probably never insert these types of objects manually, it is possible that an XML editor or other automated tool might assume your target system supports schemas.

The phone's parser does support the XML prolog statement, which is often included as the first line of an XML file, and looks something like this:

```
<?XML VERSION="1.0"?>
```

The parser reads this, but essentially ignores it.

XML Tools

After you make it through Chapter 4 and see how the phone uses XML objects, you should see that Cisco's use of XML is simply as a convenient wrapper for object information. For the majority of your service creation projects, you do not need any sophisticated XML tools to create IP Phone objects. You might find such tools useful in more complex applications, such as when using XSLT to transform back-end database objects to displayable format. You might also appreciate having a tool that checks your documents for conformance to the IP Phone schema as you work. But don't spend money in this area needlessly—make sure you are getting some tangible value before investing in expensive tools.

A Simple Sample

Just to get your feet wet, you can create a sample Web application by following the steps laid out here. To start, you need to have access to a CallManager system and be able to administer a phone. You'll also need access to a Web server. In my case, that's my Windows 2000 Server system running IIS. The code for this sample is provided on the CD-ROM accompanying this book.

My sample application is an incarnation of a classic fortune-telling device, the Magic Cube. To implement the Magic Cube, I'm going to write an Active Server Page using some very simple JavaScript. The page simply answers a Yes/No question by serving up a random quote.

Since the focus of this book isn't to teach you JavaScript, I'll simply show you the simple ASP page I created without comment:

MagicCube.asp

```
<%@ Language=JavaScript%>
<%

var choice = Math.random() * 7 + 0.5;
choice = Math.round( choice );
var response;

switch ( choice )
{
  case 1   : response = "Try again later";                     break;
  case 2   : response = "Indications look bad";                break;
  case 3   : response = "Not today";                           break;
  case 4   : response = "When Greenspan cuts rates";           break;
  case 5   : response = "Today will be your lucky day";        break;
  case 6   : response = "Look to yourself for the answer";     break;
  case 7   : response = "When you take the pebble from my hand"; break;
  default  : response = "Ask Oprah";                           break;
}

Response.Write( response );
Response.End();
%>
```

I created this ASP file, then copied it to c:\Inetpub\wwwroot on my Web server. That means I can access it using the following URL:

```
http://server-name/MagicCube.asp
```

This page then serves up a random quote every time it is loaded. You should be able to hit the reload button on your browser repeatedly to get a random quote. The resulting page is shown in Figure 2-12.

One important thing to note about this Web page is that it is not using HTML, it is outputting unadorned ASCII text. You could just as easily serve up this data by creating a file with static text called MagicCube.txt.

Once you verify that the Web page is working, your next step is to present it to your Cisco IP Phone. To do this, go to your Cisco CallManager Administration page and click **Device > Phone**. Use the search feature to select your phone. Scroll down the page until you find the group labeled External Data Locations. Change the Services URL to point to the MagicCube Web page. See Figure 2-13 for an example of this.

Figure 2-12 *MagicCube Web Page in Action*

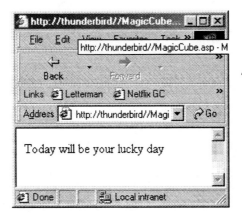

Figure 2-13 *Setting the Services URL*

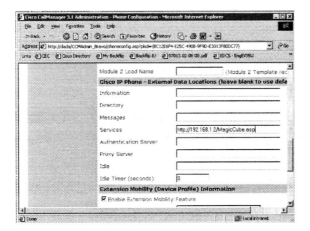

One important thing to note here is that instead of giving a server name, I input the IP address of my Web server. You won't need to do this if your Web server name can be found in the phone's DNS server, but on many networks (including mine) most desktop PCs can't be found that way. (Windows resolves names using the WINS protocol, which is not supported by the Cisco IP Phone.) It is quite common to run into this problem when testing and configuring services—so when testing it's not a bad idea to always use IP addresses for server names entered into the phones.

After saving the settings and resetting the phone, simply pressing the **services** button should invoke the Web page and feed the text to the phone. If all goes as planned, you should see the output shown in Figure 2-14.

Figure 2-14 *Service Output*

In the event that you do not see that page, the first step is to verify via the **settings** button that you have entered the URL properly in the phone. If you have, verify that you can invoke the same page from your PC. The most common cause of problems with invoking a service is failure to connect to the HTTP server.

Using XML Objects

The example in the section, "A Simple Sample," sends simple text to the phone, which is nice and simple. But when developing real services for your phone system, the odds are that you will create XML objects that the phone understands. The extra flexibility and power you get with these objects make them almost mandatory.

In this case, I took the output from MagicCube.asp and wrapped it up in a CiscoIPPhoneText XML object. The resulting JavaScript ASP page, called SonOfMagicCube.asp is shown below. Check the CD-ROM for your copy of this ASP page.

SonOfMagicCube.asp

```
<%@ Language=JavaScript%>
<%

Response.ContentType = "text/xml";
Response.Write("<CiscoIPPhoneText>\r\n");
Response.Write("<Title>Magic Cube</Title>\r\n");
Response.Write("<Text>\r");

var choice = Math.random() * 7 + 0.5;
choice = Math.round( choice );
var response;

switch ( choice )
{
  case 1  : response = "Try again later";                  break;
  case 2  : response = "Indications look bad";             break;
  case 3  : response = "Not today";                        break;
  case 4  : response = "When Greenspan cuts rates";        break;
  case 5  : response = "Today will be your lucky day";     break;
  case 6  : response = "Look to yourself for the answer";  break;
```

```
    case 7  : response = "When you take the pebble from my hand"; break;
    default : response = "Ask Oprah";                            break;
}

Response.Write( response );
Response.Write("\r</Text>\r\n");
Response.Write("</CiscoIPPhoneText>\r\n");
Response.Flush();
Response.End();
Session.Abandon();
%>
```

To see what happens when you execute this Web page, make sure that you have a copy of SonOfMagicCube.asp in a directory on your Web server. You should then be able to invoke the Web server using a browser and see the output from the Web page. If you are using an up-to-date version of Internet Explorer, it parses the XML object and produces a display looking like that shown in Figure 2-15.

Figure 2-15 *Internet Explorer Parses an XML Object*

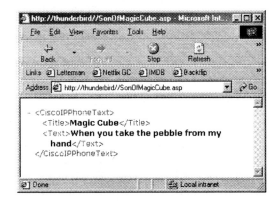

As you can see, the XML object shown here has a top-level tag of type CiscoIPPhoneText, which has predefined meaning for Cisco IP Phones. The phone then treats the text defined for the Title and Text tags and lays the information out on the phone display in the format shown in Figure 2-16.

Figure 2-16 *Result of SonOfMagicCube.asp*

You should be able to see how JavaScript was used to create this output. The only thing that might not have an immediately obvious is this:

```
Response.ContentType = "text/xml";
```

When a Web page is served up to an HTTP client (such as the Cisco IP Phone), it includes a description of the content type so the client knows how to process it. In the first script shown in this chapter, you left the content type at the default, which is simple text. In the second script, you changed it to tell the phone that the type was XML, which is what triggers the special support for the XML objects that the phone understands.

Developing Localized Services

You can develop services in any of the CallManager-supported languages as of release 3.2(1). CallManager-supported languages include Danish, Dutch, English, French, German, Italian, Norwegian, Portuguese, Spanish, Swedish, and Russian. Refer to the "HTTP Headers for Localization" section in Chapter 5 to learn how to determine what language is being used by the device making a request to your service. The services architecture is language-independent; to write a service in French, for example, you use the same object and tags, and the displayable data should be provided by the service in French (or other desired language). For example, the Name element of a MenuItem would be returned to the phone in French.

NOTE   The font used by the phone to render text is the one called for by the CallManager localization settings for that device. For example, if the phone is set to the Russian locale, it will interpret textual data as if it were coded using ISO 8859-5 character set. If you send text encoded using Unicode, or ISO-8859-1, some or all of your text will be rendered incorrectly.

Training and Support for the Cisco IP Phone Services SDK

Cisco provides an SDK to support your endeavors, and it is available free on Cisco's Web site. To reach the current copy of the SDK, you need to navigate to Cisco's Developer Support Central Web site. At the time of this writing, the Web site is located at:

```
www.cisco.com/go/developersupport
```

Knowing as we do that Web sites have a tendency to change, you should be aware that you might have to search at the main site for "Developer Support Central."

From Developer Support Central you should navigate to the area for the IP Phone Services SDK. The download link on that Web page allows you to get the current version of the SDK.

At the time of the CallManager 3.1 Prerelease, the SDK contained the following useful contents:

- Online documentation for the SDK in PDF format.
- An image conversion control that can be used to create graphics suitable for display in the Cisco IP Phone family.

NOTE	This ActiveX control is only useful on a Windows server platform. The same restriction applies to the two other controls listed in this package.

- An image filter that allows Adobe Photoshop to read and write graphics files in Cisco's proprietary format.
- An LDAP ActiveX control that can be used with Microsoft IIS to create directory listings suitable for Cisco's IP Phones.
- A Proxy control that can be used to access Web pages on the Internet by way of a local server. This is often needed when Cisco's phones are behind a firewall of some sort.
- A set of simple sample files, including a Calendar, LDAP directory tool, Speed Dial service, Stock Ticker, and Stock Chart.

While these tools are useful, they are not supported by Cisco's Technical Assistance Center. TAC is not prepared to offer developer-level support for IP Phone services.

To get support from Cisco as a service developer, you must join Cisco's Developer Support Program, which provides support for these products at an added cost. You can find more information about the program at the Developer Support Central site.

Although the program is an added cost item, you find that the support reps who work on these cases are highly experienced in SDK work and are devoted to just that product. They also have ongoing access to the engineering teams that develop the IP Phones, SDK components, and CallManager, which gives results in quick answers to difficult development questions.

Additional Resources, Further Reading

To succeed as a developer of Cisco IP Phone services, you need basic skills in several different areas.

Networking Infrastructure

It is important that you understand the basics of networking infrastructure, including the configuration and use of DNS, DHCP, and Web servers. The ultimate in this area would be a Cisco Certified Network Associate or Professional, or a Microsoft Certified Systems Engineer. These are rather arduous programs, but if you are interested you can go to either company's Web site and follow the links to certification programs.

Should you find that your normal life prevents you from taking off for a few months of certification training, you will have to hit the books. You can find an incredibly good selection of books on networking in general from Cisco Press at http://www.ciscopress.com.

Administration, Programming, and Care of Web Servers

Cisco's CallManager architecture is firmly wedded to Windows 2000 at this point, and Cisco Press is not well represented in this area. You need to be able to learn how to administer the entire Windows 2000 server, which should include the Web server, the DHCP server, the WINS server, and possibly even the DNS server. A good source for these books is O'Reilly & Associates, available on the Web at http://www.ora.com.

O'Reilly has an excellent set of books on administration of Windows systems. A good place to start is the title *Windows 2000 Administration in a Nutshell*, by Mitch Tulloch.

Another good source for more detailed information is Microsoft Press, at http://www.mspress.microsoft.com. Titles such as *Microsoft® Windows® 2000 and IIS 5.0 Administrator's Pocket Consultant*, by William R. Stanek, provide the in-depth information you need.

Administration of CallManager

In addition to the documentation included with CallManager, there are some great resources available in the Developer Support area of the Cisco Web site. Under the heading *Required Reading For IP Telephony AVVID Partners*, you'll find a set of titles such as *Cisco IP Telephony Network Design Guide*, various developer's guides, information on standards, and links to relevant books. At least skimming through all of these materials can only help get you up to speed faster.

Conclusion

This chapter skipped lightly over the high points of the skills and knowledge you need to develop IP Phone services. You got a basic outline of the CallManager architecture and where the phones fit in that. You were exposed to the basics of Web development and stepped through the development of a basic service that deployed XML objects to the IP Phones.

In the next chapter, you will learn the basics about developing services. As you try creating some services and learn more about the infrastructure, you might want to skim through this chapter again; it should help drive some of the points here home quite effectively.

CHAPTER 3

Phone Services Primer

This chapter provides information about the various aspects of the Cisco IP Phone and some of the basic elements of developing a phone service. In some cases, more detailed information is provided in another chapter later in the book.

To develop phone services, you need access to Cisco CallManager. To provide this capability, if you do not already have access, we have included CM-Sim, a CallManager Simulator, on the CD-ROM included with this book. See Chapter 12, "Cisco CallManager Simulator," for more information about CM-Sim. You also need Cisco IP Phone models 7960 or 7940 to test your service on. You can purchase phones at the following location, or by accessing Cisco Connection Online (www.cisco.com) and searching on Cisco IP Phone:

```
www.cisco.com/public/ordering_info.shtml
```

How to Do It, in a Nutshell

Building a Cisco IP Phone service is a simple thing. After reviewing Chapter 2, "The Basics," and coming to this adventure with some Web programming experience in the Web environment your company or your target company uses, you're ready to dive right in. The following is a quick guide to developing a service:

1 Brainstorm about the service you want to provide: what functions will it perform, who will use it, where will you get the data?

2 Build your service using the objects, tags, and headers defined later in this book.

3 Deploy, test, and debug your code.

4 Add the service to Cisco CallManager Administration.

5 Announce the service to users so they can subscribe to it, or use CallManager Administration to subscribe all or some phones to the service.

XML and Cisco IP Phones

In the beginning (circa 1999), there was the IP telephone; a communication device that allowed people to speak to each other across vast distances (or perhaps just the guy two cubicles away). The engineers at Cisco wanted to expand the role of the IP phone, so that it facilitated an enhanced communication. The search began for a technology that would permit this expanded capability, so that what was once a simple telephone could be supercharged into a desktop appliance that performed communications not just by speech, but in a readable format, a downloadable format, and an extensible format. We wanted to stay true to the telephone functionality, yet expand the role of the device so that it provided greater functionality central to the user. Yes, it would still be a way to talk to Grandma, but it could also be used for business, information, and entertainment applications in an enterprise environment. But first we needed a technology that would enable us to do this efficiently and cost-effectively.

Many other technologies exist besides XML. There's wireless access protocol (WAP), SHTML, HTML, embedded java, and so on. As it turns out, WAP can be pricey by the time you buy all those licenses, and the other technologies didn't make the most sense for our needs for a variety of reasons. In the end, XML over HTTP provided the greatest fit for our vision of what we wanted the phone to become.

With XML over HTTP, we can provide targeted functionality designed specifically for the device, while still keeping with our desire to maintain but expand the core phone functionality. Certain other standards can be cost-prohibitive and the technology did not naturally align itself with phone functionality. For instance, WAP is just a low-bandwidth, optimized protocol for Web page retrieval. Cisco IP Phones run over a 10/100 MB link, so we can push more data. XML provides the horsepower through Cisco IP Phone objects and tags to push that content. Plus, XML is user-readable, machine-readable, and low-cost (free is always good), plus it expands the use and value of the phone without diminishing the phone functionality. Instead it enhances the phone to the extent that it can be considered more than a phone . . . a Net appliance, if you will.

Like any good scientist, we tried the cure on ourselves first before giving it to others. Fortunately, it worked. In its original form, the Cisco IP Phone 7960 provided menus, directories, and input ability. These are considered native features of the phone. To assist you with developing services to continually expand the range, value, and importance of the Cisco IP Phone, we exposed the phone's native operations so that you could leverage them for your services. This book teaches you how to use XML to encapsulate the data for the various native operations in the phone (and then some), and then retrieve the data over HTTP. XML enables you to provide data to the native functionality of the device. Cisco IP Phones provided much of the XML services you're using today just to create the setting features—contrast, ring type, and so on. With the Cisco IP Phone Services SDK, the native functionality has been exposed for your use, and we have added more objects, including the CiscoIPPhoneGraphicMenu and CiscoIPPhoneImage objects that enable you to make enhanced services. To see the graphic menu in action, observe the simple calendar service provided on the companion CD-ROM. To see the image object, take a look at the stock charts service on the SDK. But the real question is: What can YOU do with the Cisco IP Phone?

The key to the concept is this—XML is a user- and machine-readable way of structuring and encapsulating data; this simply provides the data to the phone to use with its existing menu structure. For example, the phone can go to a Web site, such as Yahoo!, but Yahoo! does not provide XML objects. However, the phone cannot understand HTML, the language in which Web pages communicate. So instead, the phone goes to a Web server (content translation engine), which performs a translation function. It takes the HTML from Web pages and translates it to XML (or plain text) so that the phone can receive it. Be aware, content translation engines can be expensive, but their functionality is robust. Depending on your needs, it might be a worthwhile investment.

NOTE   Cisco offers a content translation engine, the Cisco CTE 1400; it reads Internet content and translates it into XML for the phone. The content translation engine takes a complicated Web page and provides a menu (links, images, text, and so on) to break down the elements on the page to help you render a sizeable Web page on the Cisco IP Phone in the format you require. You can learn more about Cisco CTE 1400 by searching on Cisco Connection Online (CCO) or by using the following link:

`www.cisco.com/warp/public/cc/pd/witc/cte1400/`

Services and Directory Architecture

Architecturally speaking, services and directories could be identical twins. Both provide functionality using HTTP to retrieve content that resides on Web servers. The phones retrieve data for directories or services from uniform resource locators (URLs) that have been entered in CallManager Administration. The URLs can be defined cluster-wide at either the enterprise level (**System > Enterprise Parameters**) or overwritten on a device-by-device basis (**Device > Phone >** *search for a phone > set values in the Phone Configuration screen*). Figure 3-1 shows the **Services** field (at the bottom of the screen) in the Enterprise Parameters Configuration page in CallManager Administration.

When a user invokes a directory or a service, the phone's HTTP client requests the associated URL. On the first request, the phone appends its device name with a query string parameter called Name. Subsequent requests can also send the device name if you re-append the device name as a query string parameter. With this information, you can identify the device making the request and return targeted content if you want.

Figure 3-1 *Enterprise Parameters Configuration*

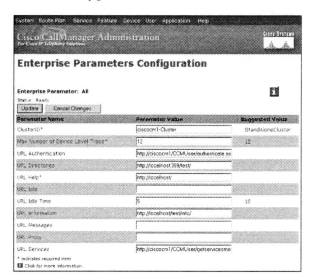

Adding a directory enables you to provide additional functionality beyond what Cisco IP Phones automatically provide when the user presses the **directories** button. You could create a multi-tenant or customized directory—for example, a directory of conference room phone numbers, a list of emergency personnel and their phone numbers, and so on.

You can also implement indirection for **services**, **directories**, or the **i/?** button (information/help). *Indirection* is the changing of the default URL to point to another URL that returns a directory menu that has the custom directories and a link back to the built-in corporate directory. See "Providing Default Services to All Phones" in Chapter 9, "Integrating a Service with Cisco IP Phones," for more information.

When you make an HTTP request, the content returned should be in either predefined XML objects or plain text. If you are using XML, the phone processes the XML data that is returned and invokes the action specified by the object. If you're using plain text, the phone processes the text by encapsulating it into the CiscoIPPhoneText object and then simply processes the XML object. See Chapter 4, "Using Cisco IP Phone XML Objects and Tags," for more information about the XML objects.

At a high-level, the existence of an HTTP server in the phone enables the phone to provide configuration and status information for use by services. The Web (HTTP) server in the phone enables an application the ability to Push a request to the phone as needed based on external stimulus, such as a service for a call center. In a call center example, the application can push a request to the phone to pull an update if there's a change in the call queue. This method is more efficient than having the phone's client continually poll the server on a timer. If the queue state changes once a minute, it can instantly update the phone when the state of the queue changes. In another example, you could build a service that notifies users when a certain event occurs. When the specified event occurs, the service is invoked and the message is displayed on the specified users' phones. For example, you want to be notified when your company stock hits a certain price or to display meeting reminders for all meeting participants.

Providing Help for Your Services or Redirecting the i Button

Like services and directories, you can also provide information or help. The simplest way to do this is to provide a **Help** soft key on your service or directory that calls help text you provide. However, if you want the help to point to a local server instead of a WAN server, you can also redirect the **i** or **?** button on the phone. The help that is called when the **i** or **?** button is pressed goes to one URL. If you overwrite this URL, you need to point to a local CallManager server. You should only do this when you are addressing network topology issues.

HTTP and Cisco IP Phones

The following sections describe Cisco IP Phones and HTTP client and server functionality.

HTTP Client

Cisco IP Phones have a HTTP 1.1-compliant client that is used for services and directories functionality. The HTTP client enables the phones to use a simple standard mechanism for retrieving data and providing input to and from standard Web servers. With the low learning curve for using the HTTP headers, you have an easy method for providing content to the phones.

All Cisco IP Phone services use the client functionality for every request. The client is used to request URLs and provides the HTTP GET functionality. You can learn more about the client functionality in Chapter 5, "Using HTTP." Chapter 5 defines the parts of the HTTP standard that are applicable for Cisco IP Phones.

HTTP Server

HTTP also provides server functionality. The most important thing we can stress in this section is that you need to know the type of Web programming used for your Web server environment. For example, if you're using IIS, you need to be able to program active server pages; if you're using Tomcat, you'll need to know how to do servlets or java server pages or perl. Chapter 5 provides an explanation of how the HTTP standard applies to the phone's actions. In addition to an explanation of the use and functionality of the headers, you'll find other information like using cookies for session management and examples on how to generate the headers. Chapter 5 provides enough information about HTTP to get you started for building Cisco IP Phone services, and you can refer to the HTTP RFC for more information.

Gathering Device Information

The HTTP server in the phone can provide information about the phone, including configuration, firmware version, device name, primary directory number, and more. This information is used for administration purposes and is provided in both HTML and XML formats. Administrators can use the HTML interface to read the device information, and you can use the XML interface to build a programmatic interface to the data. For example, if you want to build a service that aids in troubleshooting, you can use the XML data so the information is presented in its raw format.

With the information the HTTP server provides about the phone, you can determine the phone's current configuration settings. You can use the information for troubleshooting. For example, you can learn the streaming statistics for each phone call. This helps you learn, for troubleshooting purposes, what top-level URL is called when the **services** button is pressed. (This is also true for **directories** or the **i/?** button.) With this information, you can build a troubleshooting service, such as the Voice Anomaly Tracking service provided on the companion CD-ROM (which collects streaming information on demand). Consider this scenario: users complain about choppy audio or static during phone calls. To gather troubleshooting information, you can build a service (or in this case, use the one we provide on the CD) that collects the streaming information from the phone. Once all phones have been subscribed to the service, you can instruct the users that whenever they experience voice quality problems during a phone call they should invoke the Voice Anomaly Tracking (VAT) service. The VAT service automatically collects streaming information about the call and logs it on the server providing the service.

Using HTTP Post

An HTTP client can also push content to the phone using the HTTP Post method. With this functionality, you can post an XML object to the phone's Web server and have the phone execute the items listed in the object. You can push one URL and two uniform resource identifiers (URIs) in a single post, giving you the ability to navigate to a service and setup a Real-Time Transport Protocol transmit (RTPTx) and an RTP receive (RTPRx) stream. You can learn more about Push in Chapter 10, "Techniques for Advanced Services."

Creating a Screen Capture of a Phone Display

The HTTP server can also provide raw screen data encapsulated in an XML object. With the CiscoIPPhoneImage object, you can request the current display information from the phone's Web server, which returns a CiscoIPPhoneImage object. Then you can use a graphics tool (such as Adobe Photoshop or Jasc's Paint Shop Pro) to convert it to your chosen format using the CiscoIPPhoneImage import/export filter. The CD-ROM provided with this book provides a sample service that allows you to enter the IP address for a given Cisco IP Phone. The HTTP server in the phone then returns an image of its display, assuming you have the necessary credentials to access that information (see "Security" later in this chapter). This service basically captures a screen shot in XML and then converts that to GIF and outputs the result to the Web browser that made the request. You can learn more about creating a screen caption in Chapter 10.

Identifying a Requesting Client Device

If I had a dollar (US) for every time an application developer asked, "How can I tell which device is hitting my service?" let's just say I could have hired a ghostwriter for my portion of this book. The answer is coming, but first let's examine the myriad reasons why you might want to know the name of the device requesting your service.

For starters, it is always nice to gather information about who is accessing your service, whether it is for some simple "atta-boys" (for non-U.S. Southerners, this is one way of saying you're seeking recognition for your good work) or to gather and record statistical information. You might also need this information for security purposes in the event that the device behaved maliciously toward your service. Debugging is a popular reason in case the user later reports to you that there was an error when using the service (this will completely wipe out any atta-boys you have collected to this point). Sometimes you want to be able to provide targeted content to the device. For any of these reasons, you need to be able to discern which devices are hitting your services.

When a request for a service is made, the service's Web server knows the IP address of the requesting phone. You can use the Cisco URL Proxy to gather additional information from the phone's Web server, such as device name, primary directory number, and more. This provides a method to identify all the phones, assuming you have access to the phone's Web server. Only phones running firmware for Cisco CallManager release 3.1 and above have a Web server.

Push Versus Pull

Let's define *Push* and *Pull* in terms of Cisco IP Phone services, so you understand how we use those terms in this book and for the Cisco IP Phone Services SDK. Then we'll discuss the other ways you may notice Push and Pull being used in the industry. For Cisco IP Phone services, Push is the ability to invoke action on the phone by posting content to its Web server at any time, regardless of what the client is doing. We implement Push through the phone's Web server, not its client. So when we use the term Push, we are actually posting an object to the phone's Web server (performing an HTTP POST using the

CiscoIPPhoneExecute object). Pull is when the phone's HTTP client makes a request. An example of Pull is when the user presses the **services** button. The phone performs a Pull operation by retrieving the services menu.

When the term is used outside of Cisco IP Phone services, Push is often confused with bastardized versions of Pull. A lot of technologies talk about HTTP Push, but most currently implemented are truly HTTP Pull or Timed Pull. For example, Netscape implements Push, which is actually a Pull request that's left pending until the server decides to send more data resulting in a constantly open Pull connection.

Cisco IP Phones support Timed Pull by using HTTP Refresh Header. You can see this in action in the stock quote service, which updates every five seconds.

You can learn more about Push and Pull in Chapter 10.

URIs

Uniform resource identifiers (URIs) can be used in any URL tag in an XML object. URIs enable you to call native functionality based on the definition of the URI. There are different URIs that can be used with different objects. URIs enable you to invoke native functionality of the phone such as **EditDial** and **Dial**. You might be wondering why the tag is called URL when it can also invoke URIs. Originally, URLs were all that were used in the first release of the phone's firmware. However, it has since been expanded to accept both URLs and URIs. URLs are just locators within the higher subset of identifiers. URIs can invoke, transmit, or receive Real-Time Transport Protocol (RTP) streams as well as terminate them (this is also native Cisco IP Phone functionality exposed for your use).

See Chapter 4 for a section showing all the URIs.

Stream Control

Stream control is the ability to start and stop RTP streams on channel 1 (to and from the phone) using G.711μ-law. The phone is capable of streaming on two channels internally (two separate sets of TX and RX). Channel 0 is reserved exclusively for use by CallManager. Channel 1 is available for services, so that when you specify an RTPRx or RTPTx URI, it runs over channel 1 automatically. (For more information about URIs, see the section, "URIs" in Chapter 4.) Channel 1 performs a modal interaction; while streaming, no other functions can be performed without terminating the stream. For example, if the user has invoked a service that streams emails or voice mails and then receives a call and answers it, the streaming terminates. Currently, channels 0 and 1 cannot be mixed.

Services can stream music or a conference; it can also be used for an intercom service. When streaming is invoked, an animated icon displays on the right side of the display on the prompt line. The icon indicates whether it's receiving an RTP stream, transmitting an RTP stream, or both. Figure 3-2 illustrates the TX and RX icons.

Figure 3-2   *Icons for RX and TX RTP Streams*

Examine the lower right corner of Figure 3-2. When receiving an RTP stream, the top arrow points toward the handset. When transmitting an RTP stream, the bottom arrow points away from the mouthpiece.

You can setup or teardown streams using a URI—for example, RTPTx:IPaddress or RTPRx:Stop, respectively. Following is a code example of the URIs that instruct the phone to perform an RTP transmit and RTP receive.

```
RTPRx://10.0.0.1
RTPTx://10.0.0.1:20002
```

An example of a service that uses stream control is MailView, a feature in the Cisco IP Phone Productivity Services (PPS) which is a part of the Cisco Personal Assistant Release 1.2 or later (available for your purchase). MailView uses streaming to play back voice mail. Figure 3-3 illustrates a message being played using the MailView service.

Figure 3-3   *E-Mail Message Played Using MailView*

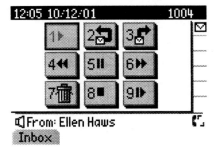

Other services that use stream control could include text-to-speech for retrieving information or an intercom service. See Chapter 10 for more information about stream control.

Soft Key Support for Directories and Services

Cisco IP Phones provide soft keys and buttons. Buttons are statically positioned on the phone's faceplate; examples include line or speed dial buttons and the **messages**, **services**, **directories**, **settings**, or **i** button. By contrast, soft keys are programmable so that button names appear on the phone's display and are associated to adjacent physical buttons on the phone. Soft keys provided by CallManager include **NewCall**, **Hold**, **Resume**, and **EndCall**.

You can create and customize soft keys for use with your service. Custom soft keys can be used either in the services or directory window. The soft keys are customized on a per-object basis so that if you return a menu, you can place custom soft keys on that menu. Custom soft keys have to be sent each time the object loads; they cannot be statically displayed.

You can define your own soft keys that call URIs or URLs. Using the softkey URIs enables you to also call the original soft key functionality but rename or relocate the soft key. For example, a soft key is provided that when pressed, exits the service. The soft key is called **Exit**. You can retain the original exit functionality, but rename the soft key to **Goodbye**. See Chapter 4 for implementation details.

New Characters for Cisco IP Phones

CallManager release 3.1 and Cisco IP Phone models 7960 and 7940 support the ISO-8859-1 character set, commonly known as Latin-1. Prior CallManager releases supported only the Basic Latin character set. ISO-8859-1 denotes Basic Latin and the Latin-1 Supplement together. Latin-1 enables you to write services and directories using the characters needed by languages spoken in Western Europe, such as French, Spanish, Dutch, German, and so on. This comes as welcome relief for developers and companies who want to build menus in their native language.

Services in previous versions of Cisco IP Phone firmware only supported Basic Latin. Support for the ISO-8859-1 character set is automatic. There are no restrictions to building a service or directory in your language, assuming all the necessary characters are provided in Latin-1 Supplement. If you use an unsupported control character, that character displays as a block (a solid rectangle that resembles a cursor) instead of the intended character.

Security

Services both send and receive information, so authentication can occur in either direction using basic authentication as defined in the HTTP 1.1 specification (RFC-2616). This section explains how a phone's HTTP client authenticates to an HTTP server and how an external HTTP client authenticates to the phone's HTTP server. For the phone's HTTP server, the credentials are always user ID and password or personal identification number

(PIN). For the external server, the external server defines the credentials although in most cases, they are also user ID and password.

Users can change their password or PIN in the Cisco IP Phone User Options Web page. The user ID is defined in the Global Directory in the User area of Cisco CallManager Administration (**User > Global Directory**).

Client Authentication

The HTTP client in the phone supports basic authentication, which enables the Web client to authenticate to a Web server. If you've ever been prompted to logon to a Web page by providing your user ID and password, then you have experienced authentication. When the Cisco IP Phone service requests a secured HTTP resource from a Web server, the phone prompts the user to enter his or her authorization credentials (user ID and password/PIN) for that resource. Once the entered information has been authenticated, the user is permitted access to the HTTP resource. If authentication fails, the user is prompted to re-enter the credentials.

Authenticating to the Phone's HTTP Server

The phone's HTTP server supports basic authentication, which enables an external HTTP client to access the phone's Web (HTTP) server. When the external HTTP client requests secured information from the phone, such as generating screen shots or for Push, the credentials required are user ID and password/PIN as defined in CallManager Administration. The user must have one of the following characteristics to be authorized:

- The user must be authorized for associated device control, which means that the user has permission to access the device profile for a given phone—just as he or she can do in the Cisco IP Phone User Options Web page to set or change speed dial settings, subscribe to services, and so on.

- For extension mobility, the user must be the same user that is currently logged in for that device. (Extension mobility is a feature introduced in CallManager release 3.1 that enables a user to configure any Cisco IP Phone to appear as that user's phone temporarily. By logging into a phone, the user can temporarily convert the phone to adopt his or her line numbers, speed dials, services, and other user-specific properties of a Cisco IP Phone.)

Authentication credentials can be tied to a user or an application so that when the Push operation is invoked, the user or the service account can provide the credentials for that application.

For example, you have a service that uses Push to display a meeting reminder to all meeting participants. The application pushing content to the phones must have credentials sufficient to authorize to all those devices.

Fail Over and Fail Back

Fail over (the process of transferring call control to a back up server when the primary server fails) and *fail back* (the process of transferring call control to the primary server when it is restored) is also known as *redundancy*. CallManager enables you to have redundant servers to maintain call processing and call features if a primary server fails; if the server on which a service is running fails, however, there is no redundancy. The service too fails.

Redundancy for your services needs to be provided externally. The only protection against failed services is to practice standard server and network techniques for redundancy. Because the system utilizes the Internet protocol (IP), you can take advantage of existing Internet redundancy schemes, such as round robin domain name system (DNS) or clustering a server using Windows 2000 Advanced Server or any other operating system that supports redundant Web services. You can also use Cisco LocalDirector and Cisco DistributedDirector.

Conclusion

In this chapter, you learned about many of the basic elements of developing a phone service, including (but not limited to):

- Architectural information
- HTTP client and server
- Push and Pull
- URIs
- Redirecting the **i** button
- Security
- Authentication
- Redundancy

The next chapter provides detailed information about the Cisco IP Phone XML objects and tags.

CHAPTER 4

Using Cisco IP Phone XML Objects and Tags

Creating interactive service applications is relatively simple once you master the XML objects and tags defined for Cisco IP Phones and the behavior that each XML object generates. The important thing to understand about services is that the phone does not have any concept of a state when it loads an XML page. Cisco IP Phones can use HTTP to load a page of content in many different places, starting with the pressing of the **services** button. Regardless of what causes the phone to load a page, the phone always behaves appropriately once it loads a page.

What is the appropriate behavior? That depends solely on the type of data that has been delivered in the page. This chapter discusses the supported XML display objects and how they work with Cisco IP Phones.

The Web server must deliver the XML pages with a multipurpose Internet mail extensions (MIME) type of text/xml. The exact mechanism required varies according to the type of Web server you are using and the server side mechanism you are using to create your pages—for example, static files, JavaScript, CGI, and so on.

This chapter provides definitions and descriptions of each Cisco IP Phone XML object:

- CiscoIPPhoneMenu
- CiscoIPPhoneText
- CiscoIPPhoneInput
- CiscoIPPhoneDirectory
- CiscoIPPhoneImage
- CiscoIPPhoneGraphicMenu
- CiscoIPPhoneIconMenu
- CiscoIPPhoneExecute
- CiscoIPPhoneResponse
- CiscoIPPhoneError

Using Soft Keys and URLs/URIs

Soft keys can be embedded in any Cisco IP Phone XML object except CiscoIPPhoneResponse and CiscoIPPhoneExecute. The soft keys that display on the phone vary depending on the XML object in use. You can supply soft keys for your service by creating your own list of soft keys, which can include native soft keys such as **Exit** or **Cancel**. The soft keys that are available for individual XML objects provide specific functionality for the IP phone. For example, the CiscoIPPhoneDirectory object contains a soft key that when pressed causes the phone to dial a directory number. You can associate a URL or URI to a soft key. When pressed, the soft key invokes the associated action; for example, if it is a URL, it requests that URL. If it is a URI, the specified URI is executed. Later in this chapter we will discuss the soft keys available for each XML object.

If you want to add new soft keys to an XML object or re-use existing soft keys provided by that object, you must redefine all soft keys in that object. For example, in the CiscoIPPhoneMenu object, the soft keys **Select** (position 1) and **Exit** (position 3) are automatically provided for you. Position 2 is blank. If all you want to do is change the word "Select" to "Choose," you have to redefine both soft keys. So the soft keys would be as follows: Choose (position 1) with a URL of SoftKey:Select and Exit (position 3) with a URL of SoftKey:Exit. Soft key positions that are not defined, such as position 2 in the preceding example, are simply blank. This is shown in the following code sample, excerpted from a XML object.

```
<SoftKeyItem>
   <Name>Choose</Name>
   <URL>SoftKey:Select</URL>
   <Position>1</Position>
</SoftKeyItem>
<SoftKeyItem>
   <Name>Exit</Name>
   <URL>SoftKey:Exit</URL>
   <Position>3</Position>
</SoftKeyItem>
```

You can code up to eight soft keys for each XML object. When needed, the Cisco IP Phone automatically inserts the **more** soft key. If you place a soft key in position 5 or higher, **more** soft key(s) are automatically provided. Remember that when choosing soft key placement the position you specify might change depending on the positions of other specified soft keys. For example, a soft key in position 4 would normally appear on the first page. But if there is a soft key in position 5 or higher, the original position 4 soft key is displaced by the **more** soft key and pushed onto the second page. Up to two **more** soft keys enable up to eight soft keys. Figure 4-1 shows the placement of the eight possible soft keys.

All user-visible XML objects, such as CiscoIPPhoneDirectory, automatically include soft keys. You can view the native soft keys for each XML object in the Definition section of each object. You can use the default soft keys or define a custom set.

Figure 4-1   *Soft Key Positioning*

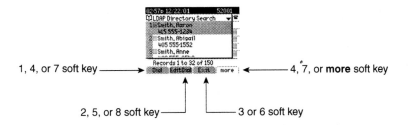

1, 4, or 7 soft key ——————→   ←———— 4, 7, or **more** soft key

2, 5, or 8 soft key ————┘   └———— 3 or 6 soft key

The `SoftKeyItem` tag includes the following tags:

- **Name**—the name you want to display on the soft key; an ANSI string (256 characters, numbered 0 to 255) up to 32 characters.

- **URL**—the URL or URI for the Cisco IP Phone object you want to display when the user presses the soft key; an ANSI string up to 256 characters.

- **Position**—the numerical position of the soft key from 1 to 8. Figure 4-1 detailed the position numbers.

The URL tag accepts URLs or URIs. Generic URIs that can be used in place of URLs is as follows:

- `Dial:xxxxx`—Where *xxxxx* represents the number to be dialed; use this tag to cause the phone to dial the *xxxxx* digit string.

- `EditDial:xxxxx`—Where *xxxxx* represents the number the user can edit; use this tag to enable a user to edit the specified digit string and then dial it. (The user can cause the edited number to be dialed by going off-hook.)

- `Init:CallHistory`—Use this tag to clear the call history list for the internal directories for Missed Calls, Placed Calls, or Received Calls.

- `Key`—Use this tag to electronically cause the same action as if you were physically pushing the specified button. Table 4-1 shows the `Key` URIs.

TIP   **Exit** and **Cancel** perform basically the same function—redisplaying the previously cached Cisco IP Phone object. Use the **Exit** soft key instead of **Cancel** if you know there is not an object in cache to redisplay. Use **Cancel** when you want to cancel the user input and allow the user to page back through previously cached objects. For guidance, consider how the native soft keys are used.

Table 4-1 *Key Tags*

URI	Description
`Key:Line1` through `Key:Line34`	Presses lines 1 through lines 34. • Cisco IP Phone 7940 uses `Key:Line1` through `Key:Line2` • Cisco IP Phone 7960 uses `Key:Line1` through `Key:Line6` • Cisco IP Phone 7914 Expansion Modules attached to a Cisco IP Phone 7960 uses `Key:Line7` through `Key:Line20` for lines on the first 7914; the second 7914 (attached to the first 7914 module) use `Key:Line21` through `Key:Line34`
`Key:KeyPad0` through `Key:KeyPad9`	Presses the specified number; for example, `Key:KeyPad4` presses the number four key on the phone's dial pad.
`Key:Soft1` through `Key:Soft4`	Presses the soft keys numbered from left to right.
`Key:KeyPadStar`	Presses the star (or asterisk) key.
`Key:KeyPadPound`	Presses the pound (or number sign) key.
`Key:VolDwn`	Presses the **Volume Down** button.
`Key:VolUp`	Presses the **Volume Up** button.
`Key:Headset`	Presses the **HEADSET** button.
`Key:Speaker`	Presses the **SPEAKER** button.
`Key:Mute`	Presses the **MUTE** button.
`Key:Info`	Presses the **i** button.
`Key:Messages`	Presses the **messages** button.
`Key:Services`	Presses the **services** button.
`Key:Directory`	Presses the **directories** button.
`Key:Settings`	Presses the **settings** button.
`Key:NavUp`	Presses the rocker bar down.
`Key:NavDwn`	Presses the rocker bar up.

Understanding Objects

Many objects are similar in their design. As you learn about the objects, notice the design pattern and relationships among the objects. For example, the CiscoIPPhoneGraphicMenu object is a combination of the CiscoIPPhoneImage and CiscoIPPhoneMenu objects.

All `MenuItems`, `SoftKeyItems`, `InputItems`, `IconItems`, and so on behave the same for all XML objects that include those items. Once you understand how those elements work in any one object, you already understand how the element works in a different object. Understanding the similar elements of different objects helps you learn how to use new objects more quickly when they are introduced.

To provide a complete reference for each XML object, the elements for each object are described in the section for each object; this results in some duplication of the same information. The object, however, is described in its entirety for your reference.

CiscoIPPhoneMenu

Use the CiscoIPPhoneMenu object to build a menu in the phone. A menu comprises a list of text items. Users select individual menu items by moving the rocker key and pressing the **Select** soft key. Users can also enter the index number using the phone's keypad. Once the user selects a menu option, the phone acts on the contents of the URL field associated with the selected MenuItem. Press the **settings** button on a Cisco IP Phone to see an example of a menu, as shown in Figure 4-2.

Figure 4-2   *Menu Example*

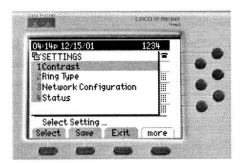

Definition

The following code example shows the structure of the CiscoIPPhoneMenu object and the tags that are used with it.

```
<CiscoIPPhoneMenu>
  <Title>Title text goes here</Title>
  <Prompt>Prompt text goes here</Prompt>
  <MenuItem>
    <Name>The name of each menu item</Name>
    <URL>The URL associated with the menu item</URL>
  </MenuItem>
  <SoftKeyItem>
    <Name>Name of soft key</Name>
    <URL>URL or URI of soft key</URL>
    <Position>Position information of the soft key</Position>
  </SoftKeyItem>
</CiscoIPPhoneMenu>
```

You can specify a title and prompt for the menu. The Title defines text that displays at the top of the display plane. If a Title is not specified, the title area of the display plane displays the Name of the previously selected MenuItem. If there is no MenuItem name to display, the default name of the plane is displayed, such as SERVICES. The Prompt tag defines text that displays at the bottom of the display plane. If a Prompt is not specified, the prompt area of the display plane is cleared.

A maximum of 100 MenuItem tags are allowed. For each MenuItem in the object, you can specify a name and an associated URL. URL tags also accept URIs. Up to three lines in a MenuItem are permitted if you embed a carriage return and line feed. For example, a person's name can display on the first line and that person's phone number can be displayed on the second line.

You can also specify soft keys for this object. See "Using Soft Keys and URLs/URIs" for general information about soft keys. Table 4-2 defines the default soft keys provided for this object.

Table 4-2 *CiscoIPPhoneMenu Soft Keys and Description*

Soft Key	Description	URIs
Select	Executes the contents of the URL field assigned to the selected MenuItem.	SoftKey:Select
Exit	Redisplays the previously cached object. If there is no previous URL in the phone's URL history, this soft key exits the SERVICES window.	SoftKey:Exit

CiscoIPPhoneText

The CiscoIPPhoneText object is used to display ordinary 8-bit ASCII text on the phone display. The text message must not contain any control characters, except for carriage returns, line feeds, and tabs. The phone's firmware controls all other pagination and word-wrap issues. Figure 4-3 provides an example of a text display. The title, *CSCO – Yahoo Finance*, appears at the top above the text.

Figure 4-3 *Text Example*

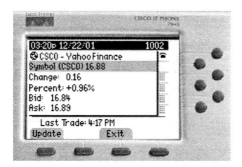

Definition

The following code example shows the structure of the CiscoIPPhoneText object and the tags that can be used with it.

```
<CiscoIPPhoneText>
  <Title>Title text goes here</Title>
  <Prompt>The prompt text goes here</Prompt>
  <Text>The text to be displayed as the message body goes here</Text>
  <SoftKeyItem>
    <Name>Name of soft key</Name>
    <URL>URL or URI of soft key</URL>
    <Position>Position information of the soft key</Position>
  </SoftKeyItem>
</CiscoIPPhoneText>
```

You can specify a title and prompt for this object. The Title defines text that displays at the top of the display plane. If a Title is not specified, the title area of the display plane displays the Name of the previously selected MenuItem. If there is no MenuItem name to display, the default name of the plane is displayed, such as SERVICES. The Prompt tag defines text that displays at the bottom of the display plane. If a Prompt is not specified, the prompt area of the display plane is cleared.

NOTE   Non-XML text—This chapter only describes the supported Cisco IP Phone XML objects. You can also deliver plain text via HTTP. Pages delivered as MIME type text/html behave exactly the same as XML pages of object CiscoIPPhoneText. The only important difference is that you cannot include a title or prompt.

NOTE   Keypad navigation—Cisco IP Phones allow navigation to a specific line in a menu by pressing numeric keys. When a menu is on the display, the far-left of each menu option displays the actual number to be pressed.

When normal text displays, the numbers are not shown on the left side of the screen, but the navigation capability is still present. So a carefully written text service display can take advantage of this capability.

You can also specify soft keys for this object. See "Using Soft Keys and URLs/URIs" for general information about soft keys. Table 4-3 defines the default soft keys provided for this object.

Table 4-3 *CiscoIPPhoneText Soft Keys and Description*

Soft Key	Description	URIs
Update	Reloads the current object. If an HTTP Refresh header was specified with a URL and a timer value of zero, the phone navigates to the URL when the **Update** soft key is pressed.	`SoftKey:Update`
Exit	Redisplays the previously cached object. If there is no previous URL in the phone's URL history, this soft key exits the SERVICES window.	`SoftKey:Exit`

CiscoIPPhoneInput

When a phone receives a CiscoIPPhoneInput object, it constructs an input form and displays it on the phone. The user then enters data into each of the `InputItem` instances and sends the data a `QueryStringParam` to the target URL. Figure 4-4 shows a sample display that is receiving input from a user.

Figure 4-4 *Sample User Input Display*

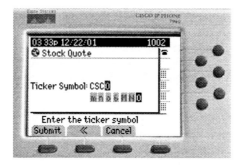

Definition

The following code example shows the structure of the CiscoIPPhoneInput object and the tags that can be used with it.

```
<CiscoIPPhoneInput>
  <Title>Directory title goes here</Title>
  <Prompt>Prompt text goes here</Prompt>
  <URL>The target URL for the completed input goes here</URL>
  <InputItem>
    <DisplayName>Name of the input field to display</DisplayName>
    <QueryStringParam>The parameter to be added to the target URL</QueryStringParam>
    <InputFlags>The flag specifying the type of allowable input</InputFlags>
    <DefaultValue>The default display name</DefaultValue>
  </InputItem>
  <SoftKeyItem>
    <Name>Name of soft key</Name>
```

```
       <URL>URL or URI of soft key</URL>
       <Position>Position information of the soft key</Position>
     </SoftKeyItem>
   </CiscoIPPhoneInput>
```

You can specify a title and prompt for this object. The `Title` defines text that displays at the top of the display plane. If a `Title` is not specified, the title area of the display plane displays the `Name` of the previously selected `MenuItem`. If there is no `MenuItem` name to display, the default name of the plane is displayed, such as SERVICES. The `Prompt` tag defines text that displays at the bottom of the display plane. If a `Prompt` is not specified, the prompt area of the display plane is cleared.

The `URL` tag defines the URL to which the input results are sent. The `URL` tag can take a URL. The actual HTTP request sent to this server is the URL with a list of parameters appended to it as a query string. The parameters are `InputItem` pairs, one for each `InputItem`.

The `InputItem` tag defines each item in the list. You can include up to five `InputItem` tags. The `InputItem` tag provides the following tags:

- `DisplayName`
- `QueryStringParam`
- `InputFlags`
- `DefaultValue` (optional)

The `DisplayName` tag provides the label text for that particular item. In a directory search where the user can specify first name and last name, the content of one of the `DisplayName` tags would be **First**, for example. The `QueryStringParam` tag provides the name of the parameter appended to the URL when it is sent out after input is complete. Table 4-4 describes the set of predefined input flags provided by the `InputFlags` tag.

Table 4-4   *Input Flags and Description*

Input Flag	Description
A	Plain ASCII text—The phone's keypad is used to enter text consisting of uppercase and lowercase letters, numbers, and special characters.
T	Telephone number—Numbers on the phone's keypad, #, and * are the only acceptable input for this field.
N	Numeric—Numbers are the only acceptable input.
E	Equation—The acceptable input includes keypad numbers (0–9) and special math symbols provided when the user presses the * or # keys.
U	Uppercase—Uppercase letters are the only acceptable input.
L	Lowercase—Lowercase letters are the only acceptable input.

continues

Table 4-4 *Input Flags and Description (Continued)*

Input Flag	Description
P	Password field—Individual characters display as they are keyed in using the standard keypad-repeat entry mode, so that users can see the characters while they page through them. When the user stops on the character, it is added to the input data as an asterisk, allowing for privacy of the entered value.

> **NOTE** P is the only InputFlag that works as a modifier with any other input flag. For example, specify a value of AP in the InputFlag field to use plain ASCII as the input type and to mask the input as a password using an asterisk (*).

The DefaultValue tag is used to set the default value to be displayed for the InputItem.

You can also specify soft keys for this object. See "Using Soft Keys and URLs/URIs" for general information about soft keys. Table 4-5 defines the default soft keys provided for this object.

Table 4-5 *CiscoIPPhoneInput Soft Keys and Description*

Soft Key	Description	URIs
Submit	The form data is added to the URL as a QueryStringParam and sent as a request to the Web server.	SoftKey:Submit
<<	Backspace within the active input field.	SoftKey:<<
Cancel	Cancels the user input and redisplays the previously cached object.	SoftKey:Cancel

CiscoIPPhoneDirectory

The CiscoIPPhoneDirectory object is already incorporated in the phone to support the Directory operation of Cisco IP Phones (accessed using the **directories** button). Because the phones already have a directory built-in, you can use this object to add more directories to the list of default directories already provided on the phones. Users press the **directories** button instead of the **services** button to access directories you build with this object. This object also works for services; it has different behavior when used in a service than when used in a directory. Refer to Chapter 8, "Building a Directory" for clarification of the differences. Figure 4-5 shows an example of a directory.

Figure 4-5 *Directory Example*

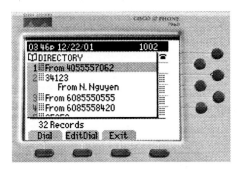

Definition

The following code example shows the structure of the CiscoIPPhoneDirectory object and the tags that can be used with it.

```
<CiscoIPPhoneDirectory>
  <Title>Directory title goes here</Title>
  <Prompt>Prompt text goes here</Prompt>
  <DirectoryEntry>
    <Name>The name of the directory entry</Name>
    <Telephone>The telephone number for the entry</Telephone>
  </DirectoryEntry>
  <SoftKeyItem>
    <Name>Name of soft key</Name>
    <URL>URL or URI of soft key</URL>
    <Position>Position information of the soft key</Position>
  </SoftKeyItem>
</CiscoIPPhoneDirectory>
```

You can specify a title and prompt for this object. The Title defines text that displays at the top of the display plane. If a Title is not specified, the title area of the display plane displays the Name of the previously selected MenuItem. If there is no MenuItem name to display, the default name of the plane is displayed, such as SERVICES. The Prompt tag defines text that displays at the bottom of the display plane. If a Prompt is not specified, the prompt area of the display plane is cleared.

A single CiscoIPPhoneDirectory object can contain a maximum of 32 DirectoryEntry tags. If more than 32 tags must be returned, use multiple CiscoIPPhoneDirectory objects in subsequent HTTP requests. The DirectoryEntry tag provides the following tags:

- **Name**—The name for the associated telephone number; an ANSI string of up to 32 characters.

- **Telephone**—The telephone number; an ANSI string of up to 32 characters.

You can also specify soft keys for this object. See "Using Soft Keys and URLs/URIs" for general information about soft keys. Table 4-6 defines the default soft keys provided for this object.

Table 4-6 *CiscoIPPhoneDirectory Soft Keys and Description*

Soft Key	Description	URIs
Dial	Causes the phone to activate a line and dial the displayed number.	`SoftKey:Dial`
EditDial	Enables the user to add or remove digits in the displayed number. The user can cause the edited number to be dialed by going off-hook.	`SoftKey:EditDial`
Cancel	Cancels the user input and redisplays the previously cached object.	`SoftKey:Cancel`

Custom Directories

Use the enterprise parameter, URL Directories, in Cisco CallManager Administration (**System > Enterprise Parameters**) and Cisco IP Phone XML objects to display custom directories. The URL Directories enterprise parameter points to a URL that returns a CiscoIPPhoneMenu object that extends the **directories** menu. The request for URL Directories must return a valid CiscoIPPhoneMenu object, even if it has no `DirectoryEntry` tags.

You can display multiple CiscoIPPhoneDirectory objects by specifying an HTTP refresh header that points to the URL of the next individual directory object, which the user accesses by pressing the **Next** soft key on the phone.

CiscoIPPhoneImage

Cisco phones have a bit-mapped display with a 133x65-pixel plane. Each pixel has four grayscale settings. A value of three (3) displays as black, and a value of zero (0) displays as white.

NOTE The palette is inverted because the phone uses a liquid crystal display (LCD).

The CiscoIPPhoneImage object lets you use the phone's display to present graphics to the user. Figure 4-6 shows an example of how this looks on the phone.

Figure 4-6   *Graphics Display on Cisco IP Phone*

Definition

The following code example shows the structure of the CiscoIPPhoneImage object and the tags that can be used with it.

```
<CiscoIPPhoneImage>
  <Title>Image title goes here</Title>
  <Prompt>Prompt text goes here</Prompt>
  <LocationX>Position information of graphic</LocationX>
  <LocationY>Position information of graphic</LocationY>
  <Width>Size information for the graphic</Width>
  <Height>Size information for the graphic</Height>
  <Depth>Number of bits per pixel</Depth>
  <Data>Packed pixel data</Data>
  <SoftKeyItem>
    <Name>Name of soft key</Name>
    <URL>URL of soft key</URL>
    <Position>Numerical position of the soft key</Position>
  </SoftKeyItem>
</CiscoIPPhoneImage>
```

You can specify a title and prompt for this object. The Title defines text that displays at the top of the display plane. If a Title is not specified, the title area of the display plane displays the Name of the previously selected MenuItem. If there is no MenuItem name to display, the default name of the plane is displayed, such as SERVICES. The Prompt tag defines text that displays at the bottom of the display plane. If a Prompt is not specified, the prompt area of the display plane is cleared.

Use LocationX and LocationY to position the graphic on the phone's display. The upper-left corner of the graphic is positioned at the pixel defined by these two parameters. Setting the X and Y location values to (0,0) positions the graphic at the upper-left corner of the display. Setting the X and Y location values to (-1,-1) centers the graphic in the services plane of the phone's display.

Width and Height define the number of pixels wide and the number of pixels high. If the values specified do not match the pixel stream specified in the object, the results are unpredictable and generally incorrect.

Depth specifies the number of bits per pixel. Cisco IP Phone models 7960 and 7940 only support a value of 1 or 2. Future Cisco IP Phones might have other values.

The Data tag defines a string of hexadecimal digits that contains the packed value of the pixels in the display. For 2-bit images in the phones, each pixel has only four possible values, which means that you can pack four pixels into a single byte. For 1-bit images in the phones, each pixel has eight possible values, which means that you can pack eight pixels into a single byte. Each byte is represented as a pair of hexadecimal digits.

Figure 4-7 provides an example of the mechanics of pixel packing. Scanning from left to right in the display, Figure 4-6 shows the process for packing pixel values. First, the pixels are converted to two-bit binary numbers. Then, the binary pairs are re-ordered in sets of four to create a single re-ordered byte, which is represented by two hexadecimal digits.

Figure 4-7 *Packed Pixel Translation Example*

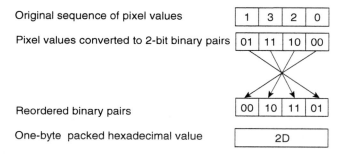

The following XML code defines a CiscoIPPhoneImage object that displays the sequence of pixels shown in Figure 4-7 as a graphic positioned at the center of the phone display:

```
<CiscoIPPhoneImage>
  <Title/>
  <Prompt/>
  <LocationX>-1</LocationX>
  <LocationY>-1</LocationY>
  <Width>4</Width>
  <Height>1</Height>
  <Depth>2</Depth>
  <Data>2D</Data>
  <SoftKeyItem>
    <Name></Name>
    <URL></URL>
    <Position></Position>
  </SoftKeyItem>
</CiscoIPPhoneImage>
```

The graphic display consists of a contiguous stream of hexadecimal digits, with no spaces or other separators. If the number of pixels to be displayed is not an even multiple of four, pad the end of the pixel data with blank (zero value) pixels so that the data is packed correctly. The phone ignores the padded data.

TIP   When displaying graphics on a Cisco IP Phone, the plane dedicated to services is always cleared before a graphic image is displayed. If a service has text or other information that must be preserved, it must be redrawn as part of the graphic. This excludes the title area. If the title is to be hidden, the graphic must be large enough to cover it.

You can also specify soft keys for this object. See "Using Soft Keys and URLs/URIs" for general information about soft keys. Table 4-7 defines the default soft keys provided for this object.

Table 4-7   *CiscoIPPhoneImage Soft Keys and Description*

Soft Key	Description	URIs
Update	Reloads the current object. If an HTTP Refresh header was specified with a URL and a timer value of zero, the phone navigates to the URL when the **Update** soft key is pressed.	SoftKey:Update
Exit	Redisplays the previously cached object. If there is no previous URL in the phone's URL history, this soft key exits the SERVICES window.	SoftKey:Exit

CiscoIPPhoneGraphicMenu

Graphic menus serve the same purpose as text menus—they enable a user to select a URL from a list. Use graphic menus in situations where the items might not be easy to display in a text list. For example, users might prefer to have their choices presented in a non-ASCII character set such as Kanji or Arabic. Figure 4-8 shows a graphic menu on a phone.

Figure 4-8   *Graphic Menu on Cisco IP Phone Display*

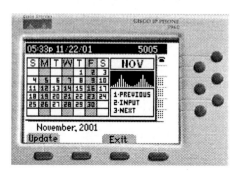

In these cases, the information is presented as a bit-mapped graphic. The user then enters a menu selection by using the keypad to enter a number that corresponds to the menu option.

Definition

The following code example shows the structure of the CiscoIPPhoneGraphicMenu object and the tags that can be used with it.

```
<CiscoIPPhoneGraphicMenu>
  <Title>Menu title goes here</Title>
  <Prompt>Prompt text goes here</Prompt>
  <LocationX>Position information of graphic</LocationX>
  <LocationY>Position information of graphic</LocationY>
  <Width>Size information for the graphic</Width>
  <Height>Size information for the graphic</Height>
  <Depth>Number of bits per pixel</Depth>
  <Data>Packed pixel data</Data>
  <MenuItem>
    <Name>The name of each menu item</Name>
    <URL>The URL associated with the menu item</URL>
  </MenuItem>
  <SoftKeyItem>
    <Name>Name of soft key</Name>
    <URL>URL of soft key</URL>
    <Position>Numerical position of the soft key</Position>
  </SoftKeyItem>
</CiscoIPPhoneGraphicMenu>
```

You can specify a title and prompt for this object. The Title defines text that displays at the top of the display plane. If a Title is not specified, the title area of the display plane displays the Name of the previously selected MenuItem. If there is no MenuItem name to display, the default name of the plane is displayed, such as SERVICES. The Prompt tag defines text that displays at the bottom of the display plane. If a Prompt is not specified, the prompt area of the display plane is cleared.

Use LocationX and LocationY to position the graphic on the phone's display. The upper-left corner of the graphic is positioned at the pixel defined by these two parameters. Setting the X and Y location values to (0,0) positions the graphic at the upper-left corner of the display.

Setting the X and Y location values to (-1,-1) centers the graphic in the services pane of the phone's display.

Width and Height define the number of pixels wide and the number of pixels high. If the values specified do not match the pixel stream specified in the object, the results are unpredictable and generally incorrect.

Depth specifies the number of bits per pixel. Cisco IP Phone models 7960 and 7940 only support a value of 1 or 2. Future Cisco IP Phones might have other values.

The Data tag defines a string of hexadecimal digits that contains the packed value of the pixels in the display. For 2-bit images in the phones, each pixel has only four possible values, which means that you can pack four pixels into a single byte. For 1-bit images in the phones, each pixel has eight possible values, which means that you can pack eight pixels into a single byte. Each byte is represented as a pair of hexadecimal digits.

Figure 4-7 provided an example of the mechanics of pixel packing.

MenuItem instances in the graphic menu have a name, just like their text menu counterparts. The Name of the MenuItem provides the default title used when the URL for the selected item is loaded. If the loaded page has a Title of its own, that is used instead. Unlike other objects with the MenuItem tag, you can have only 12 MenuItem objects in a CiscoIPPhoneGraphic object. You can have up to three lines in a MenuItem if you embed a carriage return or line feed. The URL tag can take URLs or URIs.

You can also specify soft keys for this object. See "Using Soft Keys and URLs/URIs" for general information about soft keys. Table 4-8 defines the default soft keys provided for this object.

Table 4-8   *CiscoIPPhoneGraphicMenu Soft Keys and Description*

Soft Key	Description	URIs
Update	Reloads the current object. If an HTTP Refresh header was specified with a URL and a timer value of zero, the phone navigates to the URL when the **Update** soft key is pressed.	SoftKey:Update
Exit	Redisplays the previously cached object. If there is no previous URL in the phone's URL history, this soft key exits the SERVICES window.	SoftKey:Exit

CiscoIPPhoneIconMenu

An icon menu on the phone comprises a list of MenuItem instances, one item per MenuItem. The menu can have two optional displayable items: icons and/or text. Users select individual menu items by moving the rocker key and pressing the **Select** soft key or pressing the number associated with a menu item. Press the **directories** button, then **1** to see an icon menu in action under the Missed Calls feature. The dial pad icon to the left of the phone number is created using the CiscoIPPhoneIconMenu object. Figure 4-2 shows an IconMenu. You can define up to ten custom icons and assign them to MenuItem instances.

Definition

The following code example shows the structure of the CiscoIPPhoneIconMenu object and the tags that can be used with it.

```
<CiscoIPPhoneIconMenu>
  <Title>Title text goes here</Title>
  <Prompt>Prompt text goes here</Prompt>
  <MenuItem>
    <Name>The name of each menu item</Name>
    <URL>The URL associated with the menu item</URL>
    <IconIndex> Indicates what Icon item to display</IconIndex>
  </MenuItem>
    <IconItem>
    <Index>The numeric identifier of the custom icon </IconIndex>
    <Width>Size information for the graphic</Width>
    <Height>Size information for the graphic</Height>
    <Depth>Number of bits per pixel</Depth>
    <Data>Packed pixel data</Data>
  </IconItem>
  <SoftKeyItem>
    <Name>Name of soft key</Name>
    <URL>URL of soft key</URL>
    <Position>Numerical position of the soft key</Position>
  </SoftKeyItem>
</CiscoIPPhoneIconMenu
```

You can specify a title and prompt for this object. The Title defines text that displays at the top of the display plane. If a Title is not specified, the title area of the display plane displays the Name of the previously selected MenuItem. If there is no MenuItem name to display, the default name of the plane is displayed, such as SERVICES. The Prompt tag defines text that displays at the bottom of the display plane. If a Prompt is not specified, the prompt area of the display plane is cleared.

Width and Height define the number of pixels wide and the number of pixels high. If the values specified do not match the pixel stream specified in the object, the results are unpredictable and generally incorrect.

Depth specifies the number of bits per pixel. Cisco IP Phone models 7960 and 7940 only support a value of 1 or 2. Future Cisco IP Phones might have other values.

The Data tag defines a string of hexadecimal digits that contains the packed value of the pixels in the display. For 2-bit images in the phones, each pixel has only four possible values, which means that you can pack four pixels into a single byte. For 1-bit images in the phones, each pixel has eight possible values, which means that you can pack eight pixels into a single byte. Each byte is represented as a pair of hexadecimal digits.

Figure 4-7 provided an example of the mechanics of pixel packing.

MenuItem instances in the icon menu have a name, just like the text menu counterparts. The Name of the MenuItem provides the default title used when the URL for the selected item is loaded. If the loaded page has a `Title` of its own, that title is used instead. Cisco IP Phones allow a maximum of 100 `MenuItem` instances. You can have up to three lines in a `MenuItem` if you embed a carriage return or line feed. The `URL` tag can take URLs or URIs. You can have up to 10 instances of `IconItem`.

The behavior of the phone when an icon menu is loaded is exactly the same as the menus provided by Cisco—like those you can see when you press the **settings** button (as shown in Figure 4-2). The user navigates through the list of menu items and eventually selects one using either the **Select** soft key or the phone's keypad. Once the user selects a menu option, the phone generates an HTTP request for the page with the `URL` associated with the `MenuItem`. Figure 4-9 shows an example of a `CiscoIPPhoneIconMenu` object in action.

Figure 4-9   `CiscoIPPhoneIconMenu` *Example*

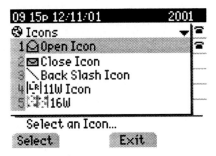

You can also specify soft keys for this object. See "Using Soft Keys and URLs/URIs" for general information about soft keys. Table 4-9 defines the default soft keys provided for this object.

Table 4-9   *CiscoIPPhoneIconMenu Soft Keys and Description*

Soft Key	Description	URIs
Select	Executes the contents of the `URL` field assigned to the selected `MenuItem`.	`SoftKey:Select`
Exit	Redisplays the previously cached object. If there is no previous URL in the phone's URL history, this soft key exits the SERVICES window.	`SoftKey:Exit`

CiscoIPPhoneExecute

Use the CiscoIPPhoneExecute object to "Push" a request to the phone via HTTP POST. This object tells the phone to execute the contents of the `ExecuteItem` instances in the object.

The case-sensitive post URL is `http://x.x.x.x/CGI/Execute`. The form that you post should have a form field called `XML` that contains the XML object that you are posting. You can post multiple requests in a single object and you receive responses for each.

Definition

The following code example shows the structure of the CiscoIPPhoneExecute object and its attributes.

```
<CiscoIPPhoneExecute>
  <ExecuteItem URL="The action you want the phone to take"/>
</CiscoIPPhoneExecute>
```

Single or double quotes can be used for the `ExecuteItem` attributes. Cisco IP Phones allow a maximum of three instances of `ExecuteItem` in one CiscoIPPhoneExecute object. Of the three items, only one can be a URL. The other two are for URIs and are used mainly for setting up transit (TX) and receive (RX) streams. You can learn more about the CiscoIPPhoneExecute object in Chapter 10, "Techniques for Advanced Services."

NOTE   If you examine the Cisco IP Phone Services schema, which defines the objects and tags, you may notice a Priority field. We do not include it here because it is not implemented and may be removed in future releases of the XML schema."

CiscoIPPhoneResponse

The CiscoIPPhoneResponse object is returned if you "Push" using HTTP POST. This object indicates the status and any additional return data for each item.

The case-sensitive post URL is `http://x.x.x.x/CGI/Execute`. The form that you POST should have a field called `XML` whose value contains the object you want to post. You can post multiple requests in a single object and get responses for each.

Definition

The following code example shows the structure of the CiscoIPPhoneResponse object and its attributes.

```
<CiscoIPPhoneResponse>
  <ResponseItem Status="the success or failure of the action" Data="the information
  associated with the request"URL=" the URL or URI specified in the Execute object"/>
</CiscoIPPhoneResponse>
```

There will be as many instances of `ResponseItem` as you send instances of `ExecuteItem`. The order differs according to completion time. The `URL` specifies the URL or URI that was sent with the request. The `Data` field contains any special data for the item. `Status` specifies a status code where zero (0) indicates no errors when processing the CiscoIPPhoneExecute object. If an execution error occurs, a CiscoIPPhoneError object is returned.

CiscoIPPhoneError

Error information is returned in a CiscoIPPhoneError object. Table 4-10 shows a list of possible error codes.

Table 4-10   *Error Codes*

Error Number	Description
1	Error parsing CiscoIPPhoneExecute object
2	Error framing CiscoIPPhoneResponse object
3	Internal file error
4	Authentication error

Definition

The following code example shows the structure of the CiscoIPPhoneError object.

```
<CiscoIPPhoneError Number="x"/>
```

XML Considerations

In your XML display definitions, do not include any tags other than those defined in this chapter. See 9=Chapter 2, "The Basics."

Mandatory Escape Sequences

By XML convention, the XML parser also requires that you escape a few special characters. Table 4-11 lists characters and their escape values.

Table 4-11   *XML Characters and their Escape Values*

Character	Name	Escape Sequence
&	Ampersand	&amp;
"	Quote	&quot;
'	Apostrophe	&apos;
<	Left angle bracket	&lt;
>	Right angle bracket	&gt;

Escaping text can be tedious, but some authoring tools or scripting languages can automate this task. See Chapter 6, "XML Conventions," to learn more about escape sequences.

Cisco IP Phone XML Object Quick Reference

Use Tables 4-12 through 4-21 as a quick reference for the XML objects discussed in this chapter.

Table 4-12 *CiscoIPPhoneMenu Object Quick Reference*

Definition	Range	SoftKey:URIs

`<CiscoIPPhoneMenu>`
`<Title>Title text goes here</Title>`
`<Prompt>Prompt text goes here</Prompt>`
`<MenuItem>`
`<Name>The name of each menu item</Name>`
`<URL>The URL associated with the menu item</URL>`
`</MenuItem>`
`<SoftKeyItem>`
`<Name>Name of soft key</Name>`
`<URL>URL or URI of soft key</URL>`
`<Position>Position information of the soft key</Position>`
`</SoftKeyItem>`
`</CiscoIPPhoneMenu>`
	CiscoIPPhoneMenu
	Title: ANSI string up to 32 characters
	Prompt: ANSI string up to 32 characters
	
	Up to 100 instances of MenuItem
	Name: ANSI string up to 64 characters
	URL: ANSI string up to 256 characters
	
	Up to 8 instances of SoftKeyItem
	Name: ANSI string up to 32 characters
	URL: ANSI string up to 256 characters
	Position: Single-digit numeric value from 1 to 8
		SoftKey:Select
		SoftKey:Exit

Table 4-13 *CiscoIPPhoneText Object Quick Reference*

Definition	Range	SoftKey:URIs

`<CiscoIPPhoneText>`
`<Title>Title text goes here</Title>`
`<Prompt>The prompt text goes here</Prompt>`
`<Text>The text to be displayed as the message body goes here</Text>`
`<SoftKeyItem>`
`<Name>Name of soft key</Name>`
`<URL>URL or URI of soft key</URL>`
`<Position>Position information of the soft key</Position>`
`</SoftKeyItem>`
`</CiscoIPPhoneText>`
	CiscoIPPhoneText
	Title: ANSI string up to 32 characters
	Prompt: ANSI string up to 32 characters
	Text: ANSI string up to 4000 characters
	
	Up to 8 instances of SoftKeyItem
	Name: ANSI string up to 32 characters
	URL: ANSI string up to 256 characters
	Position: Single-digit numeric value from 1 to 8
		SoftKey:Update
		SoftKey:Exit

Table 4-14   *CiscoIPPhoneInput Object Quick Reference*

Definition	Range	SoftKey:URIs

`<CiscoIPPhoneInput>`
`<Title>Directory title goes here</Title>`
`<Prompt>Prompt text goes here</Prompt>`
`<URL>The target URL for the completed input goes here</URL>`
`<InputItem>`
`<DisplayName>Name of the input field to display</DisplayName>`
`<QueryStringParam>The parameter to be added to the target URL</QueryStringParam>`
`<InputFlags>The flag specifying the type of allowable input</InputFlags>`
`<DefaultValue>The default display name</DefaultValue>`
`</InputItem>`
`<SoftKeyItem>`
`<Name>Name of soft key</Name>`
`<URL>URL or URI of soft key</URL>`
`<Position>Position information of the soft key</Position>`
`</SoftKeyItem>`
`</CiscoIPPhoneInput>`
	CiscoIPPhoneInput
	Title: ANSI string up to 32 characters
	Prompt: ANSI string up to 32 characters
	URL: ANSI string up to 256 characters
	
	Up to 5 instances of InputItem
	DisplayName: ANSI string up to 32 characters
	
	QueryStringParam: ANSI string up to 32 characters
	InputFlags: ANSI string up to 3 characters
	DefaultValue: ANSI string up to 32 characters
	
	Up to 8 SoftKeyItem
	Name: ANSI string up to 32 characters
	URL: ANSI string up to 256 characters
	Position: Single-digit numeric value from 1 to 8
		SoftKey:Submit
		SoftKey:<<
		SoftKey:Cancel

Table 4-15 *CiscoIPPhoneDirectory Object Quick Reference*

Definition	Range	SoftKey:URIs

`<CiscoIPPhoneDirectory>`
`<Title>Directory title goes here</Title>`
`<Prompt>Prompt text goes here</Prompt>`
`<DirectoryEntry>`
`  <Name>the name of the directory entry</Name>`
`  <Telephone>The telephone number for the entry</Telephone>`
`</DirectoryEntry>`
`<SoftKeyItem>`
`  <Name>Name of soft key</Name>`
`  <URL>URL or URI of soft key</URL>`
`  <Position>Position information of the soft key</Position>`
`</SoftKeyItem>`
`</CiscoIPPhoneDirectory>`
	CiscoIPPhoneDirectory
	Title: ANSI string up to 32 characters
	Prompt: ANSI string up to 32 characters
	
	Up to 32 instances of DirectoryEntry
	Name: ANSI string up to 32 characters
	Telephone: ANSI string up to 32 characters
	
	Up to 8 instances of SoftKeyItem
	Name: ANSI string up to 32 characters
	URL: ANSI string up to 256 characters
	Position: Single-digit numeric value from 1 to 8
		SoftKey:Dial
		SoftKey:EditDial
		SoftKey:Cancel

Table 4-16 *CiscoIPPhoneImage Object Quick Reference*

Definition	Range	SoftKey:URIs

`<CiscoIPPhoneImage>`
`<Title>Image title goes here</Title>`
`<Prompt>Prompt text goes here</Prompt>`
`<LocationX>Position information of graphic</LocationX>`
`<LocationY>Position information of graphic</LocationY>`
`<Width>Size information for the graphic</Width>`
`<Height>Size information for the graphic</Height>`
`<Depth>Number of bits per pixel</Depth>`
`<Data>Packed pixel data</Data>`
`<SoftKeyItem>`
`  <Name>Name of soft key</Name>`
`  <URL>URL of soft key</URL>`
`  <Position>Numerical position of the soft key</Position>`
`</SoftKeyItem>`
`</CiscoIPPhoneImage>`
	CiscoIPPhoneImage
	Title: ANSI string up to 32 characters
	Prompt: ANSI string up to 32 characters
	LocationX: Numeric value from -1 to 133
	LocationY: Numeric value from -1 to 65
	Width: Numeric value from 1 to 133
	Height: Numeric value from 1 to 65
	Depth: Numeric value from 1 to 2
	Data: Hexadecimal value up to 2200
	
	Up to 8 instances of SoftKeyItem
	Name: ANSI string up to 32 characters
	URL: ANSI string up to 256 characters
	Position: Single-digit numeric value from 1 to 8
		SoftKey:Update
		SoftKey:Exit

Table 4-17   *CiscoIPPhoneGraphicMenu Object Quick Reference*

Definition	Range	SoftKey:URIs

`<CiscoIPPhoneGraphicMenu>`
`<Title>Menu title goes here</Title>`
`<Prompt>Prompt text goes here</Prompt>`
`<LocationX>Position information of graphic</LocationX>`
`<LocationY>Position information of graphic</LocationY>`
`<Width>Size information for the graphic</Width>`
`<Height>Size information for the graphic</Height>`
`<Depth>Number of bits per pixel</Depth>`
`<Data>Packed pixel data</Data>`
`<MenuItem>`
`<Name>The name of each menu item</Name>`
`<URL>The URL associated with the menu item</URL>`
`</MenuItem>`
`<SoftKeyItem>`
`<Name>Name of soft key</Name>`
`<URL>URL of soft key</URL>`
`<Position>Numerical position of the soft key</Position>`
`</SoftKeyItem>`
`</CiscoIPPhoneGraphicMenu>`
	CiscoIPPhoneGraphicMenu
	Title: ANSI string up to 32 characters
	Prompt: ANSI string up to 32 characters
	LocationX: Numeric value from -1 to 133
	LocationY: Numeric value from -1 to 65
	Width: Numeric value from 1 to 133
	Height: Numeric value from 1 to 65
	Depth: Numeric value from 1 to 2
	Data: Hexadecimal value up to 2200
	
	Up to 12 instances of MenuItem
	Name: ANSI string up to 64 characters
	URL: ANSI string up to 256 characters
	
	Up to 8 instances of SoftKeyItem
	Name: ANSI string up to 32 characters
	URL: ANSI string up to 256 characters
	Position: Single-digit numeric value from 1 to 8
		SoftKey:Update
		SoftKey:Exit

Table 4-18 *CiscoIPPhoneIconMenu Object Quick Reference*

Definition	Range	SoftKey:URIs

`<CiscoIPPhoneIconMenu>`
`<Title>Title text goes here</Title>`
`<Prompt>Prompt text goes here</Prompt>`
`<MenuItem>`
`  <Name>The name of each menu item</Name>`
`  <URL>The URL associated with the menu item</URL>`
`  <IconIndex>Indicates what Icon item to display</IconIndex>`
`</MenuItem>`
`<IconItem>`
`  <IconIndex>Numeric identifier of the custom icon</IconIndex>`
`  <Width>Size information for the graphic</Width>`
`  <Height>Size information for the graphic</Height>`
`  <Depth>Number of bits per pixel</Depth>`
`  <Data>Packed pixel data</Data>`
`</IconItem>`
`<SoftKeyItem>`
`  <Name>Name of soft key</Name>`
`  <URL>URL of soft key</URL>`
`  <Position>Numerical position of the soft key</Position>`
`</SoftKeyItem>`
`</CiscoIPPhoneIconMenu>`
	CiscoIPPhoneIconMenu
	Title: ANSI string up to 32 characters
	Prompt: ANSI string up to 32 characters
	Up to 100 instances of MenuItem
	Name: ANSI string up to 64 characters
	URL: ANSI string up to 256 characters
	IconIndex: Numeric value from 0 to 9
	Up to 10 instances of IconItem
	Index: Numeric value from 0 to 9
	Width: Numeric value from 1 to 16
	Height: Numeric value from 1 to 10
	Depth: Numeric value from 1 to 2
	Data: Hexadecimal value up to 50
	Up to 8 instances of SoftKeyItem
	Name: ANSI string up to 32 characters
	URL: ANSI string up to 256 characters
	Position: Single-digit numeric value from 1 to 8
		SoftKey:Select
		SoftKey:Exit

Table 4-19 *CiscoIPPhoneExecute Object Quick Reference*

Definition	Range	SoftKey:URIs

`<CiscoIPPhoneExecute>`
`<ExecuteItem URL="The action you want the phone to take"/>`
`</CiscoIPPhoneExecute>`
	CiscoIPPhoneIconExecute
	Up to 3 instances of ExecuteItem
	URL: ANSI string up to 256 characters	

Table 4-20 *CiscoIPPhoneResponse Object Quick Reference*

Definition	Range	SoftKey:URIs

`<CiscoIPPhoneResponse>`
`<ResponseItem Status="the success or failure of the`
`action" Data="the information associated with the`
`request" URL="the URL or URI specified in the Execute`
`object"/>`
`</CiscoIPPhoneResponse>`
	`CiscoIPPhoneIconResponse`
	Up to 3 instances of ResponseItem
	`Status: Unsigned16`
	`Data: ANSI string up to 32 characters`
	`URL: ANSI string up to 256 characters`	

Table 4-21 *CiscoIPPhoneError Object Quick Reference*

Definition	Range	SoftKey:URIs
`<CiscoIPPhoneError Number="x"/>`	`Number: An error code in the range 1 to 4`	

CHAPTER 5

Using HTTP

This chapter provides an in-depth look at the Web client and the Web server capabilities of the Cisco IP Phone. The client and the server components in the Cisco IP Phone use the Hypertext Transfer Protocol (HTTP) version 1.1 to communicate with other Web entities on the network. We will look at some of the key HTTP headers that the Cisco IP Phone supports. The full HTTP 1.1 Specification is available as RFC-2616 on the Internet Engineering Task Force Web site at the following URL:

```
http://www.ietf.org/rfc/rfc2616.txt
```

HTTP headers provide functions like content refresh, content expiration, and session cookies for state management. This information helps developers understand the types of applications and solutions that can be accomplished with Cisco IP Phones.

HTTP is a simple stateless protocol that is used at the application level. HTTP is simply described as a request/response protocol. A client makes a request to a server using a request method. The client also provides additional HTTP headers that clarify the request. The client may also provide the server with information about its HTTP capabilities. If a POST request was made, the request will also contain additional data as the body of the request. The server will then respond with HTTP headers to provide details about the response and, if needed, any body data that needs to be returned. The HTTP headers may also instruct the HTTP client to make an additional request immediately or in the future. This would be the case with either a Redirect or a timed Refresh header response. The section that follows provides more definitive information about the supported HTTP headers and what they do.

HTTP Requests and Responses

HTTP requests can contain up to three types of information:

- **HTTP request methods**—Defined as a request for information that is passed from the client to the server. These methods contain the primary intent of the client, such as a GET or POST request providing the desired path as well as the version of HTTP that is supported by the client.

- **HTTP headers**—Provide more information about the request such as the content type and content length of the request.

- **Body of the request**—Contains any additional data that needs to accompany the request to the server. The body would contain HTTP form data if a POST request were made.

HTTP responses also contain three types of information:

- **Status code for the request method and the version of HTTP supported by the server**—The first items included in the HTTP response.

- **HTTP headers**—Provide more information about the response such as the content type and content length of the response.

- **Body of the response**—The type of data and the format varies depending on the type of response as well as the accompanying headers.

The HTTP headers found in both HTTP requests and responses are simple ASCII text labels that may have parameters present. The headers that are required or optional depend on what request method was made or what response is being returned. Figure 5-1 depicts a simple HTTP GET request and the accompanying response between the Cisco IP Phone's HTTP client and a Web server.

Figure 5-1   *A Sample Request and Response Between a Cisco IP Phone and a Web Server*

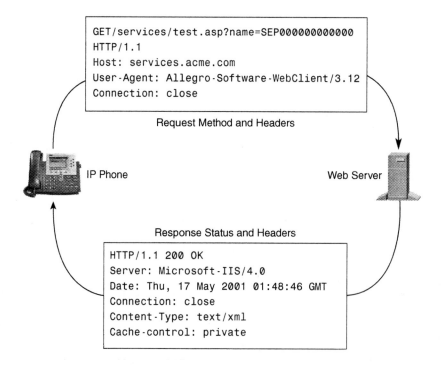

```
GET/services/test.asp?name=SEP000000000000
HTTP/1.1
Host: services.acme.com
User-Agent: Allegro-Software-WebClient/3.12
Connection: close
```

Request Method and Headers

IP Phone

Web Server

Response Status and Headers

```
HTTP/1.1 200 OK
Server: Microsoft-IIS/4.0
Date: Thu, 17 May 2001 01:48:46 GMT
Connection: close
Content-Type: text/xml
Cache-control: private
```

HTTP Client

Cisco IP Phones that support services have an integrated HTTP Client that is generically referred to as a browser or micro-browser. This browser is fully HTTP 1.1 compliant as described in RFC-2616. The Cisco IP Phone will simply ignore any unsupported headers that are received by its client. Some would argue that the Cisco IP Phone's browser is not fully HTTP 1.1 compliant due to the limited header support. However, the features that are enabled are fully compliant to the specification. Some features are limited due to the constrained resource environment that is common to most embedded devices. These limitations are concentrated to areas that require significant resources such as content caching and client-side cookies.

Cisco IP Phone Browser Request Method: GET

The GET method is the only request method that is used by the Cisco IP Phone's browser.

The client uses the GET method to request a desired Uniform Resource Identifier (URI) from a Web server. This URI is commonly referred to as the Request-URI. The request begins with the method name GET and is followed by the Request-URI. The last piece of information is the version of HTTP that is supported by the client. GET requests are usually made when the user performs any action that has a URL associated with it. Other actions that may cause a GET request include an HTTP Redirect header, an HTTP Refresh header, or a Push request.

On most GET requests, the URI is the Web server path to the data or process that will return the desired static or dynamic data. The URI may include a query string of accompanying data to the request that is appended in name and value pairs. Using query strings to pass data as part of the Request-URI is a very common technique for Web development.

A query string is formatted with multiple name value pairs. Each name is followed by an equal sign and the corresponding value. The name and value pairs are delimited with an ampersand (&) character. A sample GET request for the URI "/test.asp" with a query string containing two sample values would be made as follows:

```
GET /test.asp?DataName1=Value1&DataName2=Value2 HTTP/1.1
```

The Cisco IP Phone makes GET requests in several situations, including the following:

- When the Cisco IP Phone requests any URL that is a result of a user action.
- When the data is submitted using the CiscoIPPhoneInput object.
- When the Cisco IP Phone is directed to request a URL via the Push mechanism.
- When an HTTP Redirect header is received specifying a new location for the requested object.
- When an HTTP Refresh header is received with a timer value other than zero.

When using the CiscoIPPhoneInput object, the URL supplied with the input object will be used as the base URL for the GET request. The Cisco IP Phone will also create a query string and append the provided parameters and the data that was input for each. If a query string already exists in the supplied URL, the Cisco IP Phone will append the additional parameters properly. The Cisco IP Phone will append the first parameter using an ampersand instead of a question mark as well as subsequent parameters.

The Cisco IP Phone will also append parameters as part of a query string when the **services**, **directories**, or **messages** buttons are pressed for the first time. The Cisco IP Phone will append a parameter called "name" with the value as its device name. Appending the device name is used to identify the Cisco IP Phone quickly upon its initial request.

HTTP Client Headers

The Cisco IP Phone supports many of the common HTTP headers used by standard Web browsers. This section covers the headers that have some significance when sent to a Cisco IP Phone to affect its behavior. For a complete listing of HTTP headers and their purpose, reference the Hypertext Transfer Protocol 1.1 specification (RFC-2616).

The following HTTP headers have significant importance with regard to the Cisco IP Phone's HTTP Client:

- Content-type
- Refresh
- Location
- Expiration
- Set-Cookie

Content-type Header

The Content-type header is used to indicate the MIME type of the data that is contained in the body of a response. The Cisco IP Phone changes its behavior for one MIME type—the "text/xml" MIME type. This MIME type indicates to the Cisco IP Phone that it is receiving XML data. The Cisco IP Phone will then invoke its XML parser on the data received and process all known object types. The format for this header is as follows:

```
Content-type: text/xml
```

Any other MIME type will be ignored and the Cisco IP Phone will attempt to display the data that was returned.

Using Active Server Pages (ASP) with JavaScript, you would set the ContentType property on the Response object. This code instructs IIS to generate the appropriate Content-type header of the "text/xml" type. The code is as follows:

```
<%@ Language=JavaScript %>
<%
Response.ContentType = "text/xml";
%>
```

To generate this same header in Java Server Pages (JSP), you would use the following code:

```
<%@page contentType="text/xml"%>
```

Refresh Header

The Refresh header has multiple purposes because it has two parameters that can be returned with the header. The first parameter includes the number of seconds to wait before refreshing. If the specified number of seconds is zero, the Cisco IP Phone will not automatically refresh. The second parameter is optional and specifies the refresh URL. This URL is requested when the refresh timer expires or the user manually calls refresh with the **Update** soft key. This is a very common header to use because it enables the browser to change or update the content on the Cisco IP Phone's display after a specified number of seconds. This header is often used to redirect users to a new page location. Unlike the Redirect header, Refresh enables you to return a notice to the user that the page has moved before the user is taken to the new location upon timer expiration. The format for this header is as follows:

```
Refresh: 5; http://foo.com/newpage.asp
```

The following ASP sample will generate the Refresh header to force the Cisco IP Phone to navigate to the listed URL after the specified five seconds have elapsed.

```
<%@ Language=JavaScript %>
<%
Response.AddHeader("Refresh", "5; url=http://foo.com/nextpage.asp");
%>
```

The following JSP sample is for the most part identical.

```
<%
response.addHeader("Refresh", "5; url=http://foo.com/nextpage.jsp");
%>
```

Location Header

The Location header can be used to immediately navigate to a specified URL in conjunction with a status code 301 Moved Permanently, 303 See Other, 307 Temporary Redirect, or 302 Object Moved. This technique, combined with the User-Agent header value and some simple logic, will enable you to set up Cisco IP Phones to navigate to a main Web site address such as www.acme.com. You can then check the User-Agent value and redirect identified Cisco IP Phones to a different URL that provides appropriately formatted content. The format of a simple redirect is as follows:

```
HTTP/1.1 302 Object Moved
Location: http://services.acme.com/
```

To generate and return the 302 request status code plus the location header in ASP, you need to use the Redirect property of the Response object. The following sample instructs the client to perform an immediate request to the specified URL:

```
<%@ Language=JavaScript %>
<%
Response.Redirect("http://foo.com/nextpage.asp");
%>
```

The following sample uses JSP to perform a redirect:

```
<%
response.sendRedirect("http://foo.com/nextpage.jsp");
%>
```

Expiration Header

Use of the Expiration header has been slightly modified because the Cisco IP Phone does not cache content. The Cisco IP Phone has a URL history stack but it can only maintain ten URLs in the stack. Each URL that the Cisco IP Phone navigates to will be pushed onto the stack. The user can press the **Exit** or **Cancel** soft key to make the Cisco IP Phone navigate back one URL in the history. This action will pop the last URL off the stack and request the first URL remaining on the stack. The Expiration header can be used to instruct the Cisco IP Phone to not push the current URL onto the stack if the expiration date and time is older than that of the request date and time.

Using the Expiration header in this fashion enables a programmer to keep users from recalling URLs that are accessed throughout the life of a session. This is one of the main uses of this header for normal Web application programming techniques. Following is a sample Date and Expires Header combination:

```
Date: Tue, 5 February 2002 23:45:04 GMT
Expires: Tue, 5 February 2002 23:44:04 GMT
```

You can see that the expiration data and time is one minute older so the URL will not be pushed onto the stack. The Date header will be supplied by IIS by default when using ASP. You only need to tell IIS that you want it to return an Expiration header with the number of minutes the content is valid for. If you set the Expires property to a −1 then IIS will use the date and time of the request less one minute. Following is the code sample:

```
<%@ Language=JavaScript %>
<%
Response.Expires = -1;
%>
```

In the following JSP sample the time is set to zero. This sends the date and time of midnight January 1st 1970. The minus one date value subtracts one minute from midnight January 1st 1970.

```
<%
response.addDateHeader("Date", 0);
response.addDateHeader("Expires", -1);
%>
```

Set-Cookie Header

Cookie is a term used to describe a mechanism for the Web server to give the client a piece of data and have the client return the data with each request. The two traditional uses for cookies are:

- For Web sites to store a unique identifier and/or other information on the client's file system. This information will then be available to the server on subsequent visits.

- To track a unique identifier for state management. The client returns the cookie with each request and the server can then keep information about the current session indexed by this identifier. The identifier is commonly referred to as a session ID. Most Web servers have a built-in session management layer that uses this second type of cookie, which is commonly referred to as a session cookie.

Following is an example of the Set-Cookie header that is returned to the browser when a request method is used:

```
Set-Cookie: ASPSESSIONIDGQGQGRLS=OCPNMLFDBJIPNIOOKFNFMOAL; path=/
```

The Cisco IP Phone can receive and use a total of four cookies per host per session. Each cookie can be up to 255 bytes in size. These cookies are available until the server terminates the session or the client session has been idle for more than 30 minutes.

When using ASP on IIS the default server configuration automatically generates a session cookie and sends it to the client using the Set-Cookie header. This enables you to utilize the Session object from within ASP to store and retrieve data spanning multiple requests for the life of the session. When using JSP on Tomcat, the default configuration generates and issues a session cookie.

HTTP Client Sessions

The browser stores information for eight browser sessions at once. If a ninth session is initiated, the session that has been idle the longest is cleared and the new session is created. Each session maintains a separate set of cookies and user authentication information. The session also stores a flag indicating whether a defined proxy server is to be used. If the flag is set, all requests destined for the server will be made to the defined proxy server.

The following sections cover the areas of responsibility of the HTTP client including URL History, State Management, Session Life, Authentication, and Proxy.

URL History

As with normal Web browsers, the URL history in the Cisco IP Phone is not confined to each session, but rather a list of the last ten URLs that were accessed by the client that were not expired upon request. Exiting from services by pressing the **services** button or by repeatedly pressing the **Exit** soft key to close the services window will clear the URL history.

The URL history is shared between all applications that use the services window including Services, Messages, Push, and the Idle URL functionality. If the user is in Services and a URL is pushed to the device, the Cisco IP Phone will navigate to the URL and push it onto the stack. If the user Exits from the new URL, they will return to the last URL that was on the stack or close the services window if no URLs are remaining on the stack.

State Management

Effective state management for the Web server can be achieved with the use of session cookies. Client state management is achieved by controlling what URLs are pushed onto the URL history stack.

Session Life

HTTP sessions that are accomplished with session cookies being passed between the Cisco IP Phone and the server have a varying life span. The Cisco IP Phone keeps the session information for a maximum of 30 minutes of inactivity to any one server. If the Cisco IP Phone needs a session resource before the session has expired, it uses the session with the greatest time of inactivity. You must also consider the session inactivity timer as configured on the Web server. Check the server's documentation for more information about this topic. The server's default session time-out value may be far less than the Cisco IP Phone's default 30 minutes.

Authentication

When authenticating to a secured resource using HTTP Basic Authentication, the user ID and password will be retained for the life of the session. This authentication information will be sent to the server with each subsequent request. If the authentication fails for a resource, the user ID and password will be cleared to attempt accessing the resource anonymously. If the resource cannot be accessed with anonymous permissions, the user will be prompted to enter new credentials for accessing the resource. In Figure 5-2 you can see the window that is used to collect the authentication credentials when the phone's HTTP client requests a secured resource.

Figure 5-2   *When a Secured Resource is Requested the User is Prompted for Authentication*

While using Basic Authentication to an IIS server, a programmer can access the User Name and Password that was sent by the client using the "AUTH_USER" and "AUTH_PASSWORD" properties of the Server Variables collection in the Request object. The following code retrieves the User Name and Password from the collection into similarly named variables in the script:

```
<%@ Language=JavaScript %>
<%
var UserName = Request.ServerVariables("AUTH_USER");
var UserPassword = Request.ServerVariables("AUTH_PASSWORD");
%>
```

Proxy

When the Proxy URL is specified in a Cisco IP Phone's configuration, the phone attempts to use the proxy when any host specified in the URL contains an IP address in any form or if the host name contains a period. Without a proxy server defined, the Cisco IP Phone attempts to access all hosts directly. This method of determination allows the use of a proxy server with direct access to a non-internet host. Because of this, you need to be mindful of the proxy ramifications while writing services.

The following ASP code sample builds a base URL that refers to the directory in which the currently executing page resides. The information is obtained from two parts of the request. The path value originates as a parameter of the GET method. The host information is obtained from the Host HTTP header. The following headers are excerpted from a request:

```
GET /services/test.asp HTTP/1.1
Host: foo.com
```

The getBaseURL function builds and returns a URL of `http://foo.com/services/`. The function uses the information from the original request to insure that the Cisco IP Phone will be able to access the server on subsequent requests. This enables you to deploy a service in any virtual directory and easily generate and use URLs that are sensitive to the proxy issues. The following code implements the getBaseURL function and outputs a sample result:

```
<%@ Language=JavaScript %>
<%
function getBaseURL()
{
var scriptName = Request.ServerVariables("SCRIPT_NAME") ;
var endloc = String(scriptName).lastIndexOf("/") ;
var baseURL = "http://" + String(Request.ServerVariables("SERVER_NAME"));
baseURL += String(scriptName).substr(0, endloc + 1) ;
return baseURL ;
}
Response.Write(getBaseURL() + "nextpage.asp");
%>
```

HTTP Headers for Localization

In CallManager release 3.2(1), Cisco IP Phones began passing two new HTTP headers with every request so that service developers could identify the currently loaded locale information of a requesting device. The information passed with the two headers identifies the currently loaded language and character set.

Accept-Charset Header

The Accept-Charset header provides the ISO character set name that is currently loaded in the requesting phone. With the release of CallManager 3.2(1), the phones can support two different character sets. The phones support iso-8859-1 for all locales except Russian, which uses iso-8859-5. The following example shows the character set information for a phone with the default English locale loaded.

```
Accept-Charset: iso-8859-1
```

Knowing what character set is available solves only part of the problem. Because the iso-8859-1 character sets support so many languages' you also need to know what language the phone is using to be able to provide localized content.

Accept-Language Header

The language code that will be passed in this header is a two-letter ISO-639 language abbreviation. By default, Cisco IP Phones use English and will pass the two-letter code of "en" with every request. Here is the sample header as it is passed from a phone with locale set to English:

```
Accept-Language: en
```

Using these two headers, you can deliver content to the phone in the same language that it is configured for. For a list of supported locales and languages, refer to the Cisco CallManager documentation for the release in question.

HTTP Server

The addition of an HTTP server in supported Cisco IP Phones was introduced in the CallManager 3.1 release. This HTTP server is generically referred to as a Web server. The Web server provides HTML pages that show the current configuration and status of the device. The information provided by the Web server is very useful for troubleshooting the device. The Web server also provides the same data via XML for easy collection of data by automated systems as well as interactive applications.

The Web server also uses an internal common gateway interface (CGI) to perform more advanced functions. CGI is used to implement the ability to push requests to a Cisco IP Phone. The implementation of push using HTTP is somewhat of an oddity since it is true push. True push allows an external application to instruct a phone to perform a desired action without any initiation from the client. Most Web technologies that use the term push actually perform either a timed pull or make a client request and leave the request pending until the server wants to send data to the client.

Push

The generic term push is used to describe the capability to prepare a request and send it to the Cisco IP Phone at any time. Push enables applications to activate the display of the Cisco IP Phone based on an external stimulus, such as a call event. The Cisco IP Phone can accept an XML object via HTTP POST. A response is returned to the requestor providing detailed information about the status of the each request. The sections that follow examine the authentication process and the HTTP POST operations as they relate to Cisco IP Phones.

Authentication

Authentication to the Cisco IP Phone's server can be accomplished using standard HTTP Basic Authentication. Login credentials are based on the global directory users that are defined in Cisco CallManager Administration. By giving users rights to the device, they are also able to authenticate to secured resources on the Cisco IP Phone's Web server. A user can authenticate to an external application, and the application can then impersonate the user for requests being made to the user's Cisco IP Phone via push. The user that is currently logged into a device using extension mobility also has permission to control the device for the duration of his or her login.

HTTP POST

The Web server can accept an HTTP POST request for the /CGI/Execute path. The path and the form field XML that is being posted are case sensitive. The value of the XML field should be a CiscoIPPhoneExecute object. Upon completion of the specified execute items, the Cisco IP Phone returns a CiscoIPPhoneResponse object with the status for each item.

Accessing Device Information

Users can employ a standard Web browser to navigate to the IP address of a desired Cisco IP Phone to obtain information about the device. See Table 5-1 for a list of pages that are available from the Cisco IP Phone's Web server as HTML and XML.

Table 5-1   *Available Web Pages*

HTML Path	XML Path	Page Description
/DeviceInformation	/DeviceInformationX	Device Information
/NetworkConfiguration	/NetworkConfigurationX	Network Configuration
/EthernetInformation	/EthernetInformationX	Ethernet Information
/PortInformation?1	/PortInformationX?1	Port 1 (Network)
/PortInformation?2	/PortInformationX?2	Port 2 (Phone)
/PortInformation?3	/PortInformationX?3	Port 3 (Access)
/DeviceLog?0	/DeviceLogX?0	Debug Display
/DeviceLog?1	/DeviceLogX?1	Stack Statistics
/DeviceLog?2	/DeviceLogX?2	Status Messages
/StreamingStatistics?1	/StreamingStatisticsX?1	Channel 0 Stats
/StreamingStatistics?2	/StreamingStatisticsX?2	Channel 1 Stats

Conclusion

In this chapter, you learned about the Cisco IP Phone's HTTP client and how it interacts with Web servers using HTTP Headers. These headers are very useful in creating external content that appears to be integrated into the Cisco IP Phone's firmware. HTTP headers are easy to generate on most Web server platforms and are well worth the time and effort spent learning how to generate and use them. You can see these headers in action when you use the samples that are provided with this book on the accompanying CD-ROM.

CHAPTER 6

XML Conventions

In Chapter 2, "The Basics," you were exposed to just a small part of XML. This chapter is going to provide you with enough detail to ensure that you are fluent in the basics of XML needed to communicate with Cisco IP Phones. Make it through this chapter and you will be XML-literate. As a bonus, the XML skills you learn here should be relevant to many other applications you use in the future.

XML is a standard way of formatting tag-delimited data. This section describes the applicable portions of the XML specification and points out common errors and tips for building an application.

What Is XML?

XML is a standard that is defined by The World Wide Web Consortium (W3C), a group that is responsible for or helped create many other Internet-related standards, including:

- HTML, the markup language for Web pages
- HTTP, the Web's basic transport protocol
- DOM, the Document Object Model used when parsing XML files

The best way to start describing XML is to quote directly from the W3C:

> The Extensible Markup Language (XML) is the universal format for structured documents and data on the Web.

At first read, you might feel that the W3C is overplaying the importance of XML with this quote. After all, there are many other ways structured documents are used on the Web.

But at the same time, they may in fact be downplaying the importance of XML. Judging by its rapid acceptance throughout the world of communications, XML may some day be the universal format for structured documents everywhere, not just on the Web. Companies such as Microsoft are rapidly turning to XML as the method of choice for storing and transferring data. Word processing documents, spreadsheets, databases, and more are migrating to this new format.

Structured Documents

The W3C tells us that XML is a way to *format structured documents*. What exactly does that mean?

It helps to start with a familiar example, a Web page. Figure 6-1 shows a simple Web page as rendered by a browser such as Internet Explorer.

Figure 6-1   *A Sample Web Page*

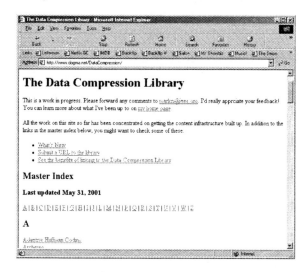

Looking at the page, you can clearly see more than just a blob of text. For example, the page has a title at the top, some highlighted links, a bulleted list, some header text, and so on.

How is it that we tell the browser (Internet Explorer in this case) what the various attributes of items on the screen are supposed to be? We use a text markup language—in this case, HTML.

A portion of the HTML text file that created the page in Figure 6-1 is shown in the following example:

```
<H1>The Data Compression Library</H1>
This is a work in progress. Please forward any comments
to <a href="mailto:markn@ieee.org">markn@ieee.org</a>. I'd
really appreciate your feedback! You can learn more about
what I've been up to on
<a href="http://www.dogma.net/markn">my home page</a>.
<p>
All the work on this site so far has been concentrated on
getting the content infrastructure built up. In addition
to the links in the master index below, you might want to
```

```
check some of these:
<UL>
  <LI><a href="WhatsNew.shtml">What's New</a>
  <LI><a href="SubmitUrl.shtml">Submit a URL to the library</a>
  <LI><a href="LinkToMe.shtml">See the benefits of linking to the Data Compression
  Library</a>
  </LI>
</UL>
<H2>Master Index</H2>
<H3>Last updated May 31, 2001</H3>
```

You can see that all the text that appears on the screen is in the HTML, but there is also a lot of hard-to-read formatting information that goes with it. For example, the phrase "The Data Compression Library" is prominently displayed at the top of the page in the browser view. However, in the preceding example it is bracketed by the strings `<H1>` and `</H1>`.

The funny bracketed strings that surround various pieces of text in the HTML file serve to mark up the text. Ordinary ASCII text takes on special meaning when marked up in this way. The term *markup* refers to the special tags and text used in a markup language. For example, tags such as `<H1>` and `<p>` are considered to be markup in an HTML document.

The creators of XML did not invent the concept of a markup language. The complex Standard Generalized Markup Language (SGML) heavily influenced XML itself. SGML is meant to be a universal language for creating device-independent documents with useful formatting and content.

SGML helped give birth to HTML, a much simpler and easy to parse markup language. HTML is used to create Web pages that can be rendered on all sorts of different computers and devices, but is not intended to do much else.

XML differs from these two forebearers in two important respects. First, it deliberately avoids the complexity of SGML and is even more regular and easy to parse than HTML. Second (and even more important), XML is not specialized for any particular type of structured document.

Cisco's developers saw that XML provided a nice tool for communicating with IP phones. Cisco created a specialized vocabulary used to pass object definitions to Cisco IP Phones using XML. The beauty of XML is that standard tools designed to work with XML will work with Cisco's vocabulary, despite the fact that Cisco IP Phone objects were created long after the XML standard or the tools used to work with those objects.

XML Basics

The subset of XML used by Cisco IP Phones is nice and simple. You can follow it completely by simply learning a few vocabulary items and concepts. The vocabulary you will learn in this section is not Cisco jargon; you will be using standard terms that XML users of all levels of experience will be familiar with.

You have already learned one important piece of vocabulary—you now know what a markup language is and perhaps have a good feel for why you might markup documents. The rest of this section gives you a few more words to keep handy and with them the sum total of XML knowledge you will need.

Tags

Just like HTML, XML marks up sections of text using tags enclosed in angle brackets, typically looking like the following:

```
<Title>Local Services</Title>
```

In this fragment of an XML document, the text "Local Services" has been marked with the tag `Title`. Note that tags must always be balanced, with both a beginning tag and an ending tag with the same name as the beginning tag. The fact that it is an ending tag is indicated by the prepended / character.

There may be some times when you want to specify a tag that encloses an empty string. (To the parser, this is quite different than not seeing the tag at all.) You might think this would be done using syntax like this:

```
<Title></Title>
```

This is perfectly valid XML, but the language defines a shortcut created by appending the slash to the beginning tag:

```
<Title/>
```

For reasons of economy and clarity, this method is probably the preferred way to use a tag with no containing text.

Attributes

Just as you have probably seen with HTML, XML tags can be adorned with attributes. An attribute has a name that is followed by an equal sign and a quoted value. Although these are only used in a couple of places by Cisco IP Phones, other XML vocabularies make frequent use of them. The choice of whether to use attributes or elements to convey information in XML documents is solely a matter of preference. In general the two approaches are equally valid.

As an example of how and where attributes are used, a hypothetical XML sequence used in a corporate HR document might look like this:

```
<Employee site="Dallas">Mark Nelson</Employee>
```

In this case the markup text is designed to define some information about an employee, including the site at which the employee works.

Note that an XML developer who did not like using attributes could just as easily have designed the document to use this format, which would be equally valid:

```
<Employee>
  <Site>Dallas</Site>
  <Name>Mark Nelson</Name>
</Employee>
```

XML allows you to define multiple attributes within a tag just as easily and will also allow you to use the special empty syntax. Those two combined might look like this:

```
<GuestList date="6/1/2002" event="mungathon"/>
```

Elements and Content

In an XML document, the combination of a tag, all of its attributes, the text and the markup that it brackets is referred to as an *element*. As an example, consider the following XML sequence used as a Cisco IP Phone menu:

```
<CiscoIPPhoneMenu>
  <Title>Local Services</Title>
  <MenuItem>
    <Name>Message of the Day</Name>
    <URL>http://Bart/motd.asp</URL>
  </MenuItem>
  <MenuItem>
    <Name>Appt Book</Name>
    <URL>http://Homer/appointments.pl</URL>
  </MenuItem>
  <MenuItem>
    <Name>Read Mail</Name>
    <URL>http://Homer/mail.pl</URL>
  </MenuItem>
  <MenuItem>
    <Name>Boss Cam</Name>
    <URL>http://streamer/cam.shtml</URL>
  </MenuItem>
</CiscoIPPhoneMenu>
```

In this complete XML document, there is just one top-level element, which is defined by the tag CiscoIPPhoneMenu. A well-formed XML document can only have one top-level element, and all text and other elements in the document must be contained within that element.

NOTE   The top-level element in an XML document is the same as an "object." For example, the tag name CiscoIPPhoneMenu is the same as the object name.

You normally refer to whatever is found between the tags as *content*, with plain text being referred to as text content or data content.

You can plainly see from the example above that some elements contain other elements. The CiscoIPPhoneMenu top level element contains a Title element and three MenuItem elements. Each of the MenuItem elements contains a Name element and a URL element.

This type of nesting is *de rigueur* in XML, but be sure to avoid any attempt to illegally nest elements. The opening and closing tags have to be nested at the same depth within any enclosing tags. You cannot have two elements that have overlapping tag definitions, as in this illegal example:

```
<Book>
  <Title>Learning XML the Hard Way</Title>
  <Author>
    Page Turner
    <ISBN>123-456789-0-x
  </Author>
  </ISBN>
</Book>
```

It really does not matter what the tags are in this example, what is important is that the opening and closing tags named ISBN are not in the same element. The opening tag for ISBN appears in element Author, the closing tag is in element Book. This is not valid XML, and any application that properly parses XML will reject it.

Objects

The previous vocabulary words you have learned in this section are ones that you will see used when talking about XML in any context. The final term you will use with Cisco IP Phone services is "object."

Object is a term that programmers use to mean many different things. Some of the uses are rigorously defined, some loosely, and some are just impulsive.

When talking about Cisco IP Phone services, an *object* is something we send from a server to the phone. It could just as easily be called a widget, a doodad, or a thingy. Regardless of the specific word, the object sent to the phone is simply a collection of various pieces of text and data that the phone uses to perform some sort of behavior.

The XML document sent from the server to the phone is not the actual embodiment of the object, but it does seem convenient to think of it that way. So in this book if a figure shows an XML document, you may see it referred to as an object. References to documents and objects can be interchanged freely with no worries.

An XML Browser that Ships with Windows

This chapter has gone through a fairly dense visitation of XML and what you need to know about it. Absorbing all of this is somewhat difficult, particularly when faced with nothing but droll text.

To move the learning process to a more visual phase, it might help to work with an XML tool you might not even know you have: Microsoft's Internet Explorer.

In version 5, Microsoft added the ability to browse XML files to Internet Explorer (IE5). For example, consider the XML file shown here:

```
<?xml version="1.0"?>
<Suppliers>
  <Company BusinessType ="Software Publisher">
    <Name>Microsoft</Name>
    <Product>Office XP</Product>
    <Product>Windows XP</Product>
    <Product>Bob</Product>
  </Company>
  <Company>
    <Name>Spacely Sprockets</Name>
    <Product>T-135A Flange</Product>
  </Company>
  <Company>
    <Name>Slate Gravel</Name>
    <Product>Rocks</Product>
    <Product>Mud</Product>
  </Company>
</Suppliers>
```

This is a fairly typical XML file that might be used to exchange information between a couple of programs. (It is not a CiscoIPPhone object, but you should be comfortable with this abstraction at this point.) If I use Internet Explorer to browse this file, instead of seeing raw text as you might expect, I get a color-coded (which you cannot see here) display screen of the parsed XML, as shown in Figure 6-2.

Internet Explorer presents the XML file as a tree and you can collapse and expand the nodes of the tree. This can be quite useful when examining a big file, as it allows you to limit the display to just the content in which you are interested. Figure 6-3 shows a browser looking at the same file after collapsing some of the nodes.

Best of all, IE will report parser errors when it reads XML data. (You will get more information about validation later in this chapter.) Changing the closing Company tag in the Microsoft element causes the browser to display the screen shown in Figure 6-4.

Figure 6-2 *IE5 Browsing an XML File*

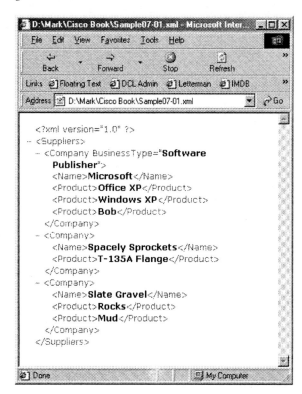

Figure 6-3   *IE5 with Some Elements Collapsed*

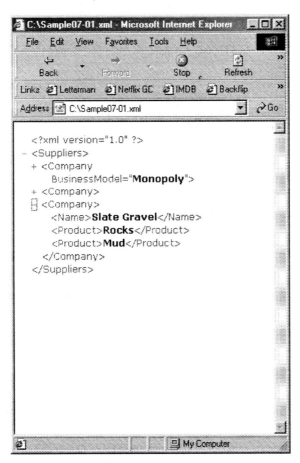

Figure 6-4   *IE5 Reporting a Parsing Error*

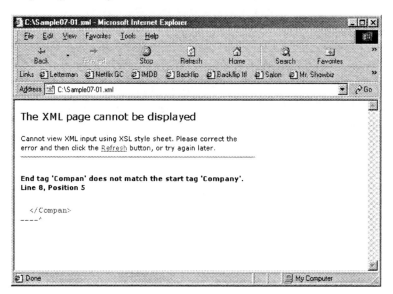

These capabilities make Internet Explorer a great free tool for examining and validating your Cisco IP Phone objects. It does not let you to actually edit your XML files, but validation is the next best thing; you can do your editing in Microsoft Notepad if necessary.

Nitty-gritty

There are a few more details that you need to be aware of when working with XML, in particular when feeding data to the Cisco IP Phone parser.

The Prolog

Most XML files have a prolog statement, looking something like this:

```
<?xml version="1.0" standalone="yes" encoding="UTF-8"?>
```

The prolog always starts and ends with the same set of brackets and question marks, and has the xml tag. It has to appear before the first element in the file. It can contain a variety of attributes, including:

- **Version**—the version of XML used to encode this document.
- **Standalone**—an indicator as to whether this file needs other files to be parsed.

- **Encoding**—a description of the encoding method used to represent characters in the file. (UTF-8 is the most common character encoding used in XML, but you may see documents encoded in UTF-16, ISO-8859-1, and many other schemes. Objects sent to Cisco phones must use UTF-8.)

The Cisco IP Phone will passively ignore a prolog with the following text:

```
<?xml version="1.0" encoding="UTF-8"?>
```

Other attributes in the prolog are likely to confuse the parser and should be avoided.

Escape Sequences

Certain characters are going to confuse the parser if they are encountered in normal text. The most obvious is the left angle-bracket character, which is normally used to start a new element. What happens if you want to include an angle bracket in the content of an element?

```
<Title>The best punctuation character: <, the left angle bracket</Title>
```

Imagine the parser's confusion as it starts reading this element. Once it gets past the opening `<Title>` tag, it starts reading content. Everything goes great as it reads "My favorite punctuation character:" It runs into trouble, however, when it hits that left angle bracket.

The trouble is caused by the fact that the parser assumes that the bracket is supposed to indicate the start of a new tag, not realizing that this character is part of my content.

The XML standard gets around this problem with the concept of an escape sequence. You may be familiar with this concept from HTML. An XML escape sequence is any sequence of characters that start with an ampersand (the "escape" character) and ends with a semicolon.

The first escape sequence you may be familiar with is the one used to encode a left angle bracket:

```
&lt;
```

This odd looking sequence is read by the parser and converted to an angle bracket that is part of the content, not part of a tag.

There is an obvious repercussion to the escape sequence used to enter the left angle bracket. It suddenly makes the ampersand into a special character as well. As a result of this problem, you will now need to use an escape sequence to enter an ampersand:

```
&amp;
```

The final escape sequence you need to know is for the right angle bracket:

```
&gt;
```

You might think that you could leave your right angle brackets "unescaped" in your XML documents, but unfortunately there is one special place where a right angle bracket can hurt you. Because of some special XML syntax (which is not important to Cisco IP Phone developers), the sequence *]]>* has special meaning. Because of this, you absolutely must escape that bracket if you have a right angle bracket following two right brackets. To see what happens, consider what will occur when you try to parse this XML sequence with Internet Explorer:

```
<?xml version="1.0"?>
<Text>
 <A>Right bracket: >>>> No Problem</A>
 <B>Funny sequence: ]]> Big Problem!</B>
</Text>
```

Internet Explorer gives you the display shown in Figure 6-5.

Figure 6-5 *Error Produced by the Right Angle Bracket in Just the Wrong Place*

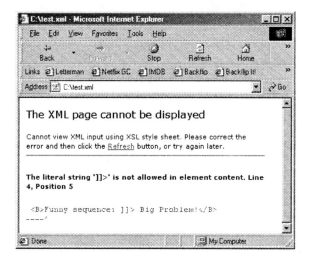

Escaping the right angle bracket so the input looks like the following will parse properly, with the end result shown in Figure 6-6.

```
<?xml version="1.0"?>
<Text>
 <A>Right bracket: >>>> No Problem</A>
 <B>Funny sequence: ]]&gt; No More Problem!</B>
</Text>
```

Figure 6-6   *The Situation Improves*

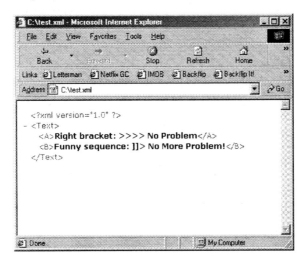

Comments

You can put comments in XML for the purposes of documentation. There are times when this can be useful for human readers of the document. A comment is any text that is enclosed by a very specific start and end sequence. The comment starts with a `<!--` set of four characters and finishes with a `-->` set of three characters. This means a typical comment looks something like this:

```
<!-- All work Copyright Norman Conquest, 1066 -->
```

You might even like to create an elaborate sequence of lines all enclosed within a single comment block:

```
<!--
You are free to use this XML file for any
project which advances the cause of world
peace, or is useful in the pursuit of
improved agronomy. You may not use this
XML file to implement any weapons of mass
destruction, or as foodstuff.
-->
```

Depending on the type of files you are creating, you may or may not find comments to be useful. In any case, the Cisco IP Phone parser will be happy to ignore any comments in the XML files it receives, which is exactly what you want. Note also that the XML standard dictates that you are free to omit the normal escape sequences for text in your comments.

XML Structure Rules—Your Friend the Schema

One thing you have probably noticed about XML so far is that you have not read anything about how the structure and content of an XML file are defined. You have read in this chapter and others about tags, attributes, and content, but very little about the rules regarding those tags and attributes.

What you have learned about so far has all been meta-language rules. XML lets you create new languages for marking up documents and you know quite a bit about how those rules must be structured. You know that tags have to be evenly matched and nested and how attributes are defined.

At some point, developers such as those at Cisco take XML and actually create a specific set of tags, attributes, and rules for their applications. The result is a new language, and the one you are learning about in this book is the Cisco IP Phone XML Services language.

The rules that define how an XML language such as the one used by Cisco IP Phone services are defined are collectively referred to as a schema. Database programmers have used this term for years, and in this section you will learn what it means to XML users.

Rules—Who Needs Them?

The designers of XML created it partially in response to the complexity of SGML. SGML was powerful but difficult to use and particularly difficult to employ in applications. So one design goal was to keep XML simple and not to impose too many requirements on casual users.

One way the developers of XML chose to make this happen was to allow for two completely different ways of using XML files. Under the simpler regime, a developer creates XML file using the tags and content of his or her choice. Whatever program or process is using those tags and content probably has a good idea of what it expects, but those rules are not necessarily formally defined anywhere. In other words, the XML definition has not been formalized in a schema of any sort.

An XML file that obeys the meta-language rules regarding XML but does not have a formal definition is referred to as a well-formed file. This means the tags are properly nested and the attributes are formatted properly.

Two Varieties of Schema

Creating and parsing well-formed XML files is pretty easy. But they have one significant problem: because there are no defined rules regulating the tags, attributes, and content of the XML files, there is usually no good way to ensure that they will be acceptable to the programs that read them.

For this reason, the inventors of XML gave developers the ability to strictly define a given XML vocabulary using a Data Type Definition (DTD). A DTD has the ability to tightly define which tags can be used where, what type of content can compose an element, and the order in which elements appear. The DTD is a control freak's dream.

The DTD is typically defined in a separate file and referenced from the XML file. This is usually defined at the start of the XML file, with some lines that look something like this:

```
<?xml version="1.0"?>
<!DOCTYPE Nematode-catalog SYSTEM "worms.dtd">
```

This declaration gives the XML parser that is using the data the opportunity to check the data as it reads it in. This process of validation gives name to the second type of XML file: a valid file.

XML supports both valid and well-formed files and lets system architects choose which they prefer.

DTD Out—XML Schema In

The original definition of the DTD that was promulgated with early XML specifications was not well accepted by the XML community. There are various reasons for this, including the fact that DTDs used a non-XML format to define schemas. A general wave of dissatisfaction has lead to the growing acceptance of something called XML Schema. *XML Schema* has much the same aims as DTDs, but is better defined and (best of all) uses XML as its method of defining the schema.

As of this book's writing, the 1.0 specification of XML Schema is in the final stages of acceptance by the W3C, the same standards body that sanctioned XML. It would appear that support for XML Schema is where the industry is headed.

Accordingly, Cisco has created a schema for the IP Phone XML language. This schema is shipped with the Cisco IP Phone Services SDK and can be used with automated tools to validate your XML files as they are created.

This book will not try to teach you anything about XML Schema, but a representative segment of the Cisco IP Phone Services schema is shown here as an interesting sample:

```
<xsd:complexType name="CiscoIPPhoneImageType">
  <xsd:sequence>
    <xsd:element name="Title" minOccurs="0">
      <xsd:simpleType>
        <xsd:restriction base="xsd:string">
          <xsd:maxLength value="32"/>
        </xsd:restriction>
      </xsd:simpleType>
    </xsd:element>
    <xsd:element name="Prompt" minOccurs="0">
      <xsd:simpleType>
        <xsd:restriction base="xsd:string">
          <xsd:maxLength value="32"/>
        </xsd:restriction>
```

continues

(continued)

```
          </xsd:simpleType>
      </xsd:element>
      <xsd:element name="LocationX" type="xsd:unsignedShort" minOccurs="0"/>
      <xsd:element name="LocationY" type="xsd:unsignedShort" minOccurs="0"/>
      <xsd:element name="Width" type="xsd:unsignedShort" minOccurs="0"/>
      <xsd:element name="Height" type="xsd:unsignedShort" minOccurs="0"/>
      <xsd:element name="Depth" type="xsd:unsignedShort" minOccurs="0"/>
      <xsd:element name="Data">
        <xsd:simpleType>
          <xsd:restriction base="xsd:hexBinary">
            <xsd:maxLength value="2200"/>
            <xsd:minLength value="1"/>
          </xsd:restriction>
        </xsd:simpleType>
      </xsd:element>
      <xsd:element name="SoftKeyItem" type="CiscoIPPhoneSoftKeyType" minOccurs="0"
                   maxOccurs="16"/>
    </xsd:sequence>
  </xsd:complexType>
```

Some tools, such as XMLSpy, enable you to design schemas in a graphical fashion, which many people find easier to work with. Figure 6-7 shows a typical schema design screen, which arranges the information in a way you might find more palatable.

Figure 6-7   *A Schema View from XMLSpy 4.0*

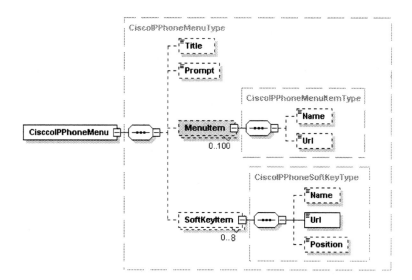

Some of the schema information here might make sense to you and some might not, but the important thing to know is that this format is clearly understood by validating parsers. It gives a clear set of rules for the creation of XML files.

Validating

If you are using a validating parser, you can tell it which schema to use by adding some text at the start of your XML file. A typical reference to a schema might look like this:

```
<?xml version="1.0" encoding="UTF-8"?>

<CiscoIPPhoneImage xmlns:xsi="http://www.w3.org/2001/XMLSchema-instance"
xsi:noNamespaceSchemaLocation="CiscoIPPhone.xsd">
```

You will put this information in your XML files that you send to the Cisco IP Phone, however, it does not have a validating parser, so this additional text will not do you any good.

However, there are some tools that you can use to validate your XML objects. The Cisco IP Phone Services SDK ships with a tool called Validator that has the ability to validate XML objects found in static files or returned from Web pages. Validator uses Microsoft's MSXML 4.0 parser to read in XML objects and validate them against the copy of the schema shipping with Cisco IP Phone Services SDK. It prints out Microsoft's error messages, with a typical example shown here:

```
Error in line 3 at position 40
MS Parser says this is the source text where the error occurred:

        <Title>Cisco Phones are xml-enabled.</title>


MS Parser reported this error:
End tag 'title' does not match the start tag 'Title'.
```

This example shows the type of mistake that might slip past a quick look on your part; the closing `Title` tag was not capitalized, which might not matter to you but will definitely matter to an XML parser.

The schema file that accompanies Validator enables the program to accurately check XML files. The parser inside the Cisco IP Phone has a hard-coded parser that will accept and reject files exactly as Validator does. You can learn more about Validator in Chapter 11.

Debugging XML Problems

The Cisco IP Phone XML parser is terse and unforgiving. Unfortunately when it receives an XML file that it does not like or understand, it is limited in the quality of response that it can give. Depending on the exact nature of the error, the phone may display a generic error (such as Parser Error) or simply show a blank screen when an XML service is invoked. This sort of behavior can be extremely frustrating to both end users and developers.

Fortunately, you have a couple of useful tools at your disposal for tracking down these problems. The first is Validator, mentioned in the previous section. As shown in the previous section, Validator can scan a file that captures an XML sequence, parsing it against the schema and informing you of parsing errors.

Validator can also be pointed to the Web server that is actually feeding XML objects to the telephone. If Validator sends the same arguments that the phone sends, it should receive XML objects that are identical as well. It can then quickly parse those files and identify any problems.

Note that the most common problem seen in the development of Cisco IP Phone services is exceeding the allowed element size. Fields such as Titles, Prompts, and Menu labels typically have relatively stringent size limits, often in the range of 32 characters. The parser in the phone cannot accept longer fields, and will generate an error upon receiving the XML.

Fortunately, the XML schema supplied in the Cisco IP Phone Services SDK has the size of all fields properly defined, so you can use Validator to quickly identify these problems. But remember, it is quicker to never even see the problem. Learn more about Validator in Chapter 11.

Need More?

XML is big and beautiful, and this chapter only gave you a peek at its majesty. To learn more, the best place to start is at the W3C Web site. Their site, devoted to XML, can be found at:

`http://www.w3c.org/XML`

There you can find links to standards documents, tutorials, and archives from discussion groups. You can also find links to software and reference books.

The XML FAQ (Frequently Asked Questions) document on the Web is very helpful to developers who are new to XML. The document is available in many places and with many translations. The following link is one such example:

`http://www.ucc.ie/xml/`

There are also many books available that attempt to teach you everything you need to know about XML. The ultimate source for information is the W3C specification. The current version of the specification is online at:

`http://www.w3.org/TR/REC-xml`

Above all, a specification needs to be precise, which often leads to a specification that is difficult to read. To help you get through the XML specification, you can get help from Bob DuCharme's book *XML: The Annotated Specification,* ISBN 0-13-082676-6, Prentice Hall. Bob includes the entire text for the 1.0 XML specification, then provides explanations that help cut through the dense language found in the official standards that can be so hard to get through.

Bob also provides a free sample chapter online via his Web page at:

`http://www.snee.com/bob/xmlann`

Follow the links shown above to the free copy of Chapter 2 of Bob's book and you will have an opportunity to study XML in much more depth than can be done here.

At this writing, Windows developers have an excellent tool for creating, reading, and validating XML files, including schema files and more. This tool, XMLSpy, is available for a free trial on the Web at:

`http://www.xmlspy.com`

Conclusion

You do not need to be an XML expert to work with Cisco IP Phone service XML objects, so this chapter should give you all the information you need. You should now understand how to create a well-formed XML document, construct XML elements, add XML attributes, and use escape special characters. If you want to learn more, follow the links given in this chapter and strive for total mastery of the language. XML is going to be with us for a long time and any knowledge you pick up will be well used.

CHAPTER 7

Building a Service

In this chapter we begin to examine some general recommendations for enhancing the end user's experience. This chapter also has an in-depth sample that creates a service using many pieces of the services infrastructure, as well as a Cisco IP Phone Services Software Developer Kit (SDK) component. The sample service demonstrates some of the recommended techniques for service behavior. Some of the recommended methods are explained in further detail with the sample service walkthrough.

Enhancing the End User's Experience

This section provides suggestions for creating a user experience that will be familiar and comfortable to the user. You can enhance the user experience by defining custom soft keys, changing the default error messages on your services Web server, and explaining how to identify what version of the Cisco IP Phone Services SDK objects are supported by the requesting phone.

Guidelines for Custom Soft Keys

There are some simple rules that you can follow to make the user interface easy to use when enabling custom soft keys:

- Place soft keys in the same position as their native counterparts. Even though you can place a soft key labeled **Exit** in any one of the possible positions, the best position is three because that is where **Exit** is located in the native Cisco IP Phone menu. The third position is also the default placement for the CiscoIPPhone objects that include the **Exit** key. You do not have to follow this rule, but frequent users of the Cisco IP Phone and services will be very comfortable with this position.

- Only display keys that are valid in the present context. Do not present soft keys with no actions associated with them. By default, a CiscoIPPhoneGraphicMenu object has both **Update** and **Exit** soft keys. You may be inclined to disable the **Update** soft key by not defining a URL. Pressing the **Update** soft key will work as you desire by doing nothing, but that results in a soft key that does not perform an action. It would be better to define only the keys the application requires so that the user is only presented with valid choices.

- Customized soft key labels should be placed based on their action. The soft key labels are not sacred by any means. Feel free to change the labels as desired. Changing the **Exit** soft key label to **Goodbye** can be a more friendly approach to the function of leaving your application. The recommended position would still be position three. If you use a **SoftKey** URI to evoke built-in functionality in a soft key set, keep in mind what the default position is for that key and use it if possible.

Web Server Error Messages

Most Web servers have a set of error pages that are returned to HTTP clients in the event of an HTTP error. As an example, there is a set of pages for IIS that are very verbose HTML-based error pages. These pages should be converted to plain text pages to accommodate for easy display on the phone if it needs to display one of the pages.

An example is the "HTTP 404 - File Not Found" page that every server has. If the phone requests a URL for a path that cannot be found on the server, it will be served an HTML page indicating the HTTP 404 error. By replacing this default page with one that is plain text you can easily view the error message on the phone's display. Otherwise, you have to navigate down looking for the relevant text hidden inside all the HTML content.

By returning plain text error messages, your Web server will be compatible with any device that is making a request from the server. If the server is only used to serve content to Cisco IP Phones, you can return an XML page containing a CiscoIPPhoneText object. Using a CiscoIPPhoneText object makes for a better end user experience even when errors occur by presenting the error message with the full capabilities of the phone's services display.

Version Compatibility

There are several ways that you can determine what version of the CiscoIPPhone objects are supported by the requesting device. The newer versions of the firmware identify what objects are supported as well as what version of the XML schema is supported. The earlier versions of the firmware can only be identified by lack of self-identification.

Cisco IP Phone firmware from Cisco CallManager 3.1 or greater uses the HTTP Accept header to identify what objects are supported. The phone passes the following Accept header to the Web server when the phone's HTTP client makes a request.

```
Accept: x-CiscoIPPhone/*;version=2.0, text/*
```

The CiscoIPPhone/* indicates that all objects in the Cisco IP Phone Services schema are supported for the listed version. The version parameter indicates that the phone supports version 2.0 of the Cisco IP Phone Services schema. The text/* indicates that the phone can receive and display MIME types that are of sub type text. A perfect example is "text/xml" because we use that for all of the service and directory objects. The phone can receive and display other MIME types such as "text/plain" or "text/html," but you need to remember that everything that is sent to the phone with these MIME types will be displayed. In the case of "text/html" if you send HTML tags they will be displayed, too.

The following sample checks the contents of the HTTP Accept header to see if "x-CiscoIPPhone" is present. If this string is present, the sample parses the version number from the header. Either the supported version of the schema or the string "Unknown" will be output. If the string "Unknown" is returned, you can assume that the phone's firmware only supports version 1.0 of the schema or that the requesting device is not a Cisco IP Phone.

```
<%@ Language=JavaScript %>
<%

var version, rawdata ;
rawdata = String(Request.ServerVariables("HTTP_ACCEPT")) ;
if (rawdata.search(/x-CiscoIPPhone/g) != -1)
{
  version = rawdata.substr(rawdata.search(/x-CiscoIPPhone\/\*;version=/g) +
    25, 3) ;
}
else
{
  version = "Unknown" ;
}
Response.Write("Schema Version: " + version);
%>
```

Another method of determining if the requesting phone supports at least version 2.0 of the Cisco IP Phone Services schema is to attempt to set a session cookie on the first page of your application. If the cookie is available on the second page, you know that the phone supports at least version 2.0. The preferred solution is to read and parse the Accept header because this information will be available on the first request from capable phones.

These guidelines are provided for your consideration. You do not have to follow them, but you will likely agree that they are to the benefit of the end user. The next section provides an example service, starting with the definition and going all the way to the final code. While you read though this next section, try to get some ideas for how you can leverage this sample design to enhance the services you develop.

Voice Anomaly Tracking (VAT) Service

This section provides an in-depth look into creating a service for Cisco IP Phones. This service uses a combination of XML objects, HTTP headers, the CiscoURLProxy, and the file system to provide a well-rounded service creation example.

VAT Service Overview

The VAT service can be invoked if the user is experiencing any anomalies with their current call. When invoked by the user, the VAT service gathers and logs the streaming statistics every 30 seconds to a comma-delimited file while the call is in progress. When either the streaming or the service has terminated, the VAT service ends the logging.

Designing the Service Using Primitives and HTTP Headers

In Figure 7-1 you can see the application flow as well as the possible events and the HTTP headers being used. Figure 7-1 was drawn as a blueprint for the service before it was created. Drawing the flowchart and creating the screen mock-ups used in the figure helped to clearly define the service Web page requirements. Review the figure and then read the detailed description provided after the figure.

The first page of the VAT service is the VAT-Welcome.asp page. This page uses a CiscoIPPhoneText object to provide the user with the service Title, a brief description, and instructions to begin tracking. Figure 7-2 shows the VAT-Welcome.asp page output.

When the custom soft key **Start** is pressed, the application navigates to the VAT-Track.asp page. This page also uses a CiscoIPPhoneText object to display the title of the service, instructions for the user explaining how to end the tracking service, and the time of the last entry written. The page automatically reloads itself using the HTTP Refresh header every 30 seconds.

Figure 7-1   *Application Primitives and Control Flow*

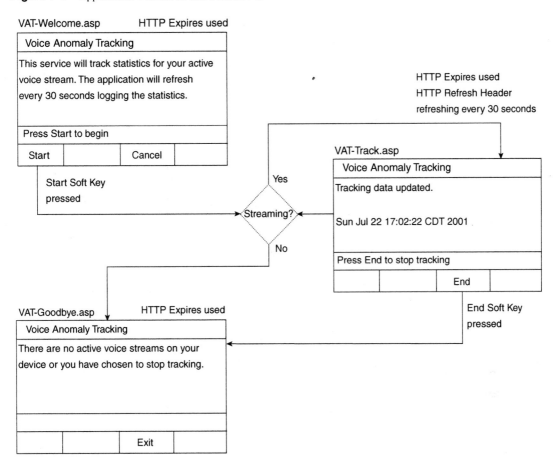

Figure 7-2   *Voice Anomaly Tracking Welcome Screen*

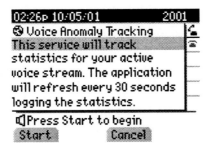

The core of the service work is done with the VAT-Track.asp page. This is where the information is gathered from the phone and collected in files on the Web server for administrator review. This page uses the CiscoURLProxy to get the statistics from the phone's Web server. There is a small amount of code that parses the XML into comma-delineated data and then writes it into a file. This sample does not use a real XML parser because it is not necessary for this example due to its simplicity. Figure 7-3 shows the VAT-Track.asp page in action.

Figure 7-3   *Voice Anomaly Tracking in Action*

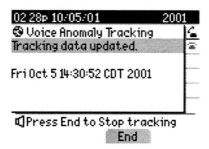

After the custom soft key **End** is pressed, the service navigates to the VAT-Goodbye.asp page. This page uses a CiscoIPPhoneText object to provide the service title as well as a message stating that tracking is complete. There is also a custom **Exit** soft key provided to exit the service and return to the services menu. Figure 7-4 shows the VAT-Goodbye.asp page output.

Figure 7-4   *Voice Anomaly Tracking Goodbye Screen*

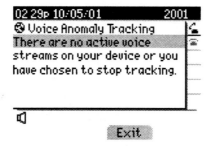

All the pages in this server utilize the HTTP Expires header functionality of the Cisco IP Phones to prevent the URLs from being added to the URL stack in the phone (Browser History). This returns the phone to the previously unexpired page when **Exit** is pressed.

Sample Service Source

This section explains the VAT source code so that you can understand how to create a service using the same techniques. This first section of code begins by specifying the default language used on the page as JavaScript. The function getBaseURL() is used to collect the Web server host reference and path that was used by the phone when making its request. This function is important for environments where the phones are configured to use a proxy server. If the phone requests the page by specifying the host by name, it will create the base URL using the host name. This also holds true if an IP address was used when making the request to the Web server. The URL returned from the getBaseURL function also has the full path to the directory that the current script is executing in. This enables you to place these files in any directory available on your Web server and run the service successfully. The URLs that are used will be generated appropriately for the service to function.

```
<%@ Language=JavaScript %>
<% // VAT_Welcom.asp

function getBaseURL()
{
  scriptName = Request.ServerVariables("SCRIPT_NAME") ;
  endloc = String(scriptName).lastIndexOf("/") ;
  baseURL = "http://" + String(Request.ServerVariables("SERVER_NAME")) +
    String(scriptName).substr(0, endloc + 1) ;
  return baseURL ;
}
```

This next fragment sets the MIME type of the response to "text/xml" using the Content-Type HTTP header. An expiration header is also being generated to the date and time of the request less one minute. The inline XML for the CiscoIPPhoneText object will be returned as is with exception of the dynamically generated URL field in the first SoftKeyItem.

```
Response.ContentType = "text/xml";
Response.Expires = -1;

%>
<CiscoIPPhoneText>
  <Title>Voice Anomaly Tracking</Title>
  <Text>This service will track statistics for your active voice stream. The
application will refresh every 30 seconds logging the statistics.</Text>
  <Prompt>Press Start to begin</Prompt>
  <SoftKeyItem>
    <Position>1</Position>
    <Name>Start</Name>
    <URL><% = getBaseURL() + "VAT-Track.asp" %></URL>
  </SoftKeyItem>
  <SoftKeyItem>
    <Position>3</Position>
    <Name>Cancel</Name>
    <URL>SoftKey:Exit</URL>
  </SoftKeyItem>
</CiscoIPPhoneText>
```

This next fragment of code begins with the same default language declaration of JavaScript. The variables are all being defined and ForAppending is being set to a value of 8. The ForAppending value is a constant for use with the FileSystemObject. The logTime is being set to the current date and time at which the script is executing. The function `getBaseURL()` is used again for creating the appropriate URLs.

```
<%@ Language=JavaScript %>
<% // VAT_Track.asp

var Inet1, statsURL, rawdata, devrawdata, logTime, deviceName, fs, a, ForAppending;
ForAppending = 8;
logTime = new Date();

function getBaseURL()
{
  scriptName = Request.ServerVariables("SCRIPT_NAME") ;
  endloc = String(scriptName).lastIndexOf("/") ;
  baseURL = "http://" + String(Request.ServerVariables("SERVER_NAME")) +
    String(scriptName).substr(0, endloc + 1) ;
  return baseURL ;
}
```

The next several code fragments consist of a function called `logStats()`. The try statement indicates the beginning of the error-checking block. The try/catch statements were introduced in Microsoft Jscript version 5.0. If you are not running version 5.0, you can obtain an upgrade to the scripting engine from Microsoft's scripting Web site.

```
http://msdn.microsoft.com/scripting
```

If you do not wish to upgrade your Web server's scripting engine, you can remove the try and catch statements from the code. This first segment uses the CiscoURLProxy to request the `/DeviceInformationX` path from the requesting phone's Web server. The `deviceName` variable is then set to the parsed version of the phone's device name. The device name is the characters "SEP" concatenated with the phone's Media Access Control (MAC) address. The device name is the same unique identifier that you see in CallManager Administration.

```
function logStats()
{
  try
  {
    devrawdata = Inet1.GetURL("http://" + Request.ServerVariables("REMOTE_ADDR") +
      "/DeviceInformationX");
    deviceName = devrawdata.slice(devrawdata.search("<HostName>") +
      "<HostName>".length, devrawdata.search("<HostName>") +
      "<HostName>".length + 15);
```

This next fragment creates an instance of the `FileSystemObject`. This object is used to output the comma-separated information into a file. The device name should be fifteen characters, so the code performs a quick validation before proceeding. If there was a problem getting the device name we do not want to create a file with an incorrect name so these steps will be bypassed. If the length is correct, the file will be opened for appending. The files will be created in the C:\VATLogs directory unless you modify the script to relocate them.

```
    fs = new ActiveXObject("Scripting.FileSystemObject");

    if (deviceName.length == 15)
    {
      a = fs.OpenTextFile("c:\\VATLogs\\" + deviceName + ".csv", ForAppending,
        true);
```

The next five lines of code all perform regular expression search and replace calls. The first line replaces all white space characters with an empty string, effectively removing all white space from the data. The following two lines remove the opening and closing `StreamingStatistics` tags. The fourth line removes any remaining opening tags and places a double quote in its place. The fifth line replaces the remaining closing tags with a double quote followed by a comma. As an example, the `<Byes>1</Byes>` line in the source XML data would be changed to 1 without the outer double quotes. This chained together with the other values creates a single comma-separated value formatted string. This also causes the file to have an extra comma at the end of the line data. The sixth line shortens the data by one character using the slice method to remove the last comma. The seventh line writes the data into the text file along with the `logTime` value surrounded by double quotes. This is followed by a carriage return and line feed by using the `WriteLine` method. The file is then closed.

```
        rawdata = rawdata.replace(/\s/g, "");
        rawdata = rawdata.replace(/\<StreamingStatistics\>/,"");
        rawdata = rawdata.replace(/\<\/StreamingStatistics\>/,"");
        rawdata = rawdata.replace(/\<[a-z]{0,30}\>/gi, "\"");
        rawdata = rawdata.replace(/\<\/[a-z]{0,30}\>/gi, "\",");
        rawdata = rawdata.slice(0, rawdata.length - 1);
        a.WriteLine("\"" + logTime + "\"," + rawdata);
        a.Close();
    }
  }
```

If an error was thrown during this operation, we will end up in this catch block. First, any buffered response data is cleared. This code fragment then generates a CiscoIPPhoneText object to display the error information and provide an **Exit** soft key. Calling the End method on the response object then terminates the response. This is also the end of the `logStats` function.

```
  catch(errResponse.Clear();
    {
      Response.Clear();
      %>
      <CiscoIPPhoneText>
        <Title>Voice Anomaly Tracking</Title>
        <Text><% Response.Write("Error: (" + err.number + ") - " + err.description);
          %></Text>
        <Prompt></Prompt>
        <SoftKeyItem>
          <Position>3</Position>
          <Name>Exit</Name>
          <URL>SoftKey:Exit</URL>
        </SoftKeyItem>
      </CiscoIPPhoneText>
      <%
      Response.End();
    }
  }
```

This next code fragment begins with a try a statement to begin error checking. After the try statement, we begin by setting the content type to "text/xml" as well as setting the expiration of the content. The server is being instructed to buffer content until it is manually flushed. Buffering content is a great way to control what is sent to the phones. This enables you to flush an incomplete XML object when an error occurs and generate a valid XML object for the error message itself. This is important when you have already set the content type up front. If the content is set to "text/xml" and you do not return a valid XML object the phone will display a parsing error. You can easily control this by either not setting the content type header until after you have created the XML object or using this method of content buffering.

```
try
{
  Response.ContentType = "text/xml";
  Response.Expires = -1;
  Response.Buffer = true;
```

The next line creates an instance of the CiscoURLProxy ActiveX component. The CiscoURLProxy is available as part of the Cisco IP Phone Services SDK and must be installed on your server for this sample to work. The following line gets the remote address from the Request object and appends the path for the streaming information that is provided by the phone's Web server. The remote address is the IP address of the phone that requested the currently executing Web page from IIS. The third line uses the CiscoURLProxy to get the streaming statistics from the requesting phone's Web server.

```
Inet1 = new ActiveXObject("CiscoURLProxy.URLGrabber");
statsURL = "http://" + String(Request.ServerVariables("REMOTE_ADDR")) +
  "/StreamingStatisticsX?1";
rawdata = Inet1.GetURL(statsURL);
```

Now that we have the raw streaming data, we check for the existence of the RowStatus tag with a value of "Not Ready." If the value of the regular expression search is equal to –1, the string is not found. If the string is not found the phone has an active voice stream. The RowStatus value is set to active if the phone is streaming. When the phone is streaming, the logStats method is called to parse and log the data. If the phone is not streaming, the server instructs the phone to perform an HTTP redirect to the VAT-Goodbye.asp page. This is done with an HTTP Redirect header.

```
if (String(rawdata).search(/RowStatus\>Not Ready\<\/RowStatus/g) == -1)
{
  logStats();
}
else
{
  Response.Redirect(getBaseURL() + "VAT-Goodbye.asp");
}
```

If streaming was active, we want to add a HTTP Refresh header that instructs the phone to call the VAT-Track.asp page again after 30 seconds elapses. The getBaseURL() method is used to construct the URL with the same host name or IP address that was used by the phone while making the current request. The script then outputs a CiscoIPPhoneText object that displays the date and time that the information was logged. A soft key labeled **End** that navigates to the VAT-Goodbye.asp page is also provided. After the XML object is build the content is flushed with the Flush method on the Response object.

```
Response.AddHeader("Refresh", "30; url=" + (getBaseURL() + "VAT-Track.asp"));
%>
```

```
  <CiscoIPPhoneText>
    <Title>Voice Anomaly Tracking</Title>
    <Text>Tracking data updated.<% = ("\r\n\r\n" + logTime) %></Text>
    <Prompt>Press End to Stop tracking</Prompt>
    <SoftKeyItem>
      <Position>3</Position>
      <Name>End</Name>s
      <URL><% = getBaseURL() + "VAT-Goodbye.asp" %></URL>
    </SoftKeyItem>
  </CiscoIPPhoneText>
  <%
  Response.Flush();
}
```

If an error occurred in the try block, we will fall down to this catch block. First, the response
buffer contents are cleared because there may be invalid or incomplete XML data in the
response buffer. A CiscoIPPhoneText object is then output indicating the error that
occurred. An **Exit** soft key is also provided.

```
catch(err)
{
  Response.Clear();
  %>
  <CiscoIPPhoneText>
    <Title>Voice Anomaly Tracking</Title>
    <Text><% Response.Write("Error: (" + err.number + ") - " +
      err.description); %></Text>
    <Prompt></Prompt>
    <SoftKeyItem>
      <Position>3</Position>
      <Name>Exit</Name>
      <URL>SoftKey:Exit</URL>
    </SoftKeyItem>
  </CiscoIPPhoneText>
  <%
  Response.Flush();
}
%>
```

The next segment is the VAT-Goodbye.asp page. The page begins with the familiar
statement setting the default language to JavaScript. The page immediately sets the content
type and expiration headers. A CiscoIPPhoneText object is returned with a statement
indicating that there are no active voice streams on the device or the user has terminated the
logging. This covers the two reasons a user ends up viewing the VAT-Goodbye.asp page.
An **Exit** soft key is also provided as part of the object. This sample explicitly adds the **Exit**
soft key even though it would be available by default on a CiscoIPPhoneText object. This
is done to effectively remove the **Update** soft key that would normally appear.

```
<%@ Language=JavaScript %>
<% // VAT_Goodbye.asp

Response.ContentType = "text/xml";
Response.Expires = -1;

%>
<CiscoIPPhoneText>
  <Title>Voice Anomaly Tracking</Title>
  <Text>There are no active voice streams on your device or you have chosen to stop
tracking.</Text>
  <Prompt/>
  <SoftKeyItem>
```

```
          <Position>3</Position>
          <Name>Exit</Name>
          <URL>SoftKey:Exit</URL>
        </SoftKeyItem>
    </CiscoIPPhoneText>
```

Conclusion

In this chapter, you learned how to build a service for Cisco IP Phones. You were given guidelines for maintaining a consistent end user experience. This chapter discussed in detail and provided examples of how to collect information from the user's phone, the use of custom soft keys, and the use of HTTP headers for enhancing a service. You can load the sample VAT service from the accompanying CD-ROM to see it in action.

CHAPTER 8

Building a Directory

In this chapter you will learn the various issues and restrictions associated with building a directory using the supported Cisco IP Phone XML objects and HTTP headers. This chapter also demonstrates how to create and deploy an IP Phone directory. You will learn all the necessary techniques to build your own custom directories through the samples in this chapter. The **directories** button on the Cisco IP Phone provides a window for deploying custom content similar to that of the **services** button. When the user activates either the services or directories functionality, the phone opens a window to display the content that was requested. The differences between services and directories functionality is very minor and the details of the differences are covered in this chapter. You will find directories to be an indispensable feature of the Cisco IP Phones. It is very simple to create a directory and there are many types of directories that the users of the phone can benefit from. Following is a sample listing of directories that you can create:

- Corporate
- Personal
- Conference rooms
- Pager
- Hot list (Security, Loss Prevention, HR, Help Desk)
- Department
- Branch office
- On call (The results are based on a schedule for 24x7 supported systems)

The list is only limited to your imagination. The directories can be small static objects stored as separate files on a Web server or sophisticated applications that use back-end data repositories and business logic to provide the information. An On Call directory is a good example of a dynamic directory. The directory could provide the name and number of the "on call" individual for an IT system or server upon request. The directory application logic would provide the correct information based upon an on call schedule. If a user needs to contact the person on call for a system they would navigate to the directory and select the desired IT resource from a list. The user would then be provided with a choice of numbers to call or page the on-call individual.

Behavioral Differences with Directories Versus Services

All of the XML services objects and headers are supported in the directories window on the phone's display. There are two minor functional differences between services and directories windows:

- The CiscoIPPhoneMenu must be the first object to be returned when the phone's HTTP client requests the directories URL.

- CiscoIPPhoneDirectory object has additional behaviors when run in the directories window as compared to when it is used in the services window.

When the phone requests the directories URL that was defined in its configuration as (set in CallManager Administration), it expects a CiscoIPPhoneMenu object to be returned. Returning a CiscoIPPhoneMenu object is required because there is a built-in high-level directories menu to support the three internal directories. The menu object that is returned is appended after the internal directory items. This functionality enables you to append additional custom directories to the list at run-time. The following ASP sample returns a menu object with a menu item for "My Custom Directory."

```
<%@ Language=JavaScript %>
<%
var serverIP = Request.ServerVariables("LOCAL_ADDR");
Response.ContentType = "text/xml";
%>
<CiscoIPPhoneMenu>
  <Prompt>Select a Directory</Prompt>
  <MenuItem>
    <Name>My Custom Directory</Name>
    <URL>http://<% = serverIP %>/S/xmldirectoryinput.asp</URL>
  </MenuItem>
</CiscoIPPhoneMenu>
```

In addition to the top-level menu requirement, there is additional functionality provided with the CiscoIPPhoneDirectory object. The directory object has three main behavioral differences when it follows an input object in the program flow when it is used within the directories window.

- The **Submit** soft key has been relabeled to **Search**. When using a Uniform Resource Identifier (URI) to call this key's functionality in a custom soft key set, you still need to use the SoftKey:Submit identifier as if the input object was being used in the services window. This was done to provide a context-correct set of soft keys for performing a directory search. There are additional soft keys natively defined on the directory object when it follows an input object. Pressing the **more** soft key reveals two additional soft keys.

- The **Next** soft key is used in conjunction with the HTTP Refresh header. You can provide a URL with a timer value of zero. When the user presses the **Next** soft key, the phone calls the defined URL. This functionality is the same as the HTTP Refresh header when the **Update** soft key is pressed on other objects.

- The **Search** soft key, when pressed, loads the last CiscoIPPhoneInput object and prepopulate the last submitted request enabling users to refine their search without reentering the last search criteria. This is valuable for searching large directories. Users can simply add more criteria if the search result is too large and then search again.

The following section explains the basics of building a directory with the available XML object primitives. There are many ways to use the objects for directories. Therefore this section covers the basic types of directory application object flow.

Designing a Directory Using Primitives

This section describes how to use the defined XML objects, also referred to as application primitives, to collect data and format output for a directory. The typical application flow for directory services is diagrammed in Figure 8-1.

The first object returned to the phone will be the CiscoIPPhoneMenu object containing the menu item for "My Custom Directory." When the user selects this item, the phone will then navigate to the CiscoIPPhoneInput object to gather search criteria. Pressing the **Cancel** soft key will navigate to the previous URL in the phone's URL history. Pressing the **Search** soft key will submit the information and return a CiscoIPPhoneDirectory object. By pressing the **more** soft key followed by the **Search** soft key, the phone will navigate the user back to the input object. If the user presses the **more** soft key followed by the **Next** soft key, the refresh URL will be called to display the next set of entries with a CiscoIPPhoneDirectory object. Pressing **Exit** on a CiscoIPPhoneDirectory object will cause the phone to navigate back to the main directories URL.

A simple directory such as a corporate hot list that contains critical numbers can be a single directory object. A single directory object that does not follow an Input object in the program flow has a smaller set of soft keys. A directory object that was not preceded by an Input object behaves the same way as a Directory object does in the services window. Figure 8-2 shows a sample directory object flow based on user input possibilities.

Figure 8-1   *A Sample Directory Flow Showing Soft Key Actions for Directory Navigation*

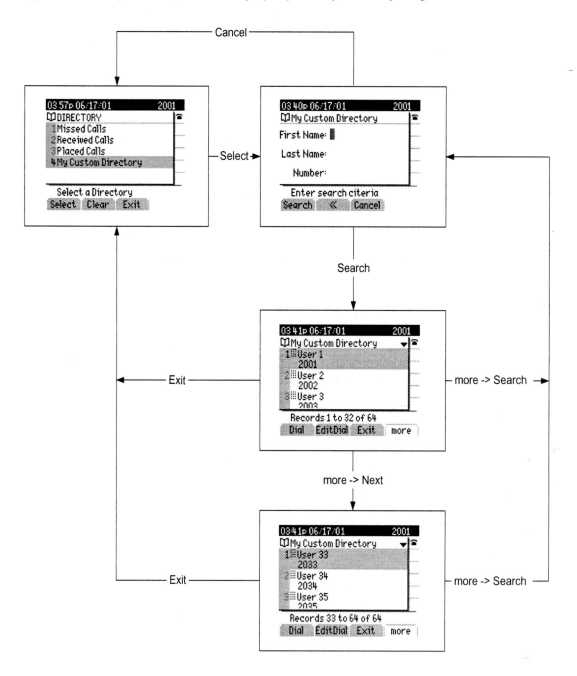

Figure 8-2   *A Sample Directory Flow Showing Soft Key Actions for a Simple Corporate Hot List Directory*

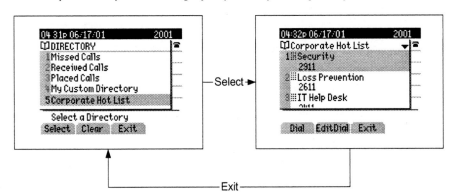

In the figure you can see that the first object returned is the CiscoIPPhoneMenu object that contains an entry for the "Corporate Hot List" directory. Navigating to this item returns a CiscoIPPhoneDirectory object. The user is then presented with the ability to **Dial** an entry, to perform an **EditDial** on an entry, or to **Exit** the directory. This single object directory is the simplest type of directory to create and can be a major convenience to your organization.

It is possible to build a directory that does not use the CiscoIPPhoneDirectory object because the phone has the ability to dial from any URL location using the Dial URI. You can create a URI in the format of Dial:2001 and place it in a URL field inside of an XML object such as a MenuItem or a SoftKeyItem. Then, by invoking the URL by selecting the item or pressing the soft key, the phone will dial the digits that followed the : character. In the sample above, Dial:2001 will cause the phone to dial the digits 2001 when executed. Figure 8-3 shows a simple directory flow for a static directory that uses a CiscoIPPhoneMenu object to list the directory entries. Selecting an entry returns a CiscoIPPhoneImage object with custom soft keys to dial the individual.

Figure 8-3   *A Sample Directory Flow Showing Soft Key Actions for a Directory Without a Directory Object*

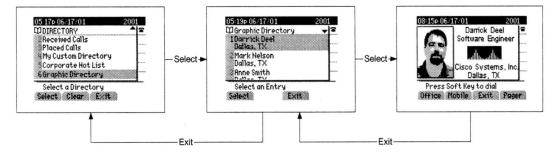

You can see in the figure that the directory flow is from the main directory menu to another menu of directory entries. This flow could also contain an Input object to enable searching of the directory similar to the first example in Figure 8-1.

Making the Directory Appear on Cisco IP Phones

This section explains common techniques used to add additional directories to the Cisco IP Phone's directories list. This includes a method that provides seamless integration with the existing corporate directory without modifying any of the Web pages on your CallManager server. Modifying the Web pages on the CallManager server is not supported and should not be done.

The following code sample returns a new Menu object that contains two directory items. The first directory represents the default "Corporate Directory" functionality. By linking to this directory, you will maintain the ability to search for users that are defined in the cluster. By default the URL Services enterprise parameter will point to the xmldirectory.asp file in the CCMCIP Web on one of the CallManager servers in the cluster. If you copy the URL that points to this file and then navigate to it with a Web browser, you get a response that includes a CiscoIPPhoneMenu object. This object will have a MenuItem for the corporate directory. The URL for this item points to the xmldirectoryinput.asp file in the Cisco CallManager Cisco IP Phone (CCMCIP) Web on one of the CallManager servers. This is the URL that you need to use for the first MenuItem URL in the following sample code.

```
<%@ Language=JavaScript %>
<%
var serverIP = Request.ServerVariables("LOCAL_ADDR");
Response.ContentType = "text/xml";
%>
<CiscoIPPhoneMenu>
  <Prompt>Select a directory</Prompt>
  <MenuItem>
    <Name>Cluster Directory</Name>
    <URL>http://callmanager.cisco.com/ccmcip/xmldirectoryinput.asp</URL>
  </MenuItem>
  <MenuItem>
    <Name>Cisco Directory</Name>
    <URL>http://<% = serverIP %>/directory/ldapdirectoryinput.asp</URL>
  </MenuItem>
</CiscoIPPhoneMenu>
```

Place this menu on one of your existing Web servers and change the URL Services enterprise parameter to point to this page at its new location. When the **directories** button is pressed, the phone navigates to this new menu. The user will be presented with the option of linking to the input page for the default CallManager directory and any other directories that you add to this page. Changing the URL Services enterprise parameter is the only thing that needs to be modified on the CallManager servers using this technique.

Making a Directory with the LDAP Search COM Object

This section demonstrates how to create a directory service that can search a Lightweight Directory Access Protocol (LDAP) directory using the LDAP Search Component Object Model (COM) object. This first page returns a CiscoIPPhoneInput object to the phone for the purposes of gathering the directory search criteria. This object enables the user to input part or all of the first name, last name, or telephone number. The search criteria that the user enters is appended to the defined URL as query string parameters. The InputFlag is set to upper case ("U") for both the first and last name fields. This is recommended over the alpha ("A") flag because it limits the possible input to only capital letters. This limits the number of characters that are presented to the user when the keypad is used for input. When the user submits this form, the information is passed to the ldapdirectorylist.asp page.

```
<%@ Language=JavaScript %>
<%
var serverIP;
serverIP = Request.ServerVariables("LOCAL_ADDR");

Response.ContentType = "text/xml";
%>
<CiscoIPPhoneInput>
  <Title>Directory Search</Title>
  <Prompt>Enter search criteria</Prompt>
  <URL>http://<% = serverIP %>/directory/ldapdirectorylist.asp</URL>
  <InputItem>
    <DisplayName>First Name</DisplayName>
    <QueryStringParam>f</QueryStringParam>
    <InputFlags>U</InputFlags>
  </InputItem>
  <InputItem>
    <DisplayName>Last Name</DisplayName>
    <QueryStringParam>l</QueryStringParam>
    <InputFlags>U</InputFlags>
  </InputItem>
  <InputItem>
    <DisplayName>Number</DisplayName>
    <QueryStringParam>n</QueryStringParam>
    <InputFlags>N</InputFlags>
  </InputItem>
</CiscoIPPhoneInput>
```

The following code is broken up into sections so that the functionality of the ldapdirectorylist.asp can be explained in detail. The script begins by setting the default language to JavaScript. The function definition for getBaseURL() follows and is used to build URLs that reference this same page for listing additional search results. Additional results need to be returned if the number of entries matched by the search exceeds the maximum number of entries that can be displayed with a single CiscoIPPhoneDirectory object. The next statement is a try block for error handling. You can also see the collection of the four possible query string parameters of "f," "l," "n," and "start." If either the last name or the first name is not provided, the value is set to an empty string. Otherwise, JavaScript will pass the string value of "undefined" around.

```
<%@ Language=JavaScript %>
<%

function getBaseURL()
{
        scriptName = Request.ServerVariables("SCRIPT_NAME") ;
        endloc = String(scriptName).lastIndexOf("/") ;
        baseURL = "http://" + String(Request.ServerVariables("SERVER_NAME")) +
                String(scriptName).substr(0, endloc + 1) ;
        return baseURL ;
}

try
{
  // Get parameters from query string

  var last = String(Request.QueryString("l"));
  var first = String(Request.QueryString("f"));
  var telephoneNumber = String(Request.QueryString("n"));
  var start = String(Request.QueryString("start"));

  // If search criteria not provided use an empty string

  if (last == "undefined"){last = "";}
  if (first == "undefined"){first = "";}
```

In the following code you can see that the maxListSize is being set to 32 entries, the
CiscoIPPhoneDirectory object maximum number of directory entries.

```
  // Get the server IP address and set the page size

  var maxListSize = 32;
```

Now the code checks to see if there was a start value received as a query string parameter.
The first request to the ldapdirectorylist.asp page has the value of the variable start set to
"undefined". Subsequent requests have the starting record number in the existing result set.
If this is the first request, a copy of the COM object will be instantiated and saved into the
Internet Information Server (IIS) Session object. The Session object in IIS enables you to
store and recall information across multiple requests to the server by the same client. The
Web server and client use a session cookie to identify the phone on subsequent requests. By
storing the COM object in the Session you can retrieve additional entries on subsequent
requests without performing another query to the LDAP source server.

```
  // If this is the first request for this criteria
  // create an instance of the COM object and perform
  // the search.

  if (start == "undefined")
  {
    Session("OBJ") = Server.CreateObject("LDAPSEARCH.LDAPSearchList.1");
    var s = Session("OBJ");
```

This next section is where you customize the script to use the appropriate settings for your
LDAP directory. Set the server, port, and searchbase properties to the appropriate values for
your environment.

```
// Set the server information

s.server = "ldap.cisco.com";
s.port = 389;
s.searchbase = "ou=people,o=cisco.com";
```

This section may need to be customized for your specific LDAP implementation. The LDAP attribute names in the sample code can be changed to return the desired information. You can also customize the format of the output and the XML tag name to be used and the maximum value length that should be returned for the tag. This makes the COM object very flexible and easy to customize for different LDAP implementations as well as different directory searches. You could easily make a directory that searches your LDAP server for other types of resources such as conference rooms.

```
// Create the return attribute content and format

s.AddReturnAttr("givenName, sn", "Name", "%2, %1", 31);
s.AddReturnAttr("telephoneNumber", "Telephone", "%1", 31);
s.SetNonemptyAttr("telephoneNumber");
```

The following section shows how to set the title and prompt of the XML object that will be returned. The size of the element value can be specified so that it will not be exceeded. Further below the sorting attributes can be set. The sorting attributes are set differently depending on whether a telephone number was provided or not. The default behavior of this script is to search based on the telephone number if it is present and ignore any name information provided. The start position is also initialized to one.

```
// Set the title and prompt format

s.SetOutputTitle("LDAP Directory Search", 32);
s.SetOutputPrompt("Records %s to %e of %c", 32);

// Set sorting criteria based on name or number search

if (telephoneNumber == "undefined")
{
    s.AddSortingAttr("sn, givenName, telephoneNumber", 1);
    s.SearchByName(last + "*", first + "*");
}
else
{
    s.AddSortingAttr("telephoneNumber, sn, givenName", 1);
    s.SearchByPhoneNumber(telephoneNumber);
}
start = 1;
}
```

The following else condition is executed if the start position was specified on the query string. If `start` was present, the object stored in the Session will be referenced to avoid another costly LDAP search. The subsequent code initializes the `listCount`, `currentStart`, and `end` values to support paging of results when more than the maximum list size was returned from a search.

```
else
{
  // Use the existing search object

  var s = Object(Session("OBJ"));
  start = Number(start);
}

var listCount = s.SearchCount;
var currentStart = start;
var end = 0;
```

The following code modifies the start and end positions depending on how many records were returned for the LDAP search as well as what the current page is based on the maximum list size. An HTTP Refresh header is created and outputted if there are additional results beyond what will be displayed on the current instance of the page.

```
// Update start if needed

if (listCount >= (start + maxListSize))
{
  start += maxListSize;
}

if (currentStart + maxListSize - 1 >= listCount )
{
  end = listCount;
}
else
{
  end = start - 1;
  Response.AddHeader("Refresh", "; url=" + getBaseURL() +
    "ldapdirectorylist.asp?" + "start=" + start);
}
```

This last section of code outputs the HTTP MIME type header of "text/xml" as well as the XML object that was generated by the COM object. By calling the Flush method on the Response object, IIS sends any pending content to the HTTP client. The catch block is executed if there is an exception thrown anywhere in the preceding try block. If an exception is caught, the error description and error number will be output to the HTTP client. The final method call of End on the Response object terminates the ASP page processor as well as the response to the HTTP client.

```
// Set the content type and output the XML from the object

Response.ContentType = "text/xml";
Response.Write(s.XMLOutput(currentStart, maxListSize));
Response.Flush();
}
catch(err)
{
  Response.Write("Error," + err.description + "," +
    err.number.toString(16));
}
Response.End();
%>
```

This directory sample is fairly short and very flexible. This COM object and sample ASP code enables sophisticated LDAP directory search support for your Cisco IP Phones with very little modification. You should now be able to develop both static and dynamic directories. Using the deployment techniques covered in this chapter you should be able to deploy your custom directories with minimal effort.

Conclusion

In this chapter, you learned how to build a directory for Cisco IP Phones. You were given the required information to integrate your custom directories into the list that is displayed when the user presses the **directories** button. This chapter discussed in detail and provided examples of how to use the LDAP search component from the Cisco IP Phone Services SDK to integrate with existing LDAP directories. Examples were provided for creating different types of directories that can be created, and hopefully this chapter sparked your imagination as to the possibilities for your organization.

CHAPTER 9

Integrating a Service with Cisco IP Phones

Once you have created a service, you need to make it available (or have the Cisco CallManager administrator make it available) to users by adding the service to Cisco CallManager Administration. Once configured in CallManager Administration, the service can be distributed to users via the User Options Web page. Users subscribe to any service in their cluster via the User Options Web page, or CallManager administrators can subscribe phones to services in CallManager Administration. CallManager administrators can also use the Bulk Administration Tool (BAT) to subscribe services to new phones.

You can define parameters when adding services in CallManager Administration. A service can have as many parameters as required. The only gotcha is the size of the URL, which including its parameters, is limited to 256 characters. This is a limitation with the Cisco IP Phone. *Parameters* are variables users can define to customize a service subscription and can be optional or required (as defined by the phone service application). A user may want to subscribe to the same service several times so they can specify different parameters for each service subscription. For example, the user might want to receive weather forecasts for the local area, as well as the city in which the user's parents live. By subscribing to the weather service twice, the user can enter the local zip code as a parameter for one service subscription, then subscribe again this time adding the zip code for the city where the parents live as a parameter for the second subscription.

Generally speaking, service subscriptions are on a per-device basis or a user device profile. However, there is a workaround, explained later in this chapter, that enables you to replace the default services menu with a modified menu that includes services you want to assign to all phones.

The core of each service is a URL. Try to keep the URL short to eliminate user error when typing the service in CallManager Administration. When a service is selected from the menu, the URL is requested via HTTP, and a server provides the content. This URL is entered in the URL Services field (**System > Enterprise Parameters**), as shown in Figure 9-1.

Figure 9-1 *Enterprise Parameters Configuration in CallManager Administration*

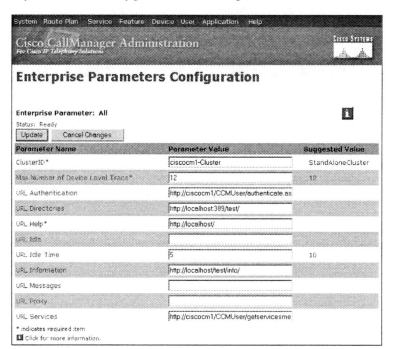

NOTE   For the services to be available, Cisco IP Phones in the CallManager cluster must have network connectivity to the server on which the service resides.

For example:

```
http://<servername>/ccmuser/sample/sample.asp
```

Where `<servername>` is a fully qualified domain name or an IP address.

WARNING   Do not add Cisco IP Phone services on any CallManager node or any server directly associated with CallManager server configuration, such as the TFTP server or Publisher database server because performance degradation on CallManager might occur.

Also make sure your services are in separate virtual Web servers to prevent any one service from affecting another Web service on the same server.

Using CallManager Administration

In addition to creating a service, which has been discussed in the chapters leading up to this one, you must integrate the service with CallManager. You can add, update, or delete services. You can also add, update, or delete service parameters in CallManager Administration.

CallManager Administration writes configuration information to the CallManager database, which can be distributed across CallManager nodes in the cluster. Once added to the database, the service is available on all CallManager nodes in the cluster.

Adding a Phone Service

You add a service to CallManager using CallManager Administration. The documentation provided with CallManager Administration, *Cisco CallManager Administration Guide*, describes the steps you'll use to add the service. For CallManager release 3.1 documentation, use the following link:

```
http://www.cisco.com/univercd/cc/td/doc/product/voice/c_callmg/3_1/sys_ad/adm_sys/
    ccmcfg/index.htm
```

For later releases, use the following link and navigate to the *Administration Guide* for your release.

```
http://www.cisco.com/univercd/cc/td/doc/product/voice/c_callmg/index.htm
```

In short, you need to perform the following tasks to make the service available to users:

1   Add and configure the service in CallManager Administration (**Feature > Cisco IP Phone Services**). The Cisco IP Phone Services Configuration page in Figure 9-2 shows a service that has been configured and inserted in the database.

2   Define parameters for the service.

Parameters, such as the Zip Code parameter shown in Figure 9-3, enable the user to set predefined values for the service. Example parameters for other services include stock ticker symbols or user IDs. Parameters are appended to the URL when sent to the server. Select the **Parameter is a Password (mask contents)** box to mask the display of the characters in the field on the Web page only. The contents of the field are transmitted in clear text; there is no hashing or digesting performed on the text.

Figure 9-2 *Adding a New Service in CallManager Administration*

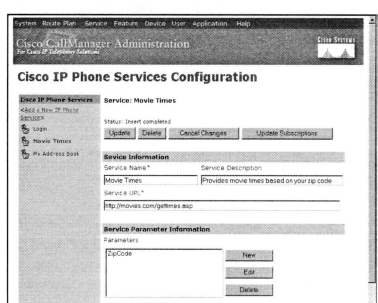

3 Once all parameters have been defined, click **Update Subscriptions** to include the parameters in the service.

TIP

If you change the service URL, remove a Cisco IP Phone service parameter, or change the name of a phone service parameter for a phone service to which users are already subscribed, you must click **Update Subscriptions** to update all currently subscribed users with the changes. If you do not do so, users must be advised to re-subscribe to the service to rebuild the URL correctly.

Figure 9-3   *Defining a Service Parameter in CallManager Administration*

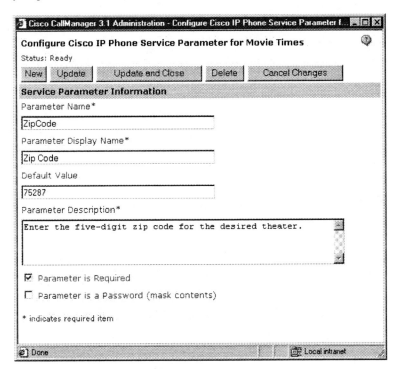

Updating or Deleting a Phone Service

Services already present in CallManager Administration can be updated or deleted. The *Cisco CallManager Administration Guide* describes the steps used to update or delete a service. For CallManager release 3.1 documentation, use the following link:

```
http://www.cisco.com/univercd/cc/td/doc/product/voice/c_callmg/3_1/sys_ad/adm_sys/
    ccmcfg/index.htm
```

For later releases, use the following link and navigate to the *Administration Guide* for your release:

```
http://www.cisco.com/univercd/cc/td/doc/product/voice/c_callmg/index.htm
```

User Subscription

Users subscribe to services in the Cisco IP Phone User Options Web page, as shown in Figure 9-4. The CallManager administrator must provide the Web address to users so they can access the Web page.

NOTE In CallManager release 3.1, the web page is called Cisco IP Phone User Options. In CallManager release 3.2, the name changed to Cisco CallManager User Options.

Figure 9-4 *User Options Web Page with Phones Services Section Highlighted*

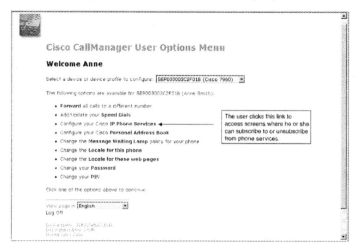

Users log on to the User Options Web page and are authenticated via the LDAP directory. Once logged on, the user selects his or her phone from the device drop down list box. If the device is a Cisco IP Phone model 7960 or 7940, then the link to **Configure your Cisco IP Phone Services** is available.

Users click the link to **Configure your Cisco IP Phone Services**. The Cisco IP Phone Services page displays, as shown in Figure 9-5.

To subscribe to a service, the user chooses a service from the **Select a Service** or **Available Services** drop-down list box. All services that have been added to CallManager Administration appear in this list. When a service is selected, the description for the service is shown in the **Service Description** box.

Users can type over the description of the service if they choose (CallManager release 3.1 only), and then click **Continue**. In the subsequent screen, users can customize the name of the service if they choose. This is particularly useful if multiple subscriptions of the same service will be added. Users also provide information for any parameters associated with the service, such as Zip Code for our example Movie Times service as shown in Figure 9-6.

Figure 9-5   *User Subscription Page in the User Options Web Page*

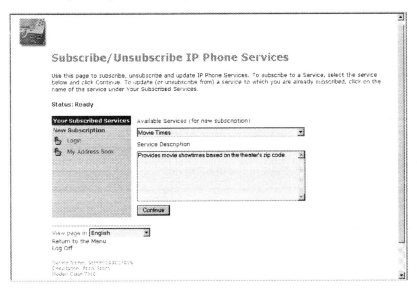

Figure 9-6   *Customize a User Subscription*

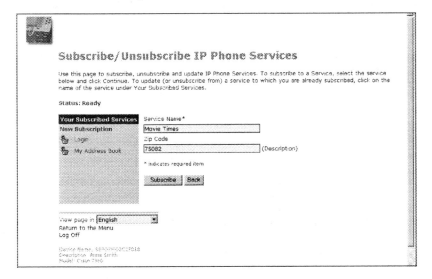

Help is provided for the parameters by clicking the **Description** link next to the parameter. This description is pulled from the **Parameter Description** field on the Configure Cisco IP Phone Service Parameter popup dialog shown in Figure 9-3.

The user clicks **Subscribe** and the service is subscribed to the phone or user device profile and displayed in the list of subscribed services on the left. At the same time, a custom URL is built and stored in the CallManager database for this subscription. The phone does not need to be reset and the newly subscribed service is available on the phone immediately. The GetServicesMenu.asp script accomplishes this. The ASP file polls the database layer to retrieve a list of all currently subscribed services.

Providing Default Services to All Phones

This section provides a workaround to the per-device subscription "rule." Using the regular methods (CallManager Administration or the User Options Web page), services can be subscribed to phones one phone at a time. Using the following workaround, however, you can build a menu of default services that you want to appear when the user presses the **services** button, followed by a submenu showing the specific services each user has individually subscribed to.

The following ASP code sample, which we call **workaround.asp**, shows two default services (cryptically named Service One and Service Two) followed by the submenu of the user's service subscriptions. The **workaround.asp** page is provided for your convenience in the Chapter 9 directory on the companion CD-ROM.

```
<%@ Language=JavaScript %>
<%

var name = String(Request.QueryString("Name").Item);
Response.ContentType = "text/xml";
%>
<CiscoIPPhoneMenu>
  <Title>SERVICES</Title>
  <Prompt>Make Your Selection...</Prompt>
  <MenuItem>
    <Name>Service One</Name>
    <URL>http://services.acme.com/one.asp</URL>
  </MenuItem>
  <MenuItem>
    <Name>Service Two</Name>
    <URL>http://services.acme.com/two.asp</URL>
  </MenuItem>
  <MenuItem>
    <Name>Service Subscriptions</Name>
    <URL>http://callmanager.yourcompany.com/CCMCIP/getservicesmenu.asp?Name=<% =
      name %></URL>
  </MenuItem>
</CiscoIPPhoneMenu>
```

To implement this workaround, set the URL Services (**System > Enterprise Parameters**) field to point to the URL for the **workaround.asp** page. When the user presses the **services** button, the phone requests the service URL passing the device name parameter on the initial request. (Other information is also passed during the initial request. For details, see Chapter 5, "Using HTTP.") This script takes the device name and returns the default menu you created along with a link to a menu of service subscriptions for the device.

The above implementation affects all Cisco IP Phones in a cluster. To implement the workaround for a single phone, the CallManager administrator must set the new URL in the **Services** field on the Phone Configuration Web page (**Device > Phone >** *find and select the phone*) as shown in Figure 9-7. This enables the pre-configured list of services to display on certain phones, such as conference room phones.

Figure 9-7   *Services URL Field on Phone Configuration Page*

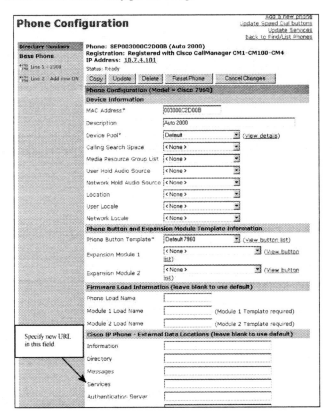

Appending the Device Name

If you want to know which devices or how many devices are hitting your service, you can append the device name to each service. The following ASP code sample, **workarounddevicename.asp**, shows the device name appended to each service. In this example, simply append **?Name=<% = name %>** to any service to pass the device name to that service (as shown in Service One in the following example). If your service has an existing query string, use an ampersand after the initial query string (as shown in Sample Two in the following example). Figure 9-8 shows a diagram of the following code sample. The **workarounddevicename.asp** page is provided for your convenience in the Chapter 9 directory on the companion CD-ROM.

```
<%@ Language=JavaScript %>
<%

var name = String(Request.QueryString("Name").Item);
Response.ContentType = "text/xml";
%>
<CiscoIPPhoneMenu>
  <Title>SERVICES</Title>
  <Prompt>Make Your Selection...</Prompt>
  <MenuItem>
    <Name>Service One</Name>
    <URL>http://services.acme.com/one.asp?Name=<% = name %></URL>
  </MenuItem>
  <MenuItem>
    <Name>Service Two</Name>
    <URL>http://services.acme.com/two.asp?Zip=75075&Name=<% = name %></URL>
  </MenuItem>
  <MenuItem>
    <Name>Service Subscriptions</Name>
    <URL>http://callmanager.yourcompany.com/CCMCIP/getservicesmenu.asp?Name=<% =
      name %></URL>
  </MenuItem>
</CiscoIPPhoneMenu>
```

Figure 9-8 *Diagram of Providing Default Services to User(s)*

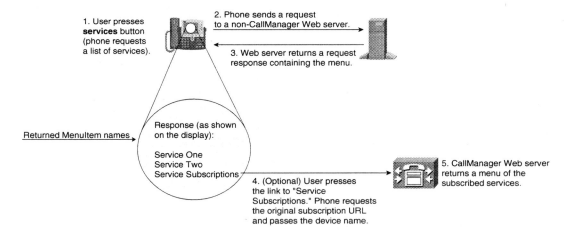

Conclusion

In this chapter, you learned the basic steps for integrating a service with Cisco CallManager, and how users subscribe/unsubscribe services for their phones in the User Options Web page. You also learned about a workaround that enables you to create a menu of default services that displays when users press the **services** button, and how to pass the name of the device that requests a service.

The next chapter exposes you to advanced techniques, including tips for working with graphics and how to capture the phone's display as an image.

CHAPTER 10

Techniques for Advanced Services

This chapter provides detailed information and samples covering some advanced techniques for runtime generation of content. This includes generating Cisco IP Phone (CIP) images. Understanding how to use the elements in this chapter helps you provide users with services that fully utilize the platform's capabilities.

The service and code samples in this chapter are written in JavaScript and can run on most Web servers from Microsoft. These samples also utilize the SDK COM objects for retrieving data from URLs and converting images from other formats to the CIP format that is understood by Cisco IP Phones.

Because these samples convey concepts that can be implemented on any platform, they should be of value to all service developers. The graphic generation and manipulation techniques that can be done in the CIP format can be performed without the use of CipImage.dll in the SDK. The more advanced sample for image navigation uses the CipImage component to do some of the heavy lifting for image resizing.

The next section covers the use of graphics in your applications. Static and dynamic content creation using the SDK components is discussed.

Adding Graphics

This section describes techniques for generating graphics for display on Cisco IP Phones in the CIP format. There are several programmatic ways to generate content using the SDK components at runtime as well as additional tools used at development time.

Generating Graphics for Applications Using Arrays

CIP image data is stored in plain ASCII text as hexadecimal (HEX) characters so it is simple to manipulate the image data as long as some issues, such as the width of the image and the color bit depth, are kept in mind during the development process. This technique has been used to develop several services that really show the capabilities of the phone's display and the XML objects that drive the behavior. A sample application that uses this technique of CIP data manipulation with arrays is the Simple Calendar, as seen in Figure 10-1.

Figure 10-1 *SimpleCalendarServiceGeneratesaGraphicCalendarImagebyManipulatingCIPImageDatain Arrays*

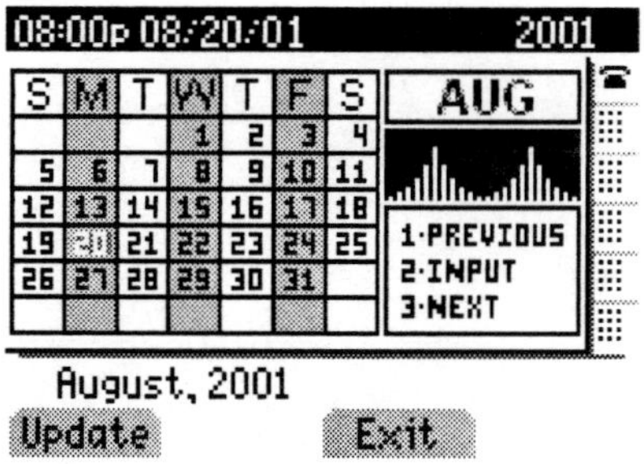

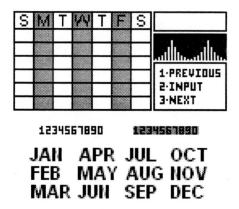

The simple calendar service generates the image at runtime, but the image subcomponents are generated at development time. This includes the month abbreviation, the font used for date values, the side menu, the Cisco logo, and the calendar background.

All the components were drawn at development time and converted to the CIP format using the Adobe Photoshop plug-in provided in the SDK. The plug-in also works with Jasc's Paint Shop Pro version 6.0 or higher. The data that made up the individual sub-image components is stored in arrays and concatenated in the data stream that is used in the CiscoIPPhoneGraphicMenu object returned to the phone. Figure 10-2 shows the components of the calendar that were drawn and then converted to CIP using the Photoshop plug-in.

Figure 10-2 *Simple Calendar Service Is Generated Using These Pre-Drawn Image Components*

The calendar base creates a framework for the other image components placed inside. There is a font with a white background and a font with a shaded background for use on the corresponding days of the week. At the bottom of the figure are the month abbreviations that appear in the box at the top right of the calendar screen. The simple calendar source is not covered in this book, but it is provided in the MiscCode directory on the accompanying CD-ROM. The sample, shown in Figure 10-4, uses the same font and array technique, but is much simpler for demonstrative purposes.

This sample takes a string containing numbers and builds a CiscoIPPhoneImage object that displays the numbers using a simple font. Each numeric digit is represented in the font array as an individual array element.

Working with CIP data, you must keep the packed pixel format in mind. The CIP format carries ramifications that must be understood and obeyed when manipulating the data in ASCII-based HEX values. The SDK documentation describes the pixel packed format for CIP images. Figure 10-3 comes from the Cisco IP Phone Services Application Development Notes provided in the SDK.

Figure 10-3 *CIP Pixel Packing Diagram*

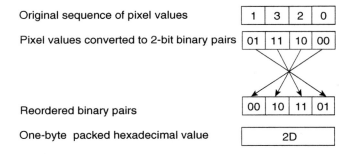

This figure shows, in detail, a sample that is four pixels wide, two bits in color depth and that packs into two HEX characters. These parameters are key to manipulating the CIP information as strings inside arrays.

In Figure 10-3, the pixel color values 1,3,2, and 0 are packed into the HEX characters "2D." These pixels can be copied, moved, and removed by manipulating the "2D" value in the Data element of the image object. In the next sample the image is built using several different arrays. The font is stored as an array for convenience in accessing the individual digits as elements. The content of each digit is colon-delimited CIP data that is placed into an array for concatenating its element values into the image array.

Figure 10-4 shows the detailed information of how the information is concatenated from individual digit arrays into the Data element of a CiscoIPPhoneImage object.

Figure 10-4 *Concatenating CIP Data Using Arrays*

A

```
Digit "1" ──→ font[1] = "0C:0F:0C:0C:3F";
Digit "5" ──→ font[5] = "3F:03:3F:30:3F";
```

B

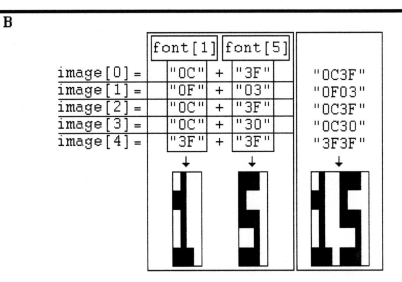

C

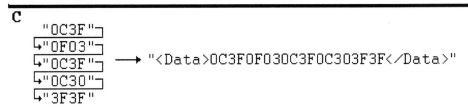

In Figure 10-4 in section A, the font array elements for digits 1 and 5 are shown. In section B, the CIP data from each font element is being concatenated into an element of the image array. On the far right the concatenated data is shown. Below the HEX data there is also a representation of the graphic pixel data for demonstrative purposes. In section C, the elements of the array are joined together (concatenated sequentially) and placed in the Data element for a CiscoIPPhoneText object.

Manipulation of the CIP data can be done with two HEX characters at a time without regard for the packing format. The color bit depth of your image determines how many pixels are being manipulated. If your image has a bit depth of two, you are manipulating four pixels. If your image has a bit depth of one, you are manipulating eight pixels. The number of pixels you are manipulating is important in the application design. This technique only works if the width of the image is evenly divisible by the number of pixels that are packed into a HEX pair. This number varies depending on the color bit depth you are using for the image.

The font used in these samples has a bit depth of two. The font characters are four pixels wide and include a single pixel space on the right side of the character. This space makes the characters exactly four pixels in width as well as provides a space between characters when they are concatenated together. After careful examination of the simple calendar service screen, you notice that the overall image width is 132 pixels. However, the display is capable of 133 pixels, but 132 are used because it is evenly divisible by four pixels. If the image is not evenly divisible by the number of pixels packed into each HEX pair, the HEX data at the right side of the image will contain data for part of the next row and will not be usable with the array technique.

The space from the left of the screen to the first column that dates appear in is four pixels in from the edge. The distance from Sunday's date values to Monday's values is also four pixels. The month abbreviation that is displayed in the top right of the simple calendar service is greater than four pixels, but it is evenly divisible by four.

Because the CIP data is HEX, you can use bitwise operators to manipulate the data. A sample of this is also contained in the simple calendar service. In Figure 10-1, the current date, in this case the $20^{th,}$ is inverted by performing a bitwise eXclusive OR (XOR) with a HEX mask of 0xFFFF. Here is the JavaScript code that performs the inversion:

```
tempImage[fc] = (eval("0x" + tempImage[fc]) ^ 0xFFFF).toString(16).toUpperCase();
```

In this sample, `tempImage` is the array containing the digits two and zero. The `eval` statement enables you to evaluate a string as the value that it translates to. This converts the contents of the `tempImage` element being referenced into the actual HEX value. Performing a bitwise XOR with the 0xFFFF mask then modifies the evaluated value. The `toString` method converts the resulting value back into a string that is base 16 (a.k.a. HEX or hexadecimal). The `toUpperCase` method converts the resulting HEX data to uppercase characters. This information is all placed back in the currently referenced `tempImage` array element. For those readers that are not familiar with bitwise operations, an eXclusive OR with a mask of all Fs (all 1s in binary) results in the exact opposite binary value. If only one of the binary digits is a 1, the result is a 1. If both of the bit values are the same, the result is a 0. This inline example shows the possible values that are a result of using XOR.

```
0011  Binary Value A
0101  Binary Value B
----
0110  Binary XOR Result
```

Numeric Digits to CiscoIPPhoneImage Sample

The sample code in this section takes the numeric string that is defined as `number` and builds a CiscoIPPhoneImage object by manipulating the font data to and from arrays.

This first code segment defines the array variables that are used for the font data, temporary data per each digit, and the final image array. The variable number is defined as the ISBN number for this book. The font array elements are defined as a colon delimited CIP data for digits zero to nine.

```
<%@ Language=JavaScript %>
<%

var font = new Array();
var temp = new Array();
var image = new Array();

var number = "1587050609"; // This book's ISBN Number

font[0] = "3F:33:33:33:3F";
font[1] = "0C:0F:0C:0C:3F";
font[2] = "3F:30:3F:03:3F";
font[3] = "3F:30:3C:30:3F";
font[4] = "33:33:3F:30:30";
font[5] = "3F:03:3F:30:3F";
font[6] = "3F:03:3F:33:3F";
font[7] = "3F:30:30:30:30";
font[8] = "3F:33:3F:33:3F";
font[9] = "3F:33:3F:30:3F";
```

The first for loop enumerates through the string value of number, incrementing once for each character. The variable temp was defined as an array. Performing a split on the string value contained in a font array element populates the array. The font array element for the currently referenced character in the variable number is used. The split method is a very handy function that creates an array as the result of parsing a string with a passed in delimiter parameter. In this case the delimiter is a colon (:). The temp array holds the array data for the current digit until it is concatenated into the image array elements. The second for loop iterates through the temp array elements and the code inside the loop concatenates the string value from temp into an image for each corresponding element. The if statement checks to see if the image element is undefined and sets the value to an empty string when appropriate. If you do not initialize the array elements and you concatenate a value into the element, it will be preceded by the string undefined.

```
for (var i = 0; i < number.length; i++)
{
  temp = String(font[Number(number.charAt(i))]).split(":");
  for (var ii = 0; ii < temp.length; ii++)
  {
    if (String(image[ii]) == "undefined")
    {
      image[ii] = "";
    }
    image[ii] = String(image[ii]) + String(temp[ii]);
  }
}
```

The next segment outputs the Content-type HTTP header of "text/xml" followed by the CiscoIPPhoneImage object. The Width element is calculated as the length of the string number multiplied by four because every character output with the font is four pixels wide. The Data element is built with the join method on the image array. The join method concatenates the contents of all of the elements into a single string using the specified delimiter. This is the opposite of the split method used earlier. The delimiter used in the preceding code sample is an empty string so that the data is contiguous without any delimiters included. All the other values are hard-coded for simplicity.

```
Response.ContentType = "text/xml";
%>
<CiscoIPPhoneImage>
  <Depth>2</Depth>
  <Width><% = (number.length * 4) %></Width>
  <Height>5</Height>
  <LocationX>0</LocationX>
  <LocationY>0</LocationY>
  <Data><% = image.join("") %></Data>
</CiscoIPPhoneImage>
```

Figure 10-5 shows the output from this sample service. The significance of this technique is not fully demonstrated by this sample. This technique allows Web programmers to create images using pre-converted image data and script. Simply outputting text as an image does not utilize the full potential. By combining images with dynamic text like that found in the simple calendar service, you can see the benefit resulting in a better user experience as compared to services that render text or static graphics.

Figure 10-5 *Number to Image Sample Service Output*

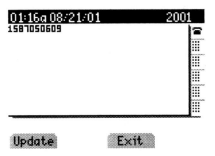

There are many types of services that can benefit from this technique, for example a weather service, graphical stock quote, current statistics for IT systems represented with graphical gauges, and so on. It would be simple to build a graphical weather service that concatenated pre-drawn weather icons like "sunny," "cloudy," and "rainy" to show a graphical four-day forecast. Another widely deployed service type that tends to be non-graphical is stock quote applications. Most of the services tend to deliver the stock quote as ASCII text in a CiscoIPPhoneText object. Some services also provide a stock chart as a CiscoIPPhoneImage object. Using this technique you can add the current stock data on top of the stock chart, providing a much richer experience by displaying text and graphical data simultaneously.

Runtime Conversion of Graphics

This section covers the runtime conversion of images to and from the CiscoIPPhoneImage format. The runtime conversions are performed using the CipImage library. The ability to retrieve an image from a URL and convert it at runtime opens up new possibilities for service development. The image-resizing sample can be used to retrieve constantly updating graphical information from other servers and display it on Cisco IP Phones. This can include weather images, stock charts, security cameras, Web cams, and so on. The image-resizing sample retrieves an image from a URL and resizes the image to fit on the phone's display while maintaining the image's original aspect ratio.

Resize an Image Maintaining its Aspect Ratio

This sample shows how to resize an image using the CipImage library in the SDK. This sample also uses the CiscoURLProxy, but is not required to perform the resize. The CiscoURLProxy is only used to retrieve an image from a URL because this is the most common use for this code.

The image is retrieved from a URL and loaded into the CipImage component. The image is then measured against the maximum display dimensions of the CiscoIPPhoneImage object. The image is then resized so that it fits on the display and maintains its aspect ratio. The image color palette is converted to grayscale and the color bit depth is reduced to two bits per pixel. The sample then returns a CiscoIPPhoneImage object to the requesting device.

This first section of code creates an instance of the CipImage and CiscoURLProxy components. The variables that are used are also declared. The getBaseURL function is used in the pages that ship with CallManager for use by the phones. This function should be used where possible or one should be written to mimic its behavior. Failure to propagate the same server name or IP that was used by the phone on its request to your service could break your service in environments that have the phones configured to use a proxy server. If the phone makes a request with an IP address and you give it a URL that references a host name, you are making an assumption that the phone is configured for DNS services and can resolve the name. By using the same name or IP address that the phone used on its request, you know that it can find your server again when calling subsequent URLs using this same information.

```
<%@ Language=JavaScript %>
<%
try
{
  var cip = new ActiveXObject("CIPIMAGE.ImageProcessor.1"); // Create my cip object
  var Inet1 = new ActiveXObject("CiscoURLProxy.URLGrabber"); // Create the proxy
                                                             // object
  var maxWidth, maxHeigth, width, height, newWidth, newHeight, rawdata;
```

```
function getBaseURL()
{
  scriptName = Request.ServerVariables("SCRIPT_NAME");
  endloc = String(scriptName).lastIndexOf("/");
  baseURL = "http://" + String(Request.ServerVariables("SERVER_NAME")) +
    String(scriptName).substr(0, endloc + 1);
  return baseURL;
}
```

The next section of code sets the URL location of the image you are trying to retrieve. The `maxWidth` and `maxHeight` values are set to the maximum size that can be displayed on the phones. The `rawdata` variable is then populated with a byte array of the JPG data that was returned with the CiscoURLProxy.

```
var url = getBaseURL() + "resize.jpg"; // Set the URL to point to a JPG Image.
maxWidth = 133;
maxHeigth = 65;
rawdata = Inet1.GetURL(url, 1); // Get the image from the url.
```

The next section loads the byte array containing the JPG data into the CipImage object. The `RGBToPalette` method converts the RGB values in the JPG image to a palette.

The `width` and `height` are taken from the properties on the CipImage component. Some simple calculations are done to determine the ratio of the original image's height and width as compared to the maximum height and width of the phone's display.

```
cip.LoadJPGFromBuffer(rawdata); // Load the byte array
cip.RGBToPalette(); // Convert the RGB image to use a palette.

width = Number(cip.width);
height = Number(cip.height);

if (width > maxWidth)
{
  widthRatio = width / maxWidth;
  newWidth = maxWidth;
}
else
{
  widthRatio = 1;
}

if (height > maxHeigth)
{
  heightRatio = height / maxHeigth;
  newHeight = maxHeigth;
}
else
{
  heightRatio = 1;
}
```

Using the ratios, the new height and new width of the image is determined. The ratios are important because we want to maintain the aspect ratio of the original image. You could easily use the `Resize` method to adjust the image to 133x65, but a vertically oriented picture's width becomes severely stretched.

```
if (widthRatio > heightRatio)
{
  newHeight = Math.round((height / widthRatio) - 1);
}
else
{
  newWidth = Math.round((width / heightRatio) - 1);
}
```

The Resize method is called, passing the new width and height of the image. The palette is converted to grayscale using the ColorToGray method. You can then reduce the number of colors in the palette with the ReducePaletteColors method passing the parameter value of 4. The phone's two-bit display is only capable of displaying a maximum of four colors.

The SetTile and SetPrompt methods are called passing a space to clear both the Title and Prompt elements of the CiscoIPPhoneImage object that is to be output. This is done in the sample code in this section because the CiscoIPPhoneImage object is output directly from the CipImage component without modification.

```
cip.Resize(newWidth, newHeight);
cip.ColorToGray();
cip.ReducePaletteColors(4);
cip.SetTitle(" ");
cip.SetPrompt(" ");
```

To end, the sample Content-Type HTTP header is set, and the BinaryWrite method is used to output the complete CiscoIPPhoneImage object to the phone.

```
Response.ContentType = "text/xml";
Response.BinaryWrite(cip.SaveCIPToBuffer());
}
catch (err)
{
  Response.Write("Error: " + err.number + ", " + err.description);
}
%>
```

The next section covers an extensive sample on manipulating graphics at runtime. This sample covers most of the techniques from this chapter to provide a robust sample that demonstrates the platform's capabilities.

Manipulating Graphics at Runtime

The advanced sample, Image View, that is dissected in this section uses a large source image and allows you to zoom in and out of the image as well as panning horizontally and vertically for image navigation. This sample uses some previously covered techniques for resizing images, getting the base URL of the execution path, and manipulating CIP data with an array.

Figure 10-6 shows the source image used for the sample on the left and some sample screen shots of the zoom capabilities.

Figure 10-6 *Image View Service Source Image and Zoom Demonstration*

The source image is a 640x480 CIP image of the Jefferson memorial in Washington, D.C. The image zoom is achieved by loading the original CIP image into an array. The desired data is then cropped and stored into a new array. This new array is then loaded into the CipImage component and resized to fit the display of the Cisco IP Phones. The level of the zoom effect is determined by the amount of data that is retained during the cropping.

The starting array element and position into the element's CIP data string determines the vertical and horizontal positioning. By manipulating these two parameters, you can perform a digital pan. In Figure 10-7, you can see a horizontal pan along the steps of the Jefferson memorial using this technique. You can see on the prompt line of the screen shots the x, y, and z values. The x parameter is the starting position in the CIP data string in each element of the image array. The y parameter indicates the first element in the array to use the CIP data from. The z parameter is used to calculate the amount of CIP data to read from each element as well as how many elements to read data from.

The Event parameter is used to indicate what manipulation is to be done to the other three parameters to impact the display of the image. All the data for the application is stored in the Session object in Internet Information Server (IIS) to increase the performance of the service as well as reduce the complexity. The parameter that is passed on the query string is the event. This enables the server to work as a CiscoIPPhoneGraphicMenu and has self-referencing URLs that pass the new event to the service. The zoom soft keys perform this same action.

Figure 10-7 *Image View Pan Demonstration*

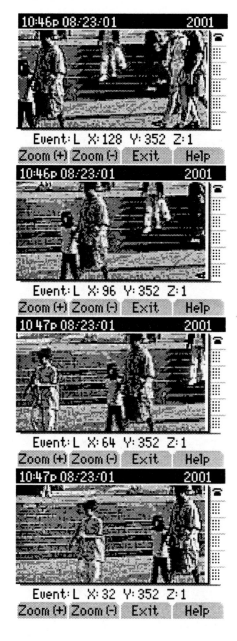

There are two additional soft keys provided for the user of the service. There is an **Exit** soft key enabling the user to exit the application. There is also a **Help** soft key that navigates to a CiscoIPPhoneImage object that provides graphical help to the user as seen in Figure 10-8.

Figure 10-8 *Image View Help Screen*

From the help screen, the user can press the **Back** soft key to return to the Image View service.

Due to the complexity of this service, the source is provided, but the commentary on the source stays at a higher level of detail to explain the overall theory of what the service is performing. The explanations reference details in the source to assist with your consumption of the code.

This first segment initializes the variables that are used throughout the service. The getBaseURL function is used to build self-referencing URLs for the service. This function is repeatedly used in the samples in this book to ensure compatibility with systems that have the phones configured to use a proxy server.

```
<%@ Language=JavaScript %>
<%
try
{
  var event, newImage, Inet1, rawdata, cip, maxWidth, maxHeight, prompt;
  var hStep, vStep, zStep, adj, newXLoc, newYLoc, clear, maxZoom;
  var tmpImage = new Array();

  //
  // Returns the base portion of the URL for building new URLs to the same path
  //

  function getBaseURL()
  {
    scriptName = Request.ServerVariables("SCRIPT_NAME");
    endloc = String(scriptName).lastIndexOf("/");
    baseURL = "http://" +
      String(Request.ServerVariables("SERVER_NAME")) +
      String(scriptName).substr(0, endloc + 1);
    return baseURL ;
  }
```

The setXLoc function is used by the service to increment or decrement the current xLoc value and store the new value in the Session object. xLoc is displayed on the phone's prompt as the value x. This function performs some validation of the requested incremental change. If the newXLoc value is less than zero, then zero is used. If the xLoc value plus the width of the data to be displayed exceeds the data available in the source image, the xLoc value reverts to its previous value.

```
//
// Increments or Decrements the "xLoc" Session variable with the passed value
//

function setXLoc(inc)
{
  Session("xLoc") = Number(Session("xLoc")) + Number(inc);
  if (Number(Session("xLoc")) >= Number(Session("imageWidth")) - (maxWidth *
    Number(Session("Zoom"))))
  {
    if (inc > 1)
    {
      Session("xLoc") = Number(Session("xLoc")) + (inc * -1);
    }
  }
  if (Number(Session("xLoc")) < 0)
  {
    Session("xLoc") = 0;
  }
}
```

The setYLoc function performs a similar functionality to the setXLoc function, but it is used to set and validate the yLoc value.

```
//
// Increments or Decrements the "yLoc" Session variable with the passed value
//

function setYLoc(inc)
{
  Session("yLoc") = Number(Session("yLoc")) + Number(inc);
  if (Number(Session("yLoc")) >= Number(Session("imageHeight")) - (maxHeight *
    Number(Session("Zoom"))))
  {
    if (inc > 1)
    {
      Session("yLoc") = Number(Session("yLoc")) + (inc * -1);
    }
  }
  if (Number(Session("yLoc")) < 0)
  {
    Session("yLoc") = 0;
  }
}
```

The setZoom function also takes an increment or decrement value and modifies the Session variable Zoom. This function also validates the value that is passed in to make sure that it is not less than a value of one and does not exceed the maxZoom value of five.

The setZoom function also handles additional issues that are encountered when you are near the edge of the image and you perform a Zoom out. Due to the normal centering of the image through the zoom process there would be a large area of white space beyond the edge of the image. This function uses setXLoc and setYLoc functions to pass the appropriate incremental values to move the image display space, removing the blank space that would normally display.

```
//
// Increments or Decrements the "Zoom" Session variable with the passed value
//

function setZoom(inc)
{
  Session("Zoom") = Number(Session("Zoom")) + Number(inc);
  if ((Number(Session("Zoom")) > maxZoom) ||
      (Number(Session("Zoom")) == 0))
  {
    Session("Zoom") = Number(Session("Zoom")) + Number(inc * -1);
  }
  else
  {
    if (Number(Session("xLoc")) > Number(Session("imageWidth")) -
      (maxWidth * Number(Session("Zoom"))))
    {
      setXLoc(Number(Session("imageWidth")) - (Number(maxWidth) *
        Number(Session("Zoom"))) - Number(Session("xLoc")));
    }
    else
    {
      setXLoc(-hStep * inc * 2);
    }
    if (Number(Session("yLoc")) > Number(Session("imageHeight")) - (maxHeight *
      Number(Session("Zoom"))))
    {
      setYLoc(Number(Session("imageHeight")) - (Number(maxHeight) *
        Number(Session("Zoom"))) - Number(Session("yLoc")));
    }
    else
    {
      setYLoc(-vStep * inc);
    }
  }
}
```

This next section gets the Jefferson.cip image file using the CiscoURLProxy from within the same path as this service. The CIP image XML data is parsed using regular expressions and the data is stored in the Session object.

```
// Get and Set the image information if it is not in the session
if (String(Session("imageSet")) != "OK")
{
  Inet1 = new ActiveXObject("CiscoURLProxy.URLGrabber");
  rawdata = Inet1.GetURL(getBaseURL() + "jefferson.cip", 0);
  Session("imageWidth") = rawdata.slice((rawdata.search(/<Width>/g) + 7),
    rawdata.search(/<\/Width>/g));
  Session("imageHeight") = rawdata.slice((rawdata.search(/<Height>/g) + 8),
    rawdata.search(/<\/Height>/g));
  Session("imageDepth") = rawdata.slice((rawdata.search(/<Depth>/g) + 7),
    rawdata.search(/<\/Depth>/g));
  rawdata = rawdata.slice((rawdata.search(/<Data>/g) + 6),
  rawdata.search(/<\/Data>/g));
  Session("imageData") = rawdata;
  Session("imageSet") = "OK";
}
```

The next section sets up the default values that are used by the service. The step values could be generated based on the height and width of the source image object to make this service work with different sized images. Making the step values dynamic based on the source image size is something that you can do to extend the functionality of this service.

An instance is created of the CipImage component. The event parameter is retrieved from the query string and set if it was not present.

```
// Set Defaults
newImage = "";
maxWidth = 132;
maxHeight = 65;
maxZoom = 5;
hStep = 32;
vStep = 32;
zStep = 1;
clear = 0;
cip = new ActiveXObject("CIPIMAGE.ImageProcessor.1");
event = String(Request.QueryString("event"));
if (event == "undefined")
{
  event = "Init";
}
```

This formatImage function is the same as the image-resizing sample earlier in this chapter. This function takes a CipImage object as input and resizes the image while maintaining its original aspect ratio. The object is then returned.

```
//
// Increments or Decrements the "Zoom" Session variable with the passed value
//

function formatImage(cipObj)
{
  cipObj.RGBToPalette();
  width = Number(cipObj.width);
  height = Number(cipObj.height);
  if (width > maxWidth)
  {
    widthRatio = width / maxWidth;
    newWidth = maxWidth;
  }
  else
  {
    widthRatio = 1;
  }

  if (height > maxHeight)
  {
    heightRatio = height / maxHeight;
    newHeight = maxHeight;
  }
  else
  {
    heightRatio = 1;
  }

  if (widthRatio > heightRatio)
  {
    newHeight = Math.round((height / widthRatio) - 1);
  }
```

```
      else
      {
        newWidth = Math.round((width / heightRatio) - 1);
      }
      cipObj.ColorToGray();
      cipObj.ReducePaletteColors(4);
      cipObj.ResizeEx(newWidth, newHeight, 1);
      return cipObj;
    }
```

This next section is a large switch statement that handles the events. You can see the events call the setXLoc, setYLoc, and setZoom functions to manipulate the image state. The case for Init and Home sets the session values directly to clear them. The Back case does not modify any image display parameters because it is used for a user returning from the help screen.

```
    //
    // This switch statement is used to initiate processing for the possible event
    // types
    //
    switch (event)
    {
      case "Init":
      case "Home":
        prompt = "H";
        Session("xLoc") = 0;
        Session("yLoc") = 0;
        Session("Zoom") = 5;
      break;
      case "UpLeft":
        prompt = "UL";
        setXLoc(-hStep);
        setYLoc(-vStep);
      break;
      case "Up":
        prompt = "U";
        setYLoc(-vStep);
      break;
      case "UpRight":
        prompt = "UR";
        setXLoc(hStep);
        setYLoc(-vStep);
      break;
      case "Left":
        prompt = "L";
        setXLoc(-hStep);
      break;
      case "Right":
        prompt = "R";
        setXLoc(hStep);
      break;
      case "DownLeft":
        prompt = "DL";
        setYLoc(vStep);
        setXLoc(-hStep);
      break;
      case "Down":
        prompt = "D";
        setYLoc(vStep);
      break;
      case "DownRight":
```

continues

(continued)

```
            prompt = "DR";
            setYLoc(vStep);
            setXLoc(hStep);
        break;
        case "ZoomIn":
            prompt = "ZI";
            setZoom(-zStep);
        break;
        case "ZoomOut":
            prompt = "ZO";
            setZoom(zStep);
        break;
        case "Back":
            prompt = "B";
        break;
        default:
            // No Default
    }
```

This next section gets local copies of the Zoom, xLoc, and yLoc session values for processing. This is where the image cropping takes place. You can see that the newWidth and newHeight values are calculated using the Zoom value as a modifier. This controls the amount of data that is cropped out of the imageData string in the Session object. All the dividing by two comes into play due to how the CIP data is packed into HEX character pairs.

Because the source image is stored as a giant string, it is possible to go beyond the edge of the image and loop into the next line of the image. This loop is allowed for the data extraction and corrected by calculating the amount that needs to be cleared, if any, doing so when the final newImage value is created.

The first if statement is checking to see if the width of the new image does not fit the width of the display. If additional padding of zeros is needed, the clear value is set to the required amount.

```
adj = Number(Session("Zoom"));
newXLoc = Number(Session("xLoc"));
newYLoc = Number(Session("yLoc"));
newWidth = maxWidth * adj;
newHeight = maxHeight * adj;

for (var i = newYLoc; i < (newHeight + newYLoc); i++)
{
    tmpImage[i-newYLoc] = String(String(Session("imageData"))).substr(i *
        (Session("imageWidth") / 2) + (newXLoc / 2), newWidth / 2);
}
if ((newXLoc + newWidth) > Number(Session("imageWidth")))
{
    clear = newWidth - Number(Session("imageWidth")) - newXLoc;
}
```

This next section takes the values stored in the elements of the tmpImage array and concatenates them into the newImage data stream. If the clear value is set, the string is split into two pieces and the second piece is cleared before they are concatenated back together. This clears the looped image data.

```
for (var i = 0; i < tmpImage.length; i++)
{
  // This code clears image to the right of the picture's edge instead of looping
  // the image

  if (clear > 0)
  {
    tmpString = tmpImage[i];
    start = tmpString.length - (clear/ 2);
    clearString = tmpString.slice(start);
    clearString = clearString.replace(/\w/gi,"0");
    tmpString = tmpString.slice(0, start) + clearString;
    newImage += tmpString;
  }
  else
  {
    newImage += tmpImage[i];
  }
}
```

This next section loads the CIP data into the CipImage object and then calls the `formatImage`
function to resize it for display on the phone. The `prompt` is set and the HTTP headers are
generated. The last portion of the sample outputs the CiscoIPPhoneGraphicMenu object.
This includes the image that was created as well as `MenuItem` and `SoftKeyItem` that use the
self-referencing URLs to cause events.

```
// Load the Image data for the selected sub Image area and resize it.

cip.LoadCIPDataFromBuffer(newImage, newWidth, newHeight);
cip = formatImage(cip);

prompt = "Event: " + prompt + " X: " + Number(Session("xLoc"));
prompt += " Y: " + Number(Session("yLoc")) + " Z: " + Number(Session("Zoom"));

Response.ContentType = "text/xml";
Response.Expires = -1;
// Build Graphic Menu

%>
<CiscoIPPhoneGraphicMenu>
  <Title> </Title>
  <Prompt><% = prompt %></Prompt>
  <LocationX>-1</LocationX>
  <LocationY>-1</LocationY>
  <Width><% = cip.width %></Width>
  <Height><% = cip.height %></Height>
  <Depth>2</Depth>
  <Data><% = cip.SaveCIPDataToBuffer() %></Data>
  <MenuItem>
    <Name>UpLeft</Name>
    <URL><% = (getBaseURL() + "view.asp?event=UpLeft") %></URL>
  </MenuItem>
  <MenuItem>
    <Name>Up</Name>
    <URL><% = (getBaseURL() + "view.asp?event=Up") %></URL>
  </MenuItem>
  <MenuItem>
    <Name>UpRight</Name>
    <URL><% = (getBaseURL() + "view.asp?event=UpRight") %></URL>
  </MenuItem>
  <MenuItem>
    <Name>Left</Name>
```

continues

(continued)

```
        <URL><% = (getBaseURL() + "view.asp?event=Left") %></URL>
      </MenuItem>
      <MenuItem>
        <Name>Home</Name>
        <URL><% = (getBaseURL() + "view.asp?event=Home") %></URL>
      </MenuItem>
      <MenuItem>
        <Name>Right</Name>
        <URL><% = (getBaseURL() + "view.asp?event=Right") %></URL>
      </MenuItem>
      <MenuItem>
        <Name>DownLeft</Name>
        <URL><% = (getBaseURL() + "view.asp?event=DownLeft") %></URL>
      </MenuItem>
      <MenuItem>
        <Name>Down</Name>
        <URL><% = (getBaseURL() + "view.asp?event=Down") %></URL>
      </MenuItem>
      <MenuItem>
        <Name>DownRight</Name>
        <URL><% = (getBaseURL() + "view.asp?event=DownRight") %></URL>
      </MenuItem>
      <SoftKeyItem>
        <Name>Zoom (+)</Name>
        <URL><% = (getBaseURL() + "view.asp?event=ZoomIn") %></URL>
        <Position>1</Position>
      </SoftKeyItem>
      <SoftKeyItem>
        <Name>Zoom (-)</Name>
        <URL><% = (getBaseURL() + "view.asp?event=ZoomOut") %></URL>
        <Position>2</Position>
      </SoftKeyItem>
      <SoftKeyItem>
        <Name>Exit</Name>
        <URL>SoftKey:Exit</URL>
        <Position>3</Position>
      </SoftKeyItem>
      <SoftKeyItem>
        <Name>Help</Name>
        <URL><% = (getBaseURL() + "viewhelp.asp") %></URL>
        <Position>4</Position>
      </SoftKeyItem>
    </CiscoIPPhoneGraphicMenu>
    <%
  }
  catch(err)
  {
    Response.Write("Error: " + err.number + " Description: " + err.description);
  }
%>
```

This sample was a pleasure to write because it fully demonstrates the capabilities of the display, custom soft keys, the versatile CiscoIPPhoneGraphicMenu object, the CiscoURLProxy, resizing images, building self-referencing URLs, and the technique of manipulating CIP images with arrays and string parsing.

The next section covers the ability to capture the contents of the Cisco IP Phone display as a CIP object. There is also a programmatic example of how to do this so you can use a Web browser.

Capturing the Phone's Display

Cisco IP Phones 7940 and 7960 have the ability to generate a CIP image of the current display contents and return the file on request. It is simple to take a manual screen capture of a phone's display. This technique was used for many of the images that you can find throughout this book.

For you to successfully request a screen shot, you must have a valid user ID and password defined in the global directory portion of Cisco CallManager Administration (CCMAdmin). The user must be associated with the target device. This privilege is the same that is used to configure the device or subscribe to services in the Cisco IP Phone User Options (CCMUser) Web pages. The authentication URL must also be configured and accessible by the phone. This can be set as an enterprise parameter or overridden on an individual device basis.

Once everything is configured, you still need the IP address of the target phone, which can either be obtained from CCMAdmin on the Device Configuration screen or via the settings menu on the phone. In the **settings** menu, select **Network Configuration** and press **6**. This takes you to the IP Address menu item.

Manually Capturing the Display

You can request the screen shot by entering the following URL into a Web browser and replacing x.x.x.x with the IP address of the phone. All URLs that are available from the phone's Web server are case sensitive.

```
http://x.x.x.x/CGI/Screenshot
```

The above URL returns a CiscoIPPhoneImage object that is 160 pixels wide and 100 pixels high with a two bit color depth. This CIP image can be converted to a standard graphics file format using the tools provided with the SDK such as the Photoshop plug-in.

Programmatically Capturing the Display

This next sample can be used to capture the phone's display and convert it to a GIF image. The sample provides an HTML form to input the phone's IP address, a user ID, and a password. The form then performs an HTTP POST back to itself with the entered data. The data is then used to perform an HTTP GET request to the /CGI/Screenshot path on the target phone's Web server.

The first section of code sets local variables with the values that are present in the Request object. If the IP address is undefined, the sample assumes that the data needs to be collected from the user and returns the HTML form.

```
<%@ Language=JavaScript %>
<%
try
{
  var phone = String(Request.Item("IP"));
  var user = String(Request.Item("USER"));
  var pass = String(Request.Item("PASS"));

  if (phone == "undefined")
  {
    %>
    <HTML>
    <BODY>
    <FORM ACTION="ScreenshotByIP.asp" METHOD="POST">
    <BR><BR><BR><BR>
    <CENTER>
    <Table>
    <tr>
    <td>Enter the phones IP Address:</td>
    <td><INPUT NAME="IP" TYPE="TEXT" SIZE="30" MAXLENGTH="30" VALUE=""></td>
    </tr>
    <tr>
    <td>User ID:</td>
    <td><INPUT NAME="USER" TYPE="TEXT" SIZE="30" MAXLENGTH="30" VALUE=""></td>
    </tr>
    <tr>
    <td>Password:</td>
    <td><INPUT NAME="PASS" TYPE="PASSWORD" SIZE="30" MAXLENGTH="30" VALUE=""></td>
    </tr>
    <tr><td></td><td><Input TYPE="Submit" VALUE="Get Screenshot"></td></tr>
    </table>
    </CENTER>
    </FORM>
    </BODY>
    </HTML>
    <%
    Response.End();
  }
```

The next section performs the actual screen shot work. The first two lines create an instance of the CiscoURLProxy and the CipImage library. Then the display information is retrieved and stored in the `rawdata` variable. The `user` and `password` are deliberately passed as part of the URL instead of the associated properties on the CiscoURLProxy. The screen shot URL redirects your HTTP client to the new URL that points to a temporary file in the phone's file system. If you use the `UserName` and `Password` properties on the CiscoURLProxy, the request fails due to the HTTP redirection. By passing these parameters as part of the URL, it completes successfully.

```
var Inet1 = new ActiveXObject("CiscoURLProxy.URLGrabber");
var cip = new ActiveXObject("CIPIMAGE.ImageProcessor.1");
var rawdata = Inet1.GetURL("http://" + user + ":" + pass + "@" + phone +
  "/CGI/Screenshot", 0);
```

The screen shot data is returned in the form of a CIP image. The raw data is loaded into the CipImage component with the `LoadCIPFromBuffer` method. The Content-Type HTTP header is set to image/gif. The Content-Disposition HTTP header is used to tell Web browsers the `filename` of the object that is being downloaded. The GIF data is then output using the `BinaryWrite` method of the IIS `Response` object because the data is binary. The binary data is returned from the CipImage component using the `SaveGIFToBuffer` method. You can change the file type that is returned from this sample by changing this line as well as the Content-Type header and the file name listed in the Content-Disposition header.

```
cip.LoadCIPFromBuffer(rawdata);

Response.ContentType = "image/gif";
Response.AddHeader("Content-Disposition", "attached;filename=ScreenShot.gif;");
Response.BinaryWrite(cip.SaveGIFToBuffer());
}
catch (err)
{
  Response.Write("Error: " + err.number.toString(16) + " Description: " +
    err.description);
}
%>
```

Both the manual and programmatic methods for capturing the phone's display were used for the screen shots throughout this book. This is a very powerful feature for making Web-based or printed documentation for detailed instruction and demonstration of a service.

Pushing Content

It is possible to push a URL or URI to supported Cisco IP Phones. (*Push* is defined as instructing the phone to perform an action via HTTP.) You can push content to the phones using the CiscoIPPhoneExecute object. The CiscoIPPhoneExecute object should be sent to the phone as an HTTP POST to the /CGI/Execute path. A CiscoIPPhoneExecute object can contain three ExecuteItem instances. Only one ExecuteItem can be a URL. All the ExecuteItems can be URIs. The sample code in this section is an HTML page that you can load with a standard Web browser. Edit the URL field of the ExecuteItem to point to a server and path that returns services data. You also need to change the IP address in the FORM action field to point to a phone's IP address.

The form has an element called XML. This form element is case sensitive. When you post the form, your Web browser prompts you to enter your user name and password. This requires the same credentials as the /CGI/Screenshot path.

```
<HTML>
<HEAD>
</HEAD>
<BODY>
<FORM action="http://10.0.0.1/CGI/Execute" Method="POST">
<TEXTAREA NAME="XML" Rows="5" Cols="60">
<CiscoIPPhoneExecute>
  <ExecuteItem URL="http://x.x.x.x/"/>
</CiscoIPPhoneExecute>
</TEXTAREA>
<BR>
<input type=submit value=POST>
</FORM>
</BODY>
</HTML>
```

After a CiscoIPPhoneExecute object is successfully posted to the phone's Web server, the phone returns a CiscoIPPhoneResponse object that contains a matching `ResponseItem` for each `ExecuteItem` that was submitted. In Figure 10-9 you can see the HTML form that is presented by the sample.

Figure 10-9 *Push HTML Page Sample*

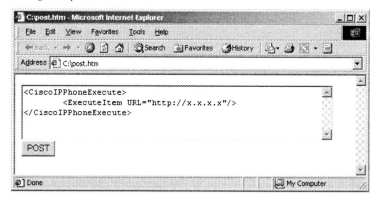

Streaming URIs for RTP

The following streaming URIs allow a service developer to control the setup and teardown of RTP audio streams to and from the phone. The phone can support both Unicast and Multicast RTP streams. The ability to stream Multicast using URIs was added in the Cisco CallManager 3.2(2) release.

RTPRx URI

The RTPRx URI instructs the phone to receive a Unicast RTP stream or to stop the reception of a Unicast or Multicast RTP stream. The supported format of the RTP stream is G.711 μ-law with 20 msec packets.

URI format: `RTPRx:i:p` or `RTPRx:Stop`

i = IP address to receive RTP stream from.

p = TCP port to receive RTP stream on. This must be an even port number within the decimal range of 20480 to 32768. If no port is specified, one will be chosen by the phone and returned when initiated via a push request.

Stop = This parameter by itself will stop any active RTP stream being received on channel one.

RTPTx URI

The RTPTx URI instructs the phone to transmit a Unicast RTP stream or to stop the transmitting of a Unicast or Multicast RTP stream. The supported format of the RTP stream is G.711 μ-law with 20 msec packets.

URI format: `RTPTx:i:p` or `RTPTx:Stop`

i = IP address to transmit an RTP stream to.

p = TCP port to transmit the RTP stream on. This must be an even port number within the decimal range of 20480 to 32768.

Stop = This parameter by itself will stop any active RTP stream being transmitted on channel one.

RTPMRx URI

The RTPMRx URI instructs the phone to receive a Multicast RTP stream. The supported format of the RTP stream is G.711 μ-law with 20 msec packets.

URI format: `RTPMRx:i:p`

i = Multicast IP address to receive RTP stream from.

p = Multicast TCP port to receive RTP stream on. This must be an even port number within the decimal range of 20480 to 32768.

RTPMTx URI

The RTPMTx URI instructs the phone to transmit a Multicast RTP stream. The supported format of the RTP stream is G.711 μ-law with 20 msec packets.

URI format: `RTPMTx:i:p`

i = Multicast IP address to transmit an RTP stream to.

p = Multicast TCP port to transmit the RTP stream on. This must be an even port number within the decimal range of 20480 to 32768.

Conclusion

Hopefully, this chapter has provided inspiration as well as the technical guidance to enable your inspired service creations. The chapter goes in-depth into using graphics with the Cisco IP Phone because this is a major capability of services as well as the phone's user interface. The ability to customize soft keys for your services can provide a higher quality interaction with your service user. The use of a **Help** soft key for services that are not self-explanatory enables you to break out of the service and assist the user. Your help page or subsystem can then return the user to the service so they can apply what they learned.

This chapter also used the CiscoURLProxy and CipImage components in several of the samples. The SDK components are not required to build services, but they help overcome hurdles. If you are using Java to build your services, the CiscoURLProxy is not needed because this functionality is available to you in the language.

The CipImage library is very powerful because it is targeted at the specific problem of converting to and from CIP as well as manipulating the images. There are Cisco partners that have created their own Java-based image conversion utilities for this purpose.

The technique of manipulating CIP data with strings and arrays applies to most development platforms. It is possible to use conventional graphics libraries to perform these actions and then convert the images from traditional formats to the CIP image format for display. Developers can use a Microsoft Windows-based PC to create the CIP images with the SDK components. Once the images are converted to CIP, services can be built using the data on any platform that can manipulate strings and use arrays.

The last sample for pushing content to the phones is the most promising feature as the Cisco IP Phone service platform matures.

CHAPTER 11

XML Development Tools

This chapter shows you how to use the tools in the Cisco IP Phone Services SDK that create XML content. These tools can be used on the server to dynamically create XML objects when needed. They can also be used during your development phase to create static XML content that will be the same each time it is served up.

The SDK ships with a few tools that help you create better applications. This chapter discusses the following SDK highlights:

- Graphics Conversion Control
- URL Proxy Control
- LDAP Search Control
- Photoshop Graphics filter
- XML Validator

The first three tools are ActiveX controls that integrate with applications running under Microsoft IIS. The last two tools are useful for service development.

Graphics Conversion Control

At this time, the Cisco IP Phone uses a proprietary format for image content, rather than using the widespread GIF and JPEG formats. This internal format is discussed in Chapter 4, "Using Cisco IP Phone XML Objects and Tags."

The reason the phone does not support GIF images is simple. At the time the Cisco IP Phone was being developed, Unisys was still actively enforcing U.S. Patent Number 4,558,302, which covers the GIF file format. For better or worse, Cisco would have been required to pay a royalty to Unisys on every phone shipped with code that could render GIF images. The royalty and associated other costs (e.g. accounting) would have substantially increased the price of the phone.

The reason the phone does not support JPEG images is different. It is a matter of processor power and code space. The task of decoding JPEG images and then properly dithering to a two-bit gray scale display is a bit much for the 25 MHz ARM processor in the Cisco IP Phone, especially because Cisco IP Phones have limited memory available for code and program data. As a result, JPEG rendering is not included in the original Cisco IP Phones.

Server-side Conversion

It's fine for Cisco to decide not to support JPEG and GIF formats in the Cisco IP Phones, but where does that leave you, the poor developer? The proprietary internal graphics format is well defined, but the idea of typing in graphics files by hand is not too appealing.

Fortunately, the Cisco IP Phone Services SDK provides you with two tools to accomplish this task. The first of these two tools is **CipImage.dll**, an ActiveX component that can be used to programmatically convert PNG, JPG, BMP, and GIF format files to Cisco's proprietary CIP format. The second tool, **Cip.8bi**, is a filter that can be used with Adobe Photoshop and other graphics manipulation programs (it is discussed later in this chapter).

Using CipImage.dll, you can set up Web pages or automated scripts to convert images to CIP format before sending them to the Cisco IP Phones.

Installation

If you install the Cisco IP Phone Services SDK, the Graphics Conversion Control is installed and registered on your system automatically. If you want to install the control on another system without going to the trouble of installing the SDK, you can do so manually.

To do a manual installation:

1   Copy the following two files to your Windows System directory:

   — CipImage.dll

   — Vic32.dll

   Both of these files can be found in the Tools directory in the Cisco IP Phone Services SDK hierarchy. By default, the root pathname for the SDK is C:\CiscoIpServices.

2   After you copy the two files, register the controls by passing the names of the files to the REGSVR32.EXE tool. Cisco recommends launching a Windows command line window to accomplish this task.

If the procedure succeeds, you will see the dialog box as shown in Figure 11-1.

Figure 11-1 *Manual Installation of the CIP Tool*

Once the DLL is registered, it is available to all programs on the PC that know how to use ActiveX controls, including JavaScript, VBScript, Microsoft Visual C++, and Visual Basic.

Methods and Properties

CipImage.dll has a long list of methods and properties, which are documented as part of the SDK. For complete details on individual methods, consult those documents. This section provides a short recap of the methods and properties you use most frequently.

Methods: LoadGIF(filename), LoadJPG(filename)

This method is used to load the contents of a graphics file into the control. There are actually five different methods for loading a file, with the string *filename* replaced with the appropriate file types: LoadGIF(), LoadJPG(), LoadPNG(), LoadBMP(), and LoadCIP(). In addition to these methods, which load graphics data from a file, there are five corresponding methods that enable you to load the data from an internal buffer: LoadJPGFromBuffer(), LoadPNGFromBuffer(), LoadBMPFromBuffer(), and LoadCIPFromBuffer().

You should find that 99 percent of the time you are using the control to convert JPG or GIF images to CIP format. Given that, the functions you most often call are LoadJPG() and LoadGIF(). When these functions return a value of 0 indicating success, you are now ready to perform the manipulations needed to create a useful CIP image.

Properties: Width, Height

These two properties return the size (in pixels) of the currently loaded image. Knowing these properties is critical because the Cisco IP Phone's limited display area of 133 by 64 pixels is quite small. Most images that you work with are going to need to be resized before saving in CIP format, and these values help you determine the correct scaling factor.

Below is a C++ code fragment that demonstrates the use of this control; it checks to see if an image needs to be resized by determining the smallest scaling factor needed to make sure both the width and height fit within the phone's display.

```
long width, height;
pProcessor->get_width( &width );
pProcessor->get_height( &height );
float scale = min( 133.0 / width, 64.0 / height );
if ( scale >= 1.0 )
    scale = 1.0;
pProcessor->Resize( width * scale, height * scale );
```

Note that in the sample C++ code, the width and height properties are returned using the `get_width()` and `get_height()` member functions.

Method: Resize(width, height)

The previous code sample calls the `Resize()` method to scale the image to the appropriate size. The previous fragment shows a typical use of the method. During the typical conversion of a JPG or GIF file to CIP, resizing to the appropriate size is a good first step.

The image conversion control does the necessary interpolation needed to scale the image without distortion, but you should be careful to not change the aspect ratio of your image when calling this method. In general, this means that you should scale the width and height by the same factor. (The pixels in the phone display are square, as are the pixels on nearly all conventional desktop PCs.)

Property: ColorBitDepth/Method: RGBToPalette()

The `ColorBitDepth` property tells you the number of bits being used for each pixel in the current image. In general it is safe to assume that JPG files have a color bit depth of 24 bits, and GIF images use eight bits or less.

The important fact to note here is that color depths of 16 or 24 bits do not use a palette—each pixel is described as an actual set of RGB values. Images that have color depths of eight bits or less do not store RGB values for each pixel; instead they simply store an index into a palette for each pixel.

The details of these two types of representation are not particularly important. What is important is that CIP images *must* use a palette—the phone hardware requires it. This means that if your image has a `ColorBitDepth` property of 16 or 24, you must call the `RGBToPalette()` member of the conversion control. The sample C++ conversion program does this without even testing the `ColorBitDepth` property, because it only converts JPG images (which are assumed to use 24-bit RGB values).

Property: ColorImage/Method: ColorToGray()

`ColorImage` is a Boolean property, which is used to determine if the image is currently a full color image or gray scale. CIP images as displayed on the Cisco IP Phone are gray scale images only. As part of the conversion process, you should call the `ColorToGray()` method, which converts the image to gray scale making it ready for display on the phone.

Property: ColorCount/Method: ReducePaletteColors()

The final property that is critical to the conversion of a JPG or GIF image to CIP format is the `ColorCount`. The Cisco IP Phone hardware only has four gray scale colors, far less than normally found in a GIF or JPG image. Calling the `ReducePaletteColors()` method with a value of four modifies the image so that it is ready to be saved as a CIP file.

Method: SetPrompt()/Method: SetTitle()

These two methods provide a way to set the prompt and title fields in the CIP image. The title and prompt are somewhat unique to the CIP format, so they do not have any preexisting value when the files are read as JPG or GIF files.

Method: SaveCIP()

This method writes the data out to a CIP file suitable for display on the phone.

An Example

The Cisco IP Phone Services SDK ships with a JavaScript sample that performs a simple conversion between any two formats supported by the image control. The code is very straightforward, is easy to modify, and can be used by invoking Windows Scripting Host or embedding the code in a Web page. The code is found in the Services\WSH\Cip directory of the SDK.

To supplement that code, the convert.cpp program is provided in this chapter. This command line C++ program reads a JPG file, resizes it, modifies the color count, sets a property, and then saves it as a CIP file. The program can be built with Visual C++ 6.0 and requires that the Image Conversion control be installed on your development system. The complete project is on the CD that accompanies the book.

```
#include <iostream>
#include <string>
using namespace std;

#import "../CipImage.dll"
using namespace CIPIMAGE;

int main( int argc, char* argv[] )
```

continues

(continued)

```
{
    try
    {
        if ( argc < 3 )
            throw "Usage: convert jpg-input-file cip-output-file";
        HRESULT hr = CoInitialize( NULL );
        SUCCEEDED( hr ) ? 0 :throw hr;
        IImageProcessorPtr pProcessor( __uuidof( ImageProcessor));
        hr = pProcessor->LoadJPG( argv[ 1 ] ) );
        if ( hr )
            throw "Failed to open file";
        long width, height;
        pProcessor->get_width( &width );
        pProcessor->get_height( &height );
        float scale = min( 133.0 / width, 64.0 / height );
        if ( scale >= 1.0 )
            scale = 1.0;
        pProcessor->Resize( width * scale, height * scale );
        pProcessor->RGBToPalette();
        pProcessor->ColorToGray();
        pProcessor->ReducePaletteColors( 4 );
        pProcessor->SetPrompt( argv[ 1 ] );
        pProcessor->SaveCIP( argv[ 2 ] );
    }
    catch ( _com_error e )
    {
        cout << "COM error: " << e.ErrorMessage() << "\n";
    }
    catch ( const char *p )
    {
        cout << "Runtime error: " << p << "\n";
    }
        return 0;
}
```

The program should be invoked from the command line with two arguments: an input JPG file and an output CIP file. Figure 11-2 shows the input and output of the program. In this case the input was a full color JPG file.

The CIP file that is output from the program is ready to be served to the telephone as an XML object. Figure 11-3 shows the image taken from the phone screen.

Using the logic shown in the preceding convert program makes it quite feasible to automate the process of image conversion; the control provides you with all the data you need in order to produce reasonable quality CIP images from any JPG or GIF source.

Figure 11-2 *Input and Output from the Conversion Program*

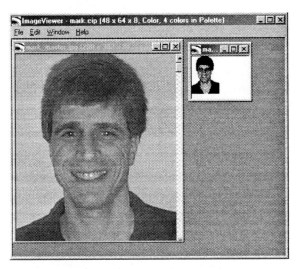

Figure 11-3 *The CIP File Displayed on the Telephone*

URL Proxy Control

The URL Proxy control is the second control that ships with the Cisco IP Phone Services SDK. Like the graphics conversion control, it is designed to run on a Win32 server and help your services create content for the phones.

And what does the URL Proxy control do to help you create services? Simply put, it pulls content from other Web pages, which enables your Cisco IP Phone service to manipulate that content, repackage it, and send it down to Cisco IP Phones.

This process, often referred to as *scraping*, has unsavory connotations to some. And in fact, if you use the URL Proxy control to repackage copyrighted material from other Web sites, you might be viewed as a bad *Netizen*.

However, there are reasonable purposes for this as well. Corporate intranets, government database, and even commercial Web sites have data that is free for the asking. Because Cisco IP Phones do not have the ability to render HTML, we have to reformat the text to a more palatable format. The URL Proxy control simply helps to make the process easier.

Installation

If you install the Cisco IP Phone Services SDK, the URL Proxy control is installed and registered on your system automatically. If you want to install the control on another system without going to the trouble of installing the SDK, you can do so manually using the approach you saw in the previous section of this chapter.

Simply copy the DLL that contains the control, **CiscoURLProxy.dll**, to a directory of your choice. If you are not sure where the DLL belongs, feel free to copy it into your Windows System directory.

Once you've copied the DLL into place, you need to register it using the REGSVR32.EXE utility. Run this utility from the command line, passing the name of the DLL as its only argument. Should things go as expected, you should see a window something like that shown in Figure 11-4.

Figure 11-4 *Successful Registration of the CiscoURLProxy Control*

Methods and Properties

The methods and properties for this control have a good set of documentation that ships with the SDK. In practice, the one method that you need to be familiar with is the GetURL() method.

GetUrl() is called with a complete URL as a string argument and returns a string containing the data returned from the Web page. Generally most of your job as a service writer is to write script that parses the returned data and identifies specific elements within the stream. You then repackage that data into XML objects that the IP Phone understands.

The Cisco IP Phone Services SDK ships with two Active Server Pages that do a good job of demonstrating how to use this control. The first page, StockChart, loads a stock chart from Yahoo's finance pages and converts the embedded GIF image to a CIP format graphic. It's a testament to the power of the toolset and the Cisco IP Phone XML objects that an application this complex can be deployed with just a couple of pages of JavaScript.

The second sample application, StockTicker, uses the URL proxy to get detailed stock quote information and display it on the phone screen. Figure 11-5 shows the output of this service.

Figure 11-5 *StockTicker Sample Service in Action*

The remaining properties and methods of this control are associated with three different areas: authentication, proxy use, and error reporting.

Authentication

Many Web pages require a user name and password. The URL Proxy control has UserName and Password properties that you can set before issuing the call to GetURL(). These two properties are then used to issue the authentication needed to access the given URL.

Error Reporting

In the event of an error, the URL Proxy control has a pair of parameters that can be queried for an error name and number. ErrorName and ErrorNumber are both string parameters that can be entered into an alarm or log file as needed.

Proxy Use

Many corporate networks require the use of a proxy server to get HTTP requests through a firewall. The URL Proxy control has a few different methods for using a proxy, which are controlled by setting the ProxyType property.

The default value of 0 tells the URL Proxy control to use the proxy settings that have been defined in the Windows control panel. For most servers and network setups, this is adequate.

A value of 1 indicates that no proxy server needs to be used, meaning that the request can go directly to the server listed in the URL.

A value of 2 instructs the URL Proxy control to use the proxy server name and port number configured in the Proxy string property. While this is only rarely needed, it gives you the complete flexibility needed to use any proxy server.

A Short Example

A simple example of how you might use the URL Proxy control is shown in the listing immediately following. This file, RFC0006.ASP, on the CD that accompanies the book, simply goes out to the Web, pulls down the contents of RFC 0006, formats it, and sends the output to the phone display:

```
<%@ Language=JavaScript%>
<%
Response.ContentType = "text/xml";
Response.Write("<CiscoIPPhoneText>\r\n");
Response.Write("<Title>RFC 0006</Title>\r\n");
Response.Write("<Text>");

Proxy = new ActiveXObject("CiscoURLProxy.URLGrabber");
var p = String( Proxy.GetURL("http://www.ietf.org/rfc/rfc0006.txt"));
for ( i = 0 ; i < p.length ; i++ )
  if ( p.charAt(i) == "&" )
    Response.write( "&amp;" );
  else
    Response.write( p.charAt(i) );
Proxy = "";

Response.Write("</Text>\r\n");
Response.Write("</CiscoIPPhoneText>\r\n");

Response.End();
Session.Abandon();

%>
```

NOTE   In this example, there is a notable lack of error checking, which is only good when creating readable examples. However, the script does go to the trouble to detect the ampersand character embedded in the text, which is necessary for this particular RFC.

A screen shot of the output of the program is shown in Figure 11-6.

Figure 11-6   *The RFC0006 Service*

LDAP Search Control

The LDAP Search control is a server side component that really only has one useful purpose—the creation of directory listings for Cisco IP Phones.

LDAP is the name of a protocol that defines the interface between directories and computer programs. The LDAP interface was invented with the goal of providing a directory structure that was simpler and easier to work with than standard X.500 directories.

Microsoft's ActiveDirectory is an LDAP server that holds information about users, devices, and other objects on an NT network. Cisco CallManager uses an LDAP directory to hold all the information regarding its users. Many large enterprises use LDAP to hold information about their users. For example, Cisco maintains a corporate LDAP directory with information about all active employees around the world.

A good place to learn more about LDAP is by visiting the OpenLDAP Web site at http://www.openldap.org. OpenLDAP is a group project whose aim is to develop an open set of professional quality LDAP tools. Naturally, they have had to collect quite a bit of information regarding LDAP.

Installation

Like the other two controls in the SDK, you can simply perform the SDK installation to get the LDAP Search control installed on your system. However, you might want to manually install the control on a different system, which is certainly feasible.

To manually install the LDAP Search control, you need to collect the following files from the Tools directory of the installed SDK:

- LDAPSearch.dll
- libnspr21.dll
- libplc21.dll
- libplds21.dll
- nsldapssl32v40.dll

The last four files are redistributable libraries that are part of Netscape's Directory SDK and are needed by the LDAP Search control.

Copy these five files to a common directory of your choice. If no better option presents itself, you can use your Windows system directory. Once the files are in place, register the DLL with your system using the following command line:

```
REGSVR32 LDAPSearch.dll
```

If the registration is correct, you should get a window from REGSVR32.EXE confirming the operation. Figure 11-07 shows an example of a successful registration.

Figure 11-7 *Successful Registration of the LDAP Search Control*

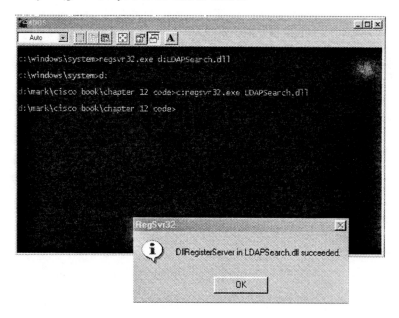

Use

Typical use of the LDAP Search control follows a straightforward pattern.

LDAP Server Properties

After creating an instance of the search object, you need to set a variety of the search properties. You should start with the Port and Server properties, which set the network parameters of the LDAP server you are trying to contact.

NOTE   If you are attempting to query the LDAP server used by your Cisco CallManager, the correct server name is your database publisher.

If you do not provide a port number, the LDAP Search control defaults to using the standard LDAP value of 389. You should be aware that CallManager uses a non-standard port value of 8404, so you need to set the parameter in the event that you are trying to access CallManager user information.

The next parameter you typically set is the SearchBase. This determines the location in the LDAP hierarchy where your search begins. Unfortunately, this value never follows any intuitive rules; you must know something about the organization of the specific directory in order to provide the correct value.

The SearchBase value on a CallManager LDAP directory typically has a value of ou=users,o=cisco.com, which means that you are searching for users in the Organization cisco.com and the Organizational Unit users.

The final two properties you often need to set are the AuthName and AuthPassword properties. These determine the user name and password that are used to bind the control to the LDAP Server. If you leave these blank (or for that matter just leave the AuthPassword property blank) you perform an anonymous binding to the server. LDAP servers are perfectly happy to talk to anonymous users, but each directory differs in the amount of data it shows to anonymous users.

Output Options

The next group of settings you need to configure are all related to controlling the various elements of the XML output object. The LDAP Search control returns a CiscoIPPhoneDirectory object with a variable number of entries, but there are a number of methods you can call to modify the default output.

SetOutputTitle is pretty conventional—simply setting the title of the display that the IP Phone user sees. Likewise, SetOutputPrompt is straightforward. However, SetOutputPrompt has the ability for you to insert some record numbers and statistics in the prompt. It's nice for your users to see a prompt such as "Records 20 to 30 of 400." Details on how to accomplish this are in the SDK documentation. The documentation for this control is in the Documentation directory of the SDK.

Search Options

The final set of options allows you some measure of control over how the search is performed and what it returns.

SetSearchOption is a method that allows you to set the maximum amount of time to spend on the search and the maximum number of records to return. It's important to set both of these parameters to fairly conservative values. For example, it's hard to imagine a scenario in which a user would want to see 1000 returned directory names on a search. The amount of time needed to scroll through more than perhaps 25 names makes it not particularly useful. Likewise, few users are going to have the patience to wait more than a few seconds for the results of their search.

The function call to AddReturnAttr is the most important method in the LDAP Search control and probably the one most likely to cause confusion. Basically when constructing the data that is returned in a CiscoIPDirectory object, you need to create three XML elements for each returned user: Name, Telephone, and Location. The difficulty arises from the fact that the LDAP attributes you use to create these differ depending on the setup of an individual LDAP directory.

To give you the flexibility you need to manage this problem, the LDAP Search control requires you to call the AddReturnAttr method three times, once for each of the three XML elements required to create the object. You should call it once to define the setup of the Name element, once for Telephone, and once for Location.

AddReturnAttr has four arguments, with the following definitions:

attrs: A list of comma separated LDAP attributes. These are the attributes that are in the LDAP server. You need to know something about the schema in use in the given server to make correct decisions about what to list here. Schema information is completely implementation specific; you will need to gather that information from the administrators of the site in question.

tag: The name of the XML element that is being defined with this function call. This needs to be Name, Telephone, or Location.

format: This is a formatting string that is used to create the value of the given element. It can be any combination of text along with attribute numbers like %1, %2, %3, and so on. When the format string is filled out attribute numbers are replaced by the values for the corresponding LDAP attributes. An example is shown in text soon to follow.

maxLen: The maximum length of the format string. Because you have no control over the length of the attributes being returned from the LDAP directory, you must impose an overall maximum length here to prevent overflow.

The formatting string in this call might seem familiar to experienced programmers, but a bit confusing to those unfamiliar with languages that use this paradigm. As an example, imagine that you make a call like this:

```
AddReturnAttr( "givenName, sn, department", "Name", "%1 %2 (%3)", 40 )
```

This tells the LDAP control to get three different attributes for each user: givenName, sn, and department. (sn is a standard LDAP attribute for a user's last name, or surname.) The actual value that is created for the Name element in the CiscoIPPhoneDirectory object then consists of a string defined by the format: "%1 %2 (%3)." For each user returned from the LDAP control, the format string has the string %1 replaced by the givenName attribute, %2 replace by the sn attribute, and %3 replaced by the department attribute.

This leads to XML output that looks like this:

```
<Name>Mark Nelson (Dallas)</Name>
```

That value then shows up in the directory listing.

If you have absolutely no idea what is returned by the LDAP server, your best bet is to skip the Location element entirely and simply use cn for the Name element, and telephoneNumber for the Telephone attribute—something like this:

```
AddReturnAttr( "cn", "Name", "%1", 40 )
AddReturnAttr( "telephoneNumber", "Telephone", "%1", 40 )
```

Search Methods

Once you've done all the prep work discussed so far, you are ready to do the actual search. The control provides quite a few different methods that enable you to perform searches based on various LDAP attributes:

- **SearchAll**—returns all records under the base position in the directory.
- **SearchByName**— only returns records that match the first and last name passed as arguments.
- **SearchByLastName**—only returns records that match the last name passed as an argument.
- **SearchByFirstName**—only returns records that match the first name passed as an argument.
- **SearchByPhoneNumber**—only returns records that match the phone number passed as an argument.
- **SearchByEmail**—only returns records that match the email argument.

Once you call the search function, you can then check the SearchCount property to see how many records have been returned.

Formatting Output

Once you've performed the search and you know how many records have been returned, you can start passing the results to the Cisco IP Phone. This is relatively easy. The XMLOutput method formats a given span of records to an output string, which your service can then pass directly to the Cisco IP Phone. The output uses the Title and Prompt you already have set up and formats the Name, Telephone, and Location elements as per your parameters.

An Example

The SDK documentation contains a few complete examples that can be used to search through your Cisco CallManager directory. To provide some alternative, this example searches across the Internet through a publicly available LDAP directory.

Novell has an LDAP directory server, NDS, which is a key part of the infrastructure they sell. As a service to LDAP developers, they have a publicly exposed directory at www.nldap.com. If you point your browser to this location, you can look through an entire organization populated with imaginary employees, divisions, and so on. (In fact, Novell even gives you your own area in the test directory, letting you store up to 1 MB of data for your own non-commercial purposes.)

The following ASP code searches through most of the Novell test server looking for users with the first name of Stan. It formats the first 32 of those into an XML object and passes them to the phone.

```
<%@ Language=JavaScript %>
<%
Response.ContentType = "text/xml";

try
{
  var s = new ActiveXObject("LDAPSEARCH.LDAPSearchList.1");
  s.Server = "www.nldap.com";
  s.SearchBase = "o=IMC,c=us";
  s.SetOutputTitle("ActiveX Directory Search", 20);
  s.AddReturnAttr( "cn", "Name", "%1", 31);
  s.AddReturnAttr( "telephoneNumber", "Telephone", "%1", 31);
  s.SearchByFirstName("Stan");
  Response.Write(s.XMLOutput(1, 32));
}

catch(err)
{
  Response.Write("Error," + err.description );
}
Response.End();
Session.Abandon();
%>
```

To see the output from this Active Server Page, you can browse directly to it with a normal browser. Microsoft Internet Explorer does a modest amount of formatting of the XML output, giving you an output screen shown in Figure 11-8.

Figure 11-8 *XML Output from the Novell Directory Search*

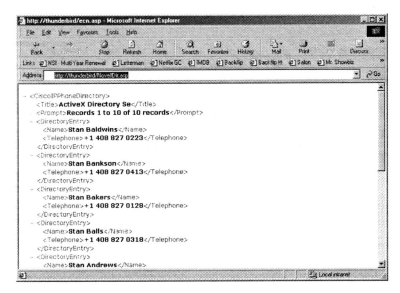

The same XML sent to the phone produces the screen shown in Figure 11-9.

Figure 11-9 *Same XML Output as Seen on the Phone*

Advanced Topics

Directory searches are a complicated business. You have just scratched the surface of what can be done with the LDAP Search control in this section of the chapter.

Reading through the SDK and Cisco CallManager documentation on the directory helps shed some light on how directories are organized, and some of the ways you can perform searches on their contents. This section skipped over a few of the methods of the control, namely:

- `SearchByDn`
- `SearchByRdn`
- `AddSortingAttr`

These methods are not likely to be used by most developers using the LDAP control. If you want to know more about these methods, see the documentation included in the SDK.

Finally, there is an excellent directory search example in the SDK LDAP examples. It covers some of the more complicated features related to directory listing, which include text input and paging the output. Walking through that entire example gives you a very good feel for what it means to write a full-fledged, LDAP-based service.

Photoshop Graphics Filter

The Cisco IP Phone Services SDK ships with a graphics filter that can be used with Adobe Photoshop and other popular graphics programs. This filter enables you to read and write CIP format graphics images. Depending on the program you are using, this might be called a plug-in, or perhaps an import filter. Regardless of what it is called, the file gives existing programs the ability to deal with CIP files.

Installation

Installation of the plug-in is usually a simple matter. However, each program has its own specific procedures for adding plug-ins, and you need to refer to your program's software manual for specifics.

Jasc's Paint Shop Pro is a popular graphics program that works well with CIP images and does well as an example of a typical installation process.

The first step in the process is to install the Cisco IP Phone Services SDK. In the Tools directory, you find a copy of the plug-in filter, named **Cip.8bi**. (The **8bi** extension is one that is commonly used for Photoshop plug-ins.)

Paint Shop Pro loads its plug-ins at startup by searching for the contents of selected folders. You can view the folders that are currently configured by choosing **File > Preferences > General Preferences**, which brings up a tabbed dialog. Select the Plug-in Filters tab to bring up the dialog shown in Figure 11-10.

Figure 11-10 *Paint Shop Pro Dialog for Configuration of Plug-in Filters*

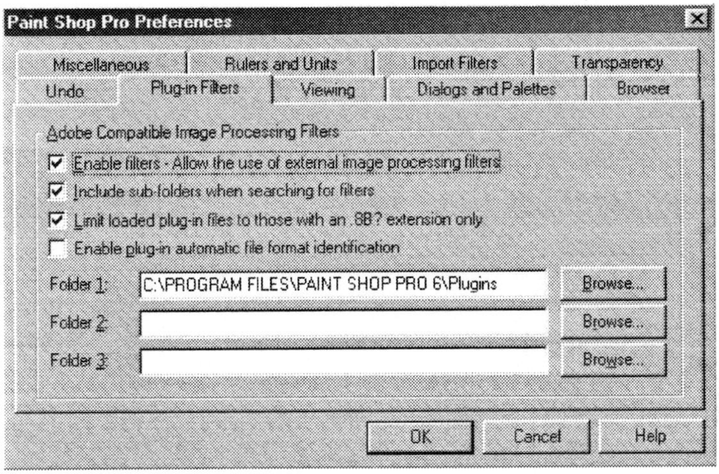

You can see that by default Paint Shop Pro stores plug-ins in a folder under the main program folder, called *Plugins*. To add the CIP format plug-in, simply create the directory if necessary and then copy the file named **Cip.8bi** into the new folder. Stop Paint Shop Pro and restart it—you should now be in business.

From that point on, Paint Shop Pro treats CIP files as standard graphics formats much like any other. Perhaps the only other non-standard thing you might notice about the CIP format is that when saving the file, you are given an opportunity to set the four parameters that are saved along with the image. Figure 11-11 shows the dialog that appears when saving, asking you for the display position, title, and prompt. (This is the only opportunity the plugin has to get these data items.)

Figure 11-11 *Saving an Image in CIP Format Using the Plug-in*

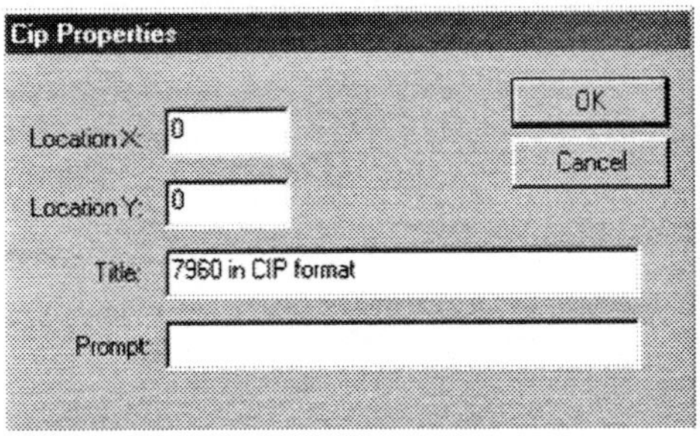

Validator

The final tool we talk about in this chapter is perhaps the simplest to use, but invaluable when you need it: **Validator.exe**. This command line tool parses the XML content of a file or Web page and checks it for validity against the schema for Cisco IP Phone XML objects.

Installation

Installation of Validator is simply a matter of copying the files from the Tools directory of the SDK to a convenient location, such as your Windows desktop. No registration or any other configuration is needed. The two files to be copied are **Validator.exe** (the program) and **CiscoIPPhone.xsd** (the schema file).

However, things are not quite as simple as you might like. Validator depends on your PC having Microsoft's MSXML Parser version 4.0 installed. At the time of this writing, this parser is only shipping with Windows XP, so there is an excellent chance you do not have it on your PC.

How will you know if you need to install MSXML Parser 4.0? You must install it when you attempt to run Validator and you see a dialog like that shown in Figure 11-12.

Figure 11-12   *The Indication that You Need to Install MSXML Parser 4.0*

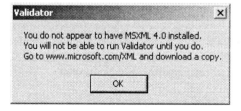

The parser uses a standard installation program that should not give you any trouble. To find the parser, go to Microsoft's XML Web site at `http://www.microsoft.com/XML` and follow their instructions to download MSXML 4. Microsoft consistently makes it easy to find their XML parsers once you get to the XML page, so you should have no trouble locating it on their site.

Using Validator

Double-clicking on Validator's icon on our desktop brings up the small dialog shown in Figure 11-13. As you can see, you are not offered too many choices in this program.

Figure 11-13 *The Initial Dialog for Validator*

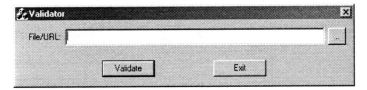

Any time you use Validator, you go through the same steps. First, you have to select either a Web page address or a file. The edit box at the top of the dialog allows you to type in either a URL, just as you would in your Web browser, or a file name.

The browse button on the right (...) enables you to browse on your PC for the XML file in question. No similar browse function exists for Web pages. (To avoid typing errors, locate the file in your Web browser and then copy and paste the URL from the browser Address box.)

Once you have either a URL or file name in the edit box, you can click the **Validate** button and find out what you have. The results are pretty simple to interpret. In the case of success, you see something like Figure 11-14, which indicates that the file was loaded properly while being compared to the schema.

NOTE The schema file **CiscoIPPhone.xsd** must be present in the same directory as **Validator.exe**.

Figure 11-14 *A Successful Validation of an XML File*

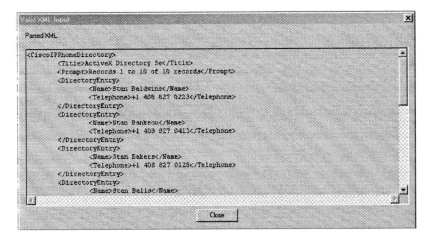

Figure 11-15 shows the output of a failed parse. Microsoft's XML parser does not attempt to continue parsing an XML object after the first error, so all the information you get is an error message and a specific location in the file. Validator points to the specific location as best it can and trusts that you are able to determine the specific problem at that point.

Figure 11-15 *An Error Located in a Web Page*

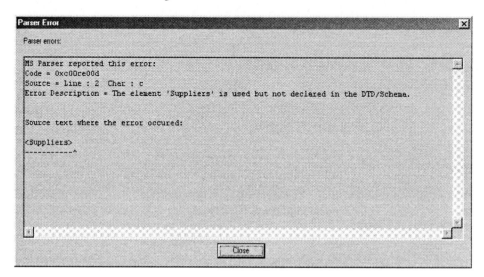

Conclusion

The Cisco IP Phone Services SDK comes with a variety of tools, all of which are designed to help you develop your Cisco IP Phone service. You should at least have a familiarity with the tools, even if you do not use all of them regularly. You never know when they might save your application.

CHAPTER 12

Cisco CallManager Simulator

Included with your purchase of this book is a useful debugging and prototyping tool called Cisco CallManager Simulator, or CM-Sim. This tool lets you work on services without the expense or hassle of providing the CallManager system for your phones to home in on. This chapter tells you most of what CM-Sim does, how to install it, and how to use it. It also gives you a bit of information about the internals of CM-Sim, which might help you use the program more effectively.

The Function of CM-Sim

CM-Sim's job is to convince a Cisco IP Phone that it is communicating with a CallManager. This enables the Cisco IP Phone to get through its boot procedure and move into its normal mode of operation. Once the Cisco IP Phone has booted, CM-Sim performs a very limited set of call processing features, generally supporting phone-to-phone calls and nothing more.

To do this, CM-Sim has to perform two important functions. First, it has to act as a Trivial File Transfer Protocol (TFTP) server, serving a valid configuration file to the Cisco IP Phone. It then opens a communications link with the Cisco IP Phone, using Cisco's Skinny Client Control Protocol (Skinny). It then uses this link to provide a fairly convincing simulation of a CallManager.

NOTE   TFTP is just what the name implies—a greatly simplified version of the File Transfer Protocol (FTP) commonly used on the Internet. TFTP is great for transferring single files across the Internet but lacks the FTP features used for browsing, directory navigation, directory creation, and so on.

Cisco IP Phones use TFTP to download configuration files from servers in a CallManager cluster. This includes the phone's configuration file, ringer files, and localization information. By using TFTP instead of FTP, Cisco's developers cut down on the amount of code that is needed in the phone, as well as on the server.

NOTE	CM-Sim is not a substitute for a real CallManager. Although you can make point-to-point calls in a very simple manner, CM-Sim does not perform any other calling features and does not work with any devices besides 7940 and 7960 phones. It is useful for working with phones during service development, but you cannot use it as a CallManager demo tool, or worse yet, a production phone system. You will be severely disappointed!

The TFTP Server Role

When you first power up a Cisco IP Phone, it begins a well-defined boot procedure. It first locates a TFTP server, using either the information retrieved from the DHCP server or the Alternate TFTP address stored in its settings, and then requests an XML configuration file. A typical XML configuration file looks something like that shown in Example 12-1.

Example 12-1 *A typical Phone XML file*

```xml
<?xml version="1.0"?>
<device>
  <devicePool>
    <callManagerGroup>
      <members>
        <member>
          <callManager>
            <ports>
              <ethernetPhonePort>2000</ethernetPhonePort>
            </ports>
            <processNodeName>192.168.1.2</processNodeName>
          </callManager>
        </member>
        <member>
        </member>
      </members>
    </callManagerGroup>
  </devicePool>
  <directoryURL>http://</directoryURL>
  <messagesURL>http://</messagesURL>
  <servicesURL>http://192.168.1.2/getservicesmenu.asp</servicesURL>
  <informationURL>http://</informationURL>
  <idleURL>http://</idleURL>
  <idleTimeout>0</idleTimeout>
  <loadInformation>P00303010013</loadInformation>
</device>
```

You do not have to be an XML expert to decode most of the information that is provided here. Some of the important things sent to the phone in its config file include a list of CallManagers the Cisco IP Phone attempts to register with, a TCP/IP port to use when communicating with each CallManager, and URLs to attach to various features on the Cisco IP Phone.

The first job of CM-Sim is to serve configuration files. When the phone first powers up, it requests a configuration file from its TFTP server. (There are a couple of different ways to configure the TFTP server, both discussed later in this chapter.) CM-Sim does not actually have a file on disk to send to the Cisco IP Phone, it simply creates an image in memory and sends that to the Cisco IP Phone.

The loadInformation element is the last one found in the XML configuration file. It contains the name of a Cisco IP Phone firmware load. During the boot process, a Cisco IP Phone has to check to see if it is actually using the load specified in the XML config file. If it is not, it requests a copy of the correct firmware BIN file, copies it into flash, and reboots. The TFTP server in CM-Sim handles the request for the firmware BIN file properly, as long as the BIN file is actually present in the same directory as the CM-Sim executable.

Once the Cisco IP Phone reads its XML config file and has the proper firmware loaded, it enters the registration process with its primary and backup CallManagers. CM-Sim config files always have just a single CallManager defined, meaning the registration process is quite a bit simpler.

The CallManager Role

In a proper CallManager system, TFTP files are served up by a TFTP service. The TFTP service might be on the same computer as CallManager, but in any event, the CallManager service has nothing to do with that portion of the boot process. This means that CM-Sim really is not simulating CallManager during this part of the phone's boot procedure. Once that process is complete, however, CM-Sim has to start acting like a CallManager. It does this by listening for phone Skinny messages on TCP/IP Port 2000. After having read in their configuration file, Cisco IP Phones send registration messages on this port, and expect CallManager to respond.

CM-Sim does respond with the appropriate registration acknowledgment, which is followed by Skinny messages that set up the Cisco IP Phone's lines, soft keys, soft key labels, and so on. After the exchange of a few messages, the Cisco IP Phone comes up in the configuration shown in Figure 12-1.

As far as the Cisco IP Phone is concerned, things are operating as normal. The only obvious difference between this and a true CallManager connection is the presence of the acronym "SIM" in the top line of the display, which is just a handy way of reminding you that this is not a live phone.

Figure 12-1 *Phone Running Under CallManager Simulator*

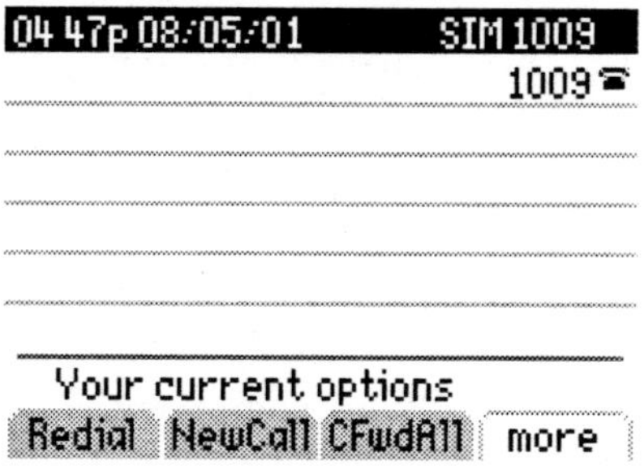

Routing Calls

Once your phone reaches this point, you are set for creating and testing services. The Cisco IP Phone is content with the environment and properly sends HTTP requests when services are invoked.

Although this is really all you need from CM-Sim, it does offer one additional bit of functionality—phone-to-phone calling. As the Cisco IP Phones come up, CM-Sim assigns line numbers to each. And just like on a true CallManager system, you can place calls from phone to phone.

When you make a call like this, CM-Sim takes care of telling the two phones that initiate the call to begin streaming RTP packets to one another, and likewise it tells the phones to stop streaming when the call ends.

Unfortunately, CM-Sim does not have the smarts it would need to do more complicated features such as conferencing, music on hold, or gateway calls. But the station-to-station calling lets you do some experimentation with interactions between your service and CallManager.

Limitations

CM-Sim works with 7940 and 7960 phones only. 7910s are not capable of executing Cisco IP Phone services, and so are not supported deliberately. The same is true of legacy Cisco IP Phones, 7935 conference stations, third party phones, and numerous other devices.

CM-Sim Installation

Installation of CM-Sim is so simple that you do not even need an install program. The entire package consists of just a few files, including the CallManager Simulator executable file and the BIN file that contains the current release of phone firmware.

In the simplest configuration of all, you do not even need to install the programs. Simply insert the CD that comes with this book, navigate to the CiscoIPPhoneServices directory, then to the CallManager directory, and double click the CallManagerSimulator.exe file, as shown in Figure 12-2.

Figure 12-2 *Running Directly from the CD-ROM*

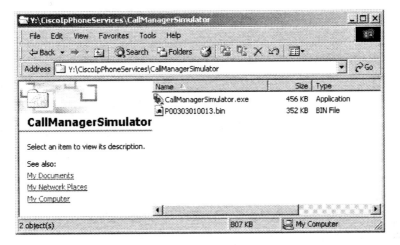

For a more conventional installation, you can drag the entire CM Simulator directory from the CD to your Program Files folder, which will place the executable and BIN file in a directory normally called C:\Program Files\CM Simulator. You can then place a link to the EXE on your desktop and execute the simulator that way.

In either case, remembering that the BIN file must be in the same directory as the EXE file is important. You should also note that the BIN file on the book's CD probably is not the same as that shown in Figure 12-2. Cisco IP Phone firmware is updated on a regular basis, and the CD contains the most current copy possible. You can check the version of your phone's firmware at any time by pressing the **settings** button, then selecting Status, and then Firmware Version.

System Requirements

CM-Sim is a well-behaved Win32 program that should run on Windows 98, XP, 2000, and ME. However, it cannot coexist with CallManager and with a TFTP server, whether it is the TFTP server that ships with CallManager or some other program. Outside of those restrictions, CM-Sim should run on any system that has a network connection and a few spare cycles.

Using CM-Sim

Figure 12-3 shows the main window of CM-Sim on startup. Despite the fact that no installation or configuration has taken place, the program is actually ready at this point to start managing phones. All that is necessary at this point is that the phones be pointed to this CallManager.

Figure 12-3 *The Main CM-Sim Screen on Startup*

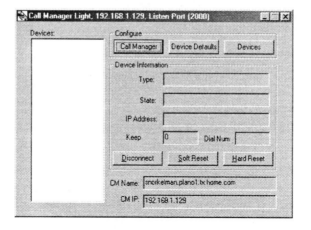

Configuring CallManager

One of the buttons in the configuration section is labeled CallManager. There are only two things you can configure for a given instance of CM-Sim—the name/address of the primary CallManager given to the phones and the next directory number (DN) that is given to phones as they register.

Figure 12-4 *Configuring CallManager Simulator*

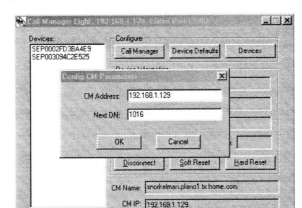

By default, the CM address is given as the IP address of the machine where CM-Sim is running. Generally there is no reason to change this, but you could conceivably use a machine name instead of an IP address (if the name is available on a DNS server accessible to the phones).

The Next DN field is used to assign directory numbers to phones as they register.

NOTE	Cisco IP Phones connected to a CallManager have varying numbers of lines that are used to make and receive calls. Lines are identified by directory numbers. Typically DNs are three-, four-, or five-digit numbers that are assigned automatically and arbitrarily as phones first register with CallManager. You do not have to worry about mapping external numbers to DNs in a CM-Sim setup, as it does not support any types of trunk or gateway interfaces. The term DN has essentially the same meaning as the term "extension," which is used on many other phone systems. Internal calls between Cisco IP Phones are usually made by dialing the DN. External calls that arrive on various types of trunk lines are mapped to DNs through CallManager Administration.

Phone Setup

To get a Cisco IP Phone to talk to CM-Sim, you need to convince the phone to use the machine running CM-Sim as its TFTP server. There are two good ways to do this.

The first choice would be to configure Option 150 on your DHCP server to contain the IP address of your CM-Sim machine. This is the best path to take, as it means every phone you bring up on your network points to CM-Sim automatically. However, this is generally only practical if you are working on a small lab setup or a home network. If this is the case, follow the instructions on your DHCP server for adding a new option, and then create Option 150 and assign it the value of your CM-Sim machine's IP address.

In the event that you do not have control of your DHCP server, every phone that you want to point to your CM-Sim will have to be manually assigned to it. Invoking the **settings** feature on the phone, enabling the Alternate TFTP server, and assigning the correct server address to the TFTP server does this.

Step 1—Enable Network Configuration Changes

To change the items described here, push the **settings** button on the Cisco IP Phone, and then select the Network Configuration menu item. This brings up the menu, listing all of the configuration items on the Cisco IP Phone.

However, by default, these settings are read-only in this page. Figure 12-5 shows what this screen looks like on the phone. Note that in the upper right hand corner of the screen there is an icon, which appears to be a small padlock. The padlock is closed, which means you are not enabled to modify settings.

Figure 12-5 *Network Configuration in Read-Only Mode*

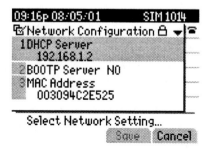

To enable changes to the network settings, you will first have to enter the unlock code, which is done by leaving the Settings menu, and then pressing ****#** on the keypad. When you now enter the Network Configuration page, the padlock is opened, as seen in Figure 12-6 meaning you are now free to make modifications at your own risk.

Step 2—Enable the Alternate TFTP Server

The next step to take is to navigate through the Network Configuration menu until you reach the Alternate TFTP menu option. This setting is set to a value of either Yes or No. A single soft key enables you to change the setting, as seen in Figure 12-6.

Figure 12-6 *Changing the Alternate TFTP Setting*

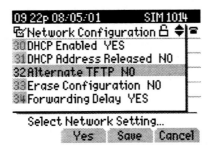

Change this setting to have a value of **Yes**.

Step 3—Enter the TFTP Address

You can now scroll back near the top of the Network Configuration menu and locate the entry for the TFTP Server. When Alternate TFTP is set to **No**, this value is read dynamically from the DHCP server when the Cisco IP Phone boots. However, now that Alternate TFTP is set to **Yes**, you can enter a value that persists through restarts of the Cisco IP Phone.

Do this by hitting the **Edit** soft key, which gives a screen similar to that shown in Figure 12-7.

Figure 12-7 *Entering a New TFTP Address*

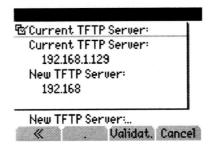

At this point you can enter the correct TFTP address, which should be the IP address of the machine running CM-Sim.

Entering the IP address (you cannot enter a host name here, you must enter an address) is done using the keypad with the period between octets entered with the * key. Note that there is a soft key that enables you to backspace.

Once you have entered the address, you can press the **Validat** soft key. This returns you to the main Network Configuration menu.

Step 4 – Save and Restart

The final step to take is to press the **Save** soft key, then exit the configuration menu. When you are back at the idle prompt, you should restart the phone by pressing the restart sequence from the keypad: ****#****

If all goes well, your Cisco IP Phone reboots, sends a TFTP request to CM-Sim (which is honored), and your Cisco IP Phone comes up.

Configuring the Default Phone Settings

CM-Simulator maintains a list of default settings that are applied to every phone that registers with it. The settings you have control over are the ones that matter to a service developer:

- Directory URL
- Information URL
- Messages URL
- Services URL
- Idle URL
- Idle Timeout

By default these settings all come up with empty values, or in the case of Idle Timeout, a "0" value. Those values are sent to a Cisco IP Phone every time it requests its XML configuration file.

You can change these values by selecting the Device Defaults button in the configuration section of the CM-Sim main window. It brings up a configuration window that looks like that shown in Figure 12-8.

Figure 12-8 *Device Defaults Configuration Dialog*

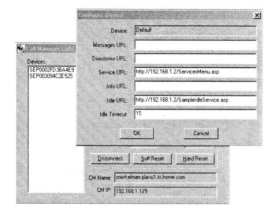

Once you set these defaults, they are applied to all devices that have not individually overridden the individual settings. However, the Cisco IP Phones do not actually acquire the settings until you reset them using the Hard Reset button on the CM-Sim dialog.

Configuring Specific Cisco IP Phone Settings

CM-Sim gives you the ability to override any of the default configuration items on a phone-by-phone basis. When you select the **Devices** button in the Configuration section of the CM-Sim main window, you are presented with a dialog that lets you select which of the devices currently in the database that you would like to configure. Figure 12-9 shows the selection box.

Figure 12-9 *Selecting a Device to Configure*

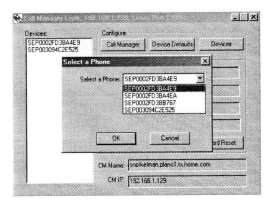

NOTE	You select the device to configure by the MAC address—not the most convenient way to do it, but this is the only way CallManager and CM-Sim know to uniquely identify a device. You can always determine the MAC address of the phone by pressing the **settings** button, then selecting Network Configuration. The MAC address is then shown as item number three in the list of settings. CM-Sim and CallManager typically prepend the string SEP to the MAC address to identify the individual instrument.

Once you select the device to configure, you are presented with a dialog box identical to that in Figure 12-8. In this case, however, you are not presented with the default configuration values for all devices. Instead, you are given the overriding values for that specific device.

After you enter (or remove) overrides for a specific device, you can perform a hard reset on the device from the CM-Sim main window and expect it to read the new settings via TFTP. All the settings configured here are visible from the Network Configuration menu of the phone settings (press the **settings** button). Therefore you should have no trouble verifying that downloading the six parameters works properly.

Seeing It In Action

Once you've done your configuration, you should be able to see CM-Sim running in normal operating mode. The main area of interest when CM-Sim is running is the list box that shows all the devices currently registered. As each new device gets its XML configuration file and then registers, its MAC address is added to the list.

Figure 12-10 shows what the main window looks like when it has a couple of live Cisco IP Phones connected. One of the phones is selected in the list box, which brings up some information about the device in the Device Information area of the main window. Information shown in this window includes the Cisco IP Phone type, state, IP address, KeepAlive count, and Directory Number.

The KeepAlive count is a counter that tells you how many times a KeepAlive message has been exchanged between CM-Sim and the phone. This message is sent at a relatively long interval, usually on the order of 30 seconds or so. The phone uses the message to be sure it is reliably connected to its chosen CallManager. In the event that CallManager does not respond to the KeepAlive message, the phone then attempts to connect to a backup CallManager.

Figure 12-10 *CM-Sim Up and Running*

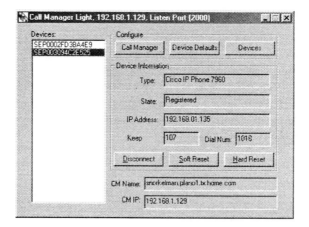

Internals

The configuration information for CM-Sim is stored in the Windows registry under the key:

```
HKEY_CURRENT_USER/Software/Cisco Systems Inc./Call Manager Simulator
```

The information stored there for the Cisco IP Phones and CallManager correspond exactly to the information shown in the configuration dialogs. Figure 12-11 shows a snapshot of the stored configuration information being viewed using the Regedit program that ships with Win32 systems.

Figure 12-11   *CM-Sim Configuration Data in the Registry*

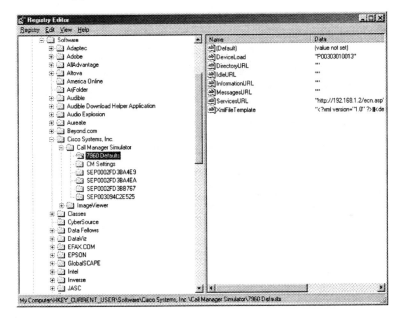

While it is normally advisable to access this information from the dialog boxes that are built into the program, looking directly at the registry values can help clear up misunderstandings or confusion about how parameters are stored.

Having access to the registry also makes it simple to move configuration information from one computer to another. By exporting and importing portions of the registry tree, you can easily copy your Cisco IP Phone configuration information from machine to machine in a relatively easy fashion.

Debugging with Command Line TFTP

One final tool that you might have available on your system to help in the debugging effort is the command line version of TFTP that ships with Windows 2000. You can use this to request XML config files from CM-Sim and actually get a copy of the same file that the Cisco IP Phone sees when it makes a request.

Figure 12-12 shows a command line session with a TFTP request for a given XML config file, followed by an invocation of NOTEPAD used to review the file.

Figure 12-12 *Using TFTP from the Command Line*

Conclusion

CM-Sim provides a convenient way to bring Cisco IP Phones up outside of a normal CallManager system. This enables you to set up development environments with nothing more than a phone or two and your desktop machine. While it certainly does not offer the complexity or depth of features given by CallManager, it does let you quickly and easily configure Cisco IP Phone settings. And (best of all) if you are reading this book, you already own it.

Glossary

This appendix provides a list of terms and acronyms applicable to the *Developing Cisco IP Phone Services* book. Additional glossary terms can be found at the following location:

www.cisco.com/univercd/cc/td/doc/product/voice/evbugl4.htm

A

AA. Auto Attendant; an application designed to distribute calls by automated means.

ad hoc. improvised, or impromptu.

API. Application programming interface; usually a set of libraries with accompanying header files that application programmers can use in their programs to interact with a third-party application.

ASP. Active server page; a Web page that uses ActiveX scripting to dynamically control the content of the Web page. Cisco CallManager Administration relies on Active server pages.

B

bandwidth. A measurement of the amount of data per unit of time that a communications interface is capable of sending or receiving.

BAT. Bulk Administration Tool; a Web-based tool that enables you to add, update, or delete large numbers of users and devices to the CallManager database. Among the values you can define when bulk-adding new phones is phone service subscriptions.

C

CCO. Cisco Connection Online; Cisco's Web site for customer support and distribution of software, www.cisco.com.

CCM. Cisco CallManager; a Cisco AVVID IP Telephony service whose primary function is the control and routing of calls from voice-enabled IP devices.

CGI. Common gateway interface; a standard method for interacting with a Web server for requests and responses.

CIP. Cisco IP Phone.

Cisco CallManager server. A Cisco-certified Windows 2000 server that is running CallManager software.

Cisco CallManager User Options/Cisco IP Phone User Options. A Web site that users can access to effect changes to their phone's configuration, including setting or canceling call forward all designations, managing speed dials, and managing service subscriptions. In CallManager release 3.1, the website was called Cisco IP Phone User Options. In CallManager release 3.2, the name changed to Cisco CallManager User Options.

CM. Another acronym for CallManager.

CM-Sim. CallManager Simulator; a stripped-down version of Cisco CallManager that performs a very limited set of call processing features, generally supporting phone-to-phone calls.

ColorBitDepth. Provides the number of bits being used to represent the color value for each pixel in the current image.

convert.cpp. A command line C++ program that reads a JPG file, resizes it, modifies the color count, sets a property, and then saves it as a CIP file.

cookie. A mechanism for the Web server to give the client a piece of data and have the client return the data with each request.

CPU. Central processing unit; the chip or chips inside a computer that execute the instructions that permit applications to function.

CSV. Comma-separated value; a type of file in which commas are used to separate individual fields of a complex data record and new lines indicate the end of an individual record.

D

DBL. Database layer; a set of software components that provide a programming interface to the SQL database containing all the CallManager configuration information.

de facto. Existing in fact, regardless if it exists in law or by regulation.

DHCP. Dynamic Host Configuration Protocol; a network service whose primary purpose is to automatically assign IP addresses to new devices that connect or existing devices that reconnect to the network.

DLL. Dynamic link library; a software component library that can be linked into another program at runtime to include the functionality provided by the software component. Dynamic link libraries are a commonly used mechanism for distributing libraries under Windows.

DN. Directory number; the numerical address assigned to an endpoint such as a phone, gateway port, or route point within an enterprise.

DNS. Domain name system; a network service whose primary function is to convert fully qualified domain names (textual) into numerical IP addresses and vice versa.

DTD. Data type definition; has the ability to tightly define which tags can be used where, what type of content can compose an element, and the order in which elements appear. A DTD defines the schema for an XML object.

DTMF. Dual tone multi-frequency; a common tone signaling method used by touchtone phones in which two pure frequencies are superimposed.

E-F-G

E.164 address. A fully qualified numerical address for a device attached to a national network. The ITU-T specification E.164 defines the framework in which nations manage their national numbering plans.

endpoint. A device or software application that provides real-time, two-way communication for users.

escape sequence. An XML escape sequence is a sequence of characters that start with an ampersand (the "escape" character) and end with a semicolon.

failover. The process whereby devices in a Cisco IP Telephony network register themselves to the backup CallManager nodes if they lose their connection to their primary CallManager. Phones open a connection to the backup CallManager at the same time they register to the primary CallManager so that they can failover faster.

fallback. The process of offering a call to a less desirable gateway after all desirable gateways have been exhausted.

FAQ. Frequently asked questions.

firewall. A computer system placed at the junction between a private computer network and other computer networks. It is designed to protect systems of a private network from users in the other networks.

GET. HTTP method used to request a desired URI from a Web server.

H-I-J-K

HTML. Hypertext markup language; a document type definition (DTD) used by Web pages and browsers on the World Wide Web that tells a Web browser how to render the content of a Web page.

HTTP. Hypertext Transfer Protocol; a simple, stateless, request/response protocol that is used at the application level.

HTTP server. Generically referred to as a Web server; the Web server provides dynamic or static content provided in varying MIME types.

hub. A nexus in a network where data arriving from one endpoint can select multiple routes of egress.

IIS. Internet Information Server; a Microsoft service designed to permit users to create and manage Internet services such as Web servers.

import filter. A component used with a graphics program such as Adobe Photoshop or Paint Shop Pro that enables the program to read or write foreign file formats. The CD-ROM supplied with this book provides an import filter to read and write Cisco IP Phone format.

Internet Explorer. Microsoft's version of a Web browser.

IP. Internet protocol; a method by which one computer can communicate packets of information to another computer on a network.

IP Telephony. The implementation of telephony over the same type of data network that makes up the Internet.

IVR. Interactive Voice Response; a voice application that provides a telephone user interface and that is capable of retrieving data and redirecting calls.

javaScript. A scripting language developed by Netscape to enable developers to design interactive sites.

JMF. Java media framework; an application programming interface (API) that enables audio, video, and other time-based media to be added to Java applications and applets.

L-M-N-O

LAN. Local area network; a group of independent computers and network appliances within a small geographic area that access common resources and each other over communications protocols.

LCD. Liquid crystal display.

LDAP. Lightweight Directory Access Protocol; a protocol that defines a programming interface that can be used to access computer-based directories. LDAP directories are a specialized format of database that is often used to hold user information in large organizations. CallManager uses an LDAP directory to store user information.

legacy. Using established, possibility outdated, methods.

line appearance. A logical entity on a phone or gateway capable of terminating calls, often associated with a particular button on a phone. Line appearances have addresses called DNs.

logical channel. A network pathway that carries a streaming data connection between two endpoints.

MCS. Media Convergence Server; a Cisco-certified server that comes preinstalled with the components that comprise Cisco AVVID IP Telephony.

Multipurpose Internet mail extensions. A specification for formatting non-ASCII messages so that they can be sent over the Internet. In addition to e-mail applications, Web browsers also support various MIME types which enable the browser to display or output files that are not in HTML format.

object. In the context of Cisco IP Phone services, an object is merely a logical collection of data that is exchanged to and from the phone. This data is in a hierarchical XML format representing application primitives that are supported with the services API.

off-hook. Literally, the action of removing the handset from the hookswitch. In modern telephony, this term indicates the phone has left the idle state. On Cisco IP Phones, off-hook can be accomplished in many ways, not limited to the following — lifting the handset, pressing the **SPEAKER** button, and pressing the **Answer** or **NewCall** soft keys. A user can go off-hook without ever placing or answering a call.

OffNet. A term applied to calls between the enterprise and another telephone network (generally the PSTN).

on-hook. Literally, the action of returning the handset to the hookswitch.

OnNet. A term applied to calls that are placed and received within the same enterprise.

OS. Operating system; a set of services running on a hardware platform that provide other applications with access to the resources (such as processor, memory, network interfaces) that the hardware platform provides.

P-Q

PA. Personal Assistant; an application that works with CallManager. This application is designed to permit a user to customize call forwarding behavior based on who is calling and to track a user down given multiple possible destinations.

parameter. Variables that can be used to customize a service subscription.

parser. A program that breaks an input stream into syntactic elements. Cisco IP Phones have an XML parser that breaks out individual element values for the phone's firmware.

PC. Personal computer.

PHP. Hypertext Preprocessor; a server-side, cross-platform, HTML embedded scripting language.

plug-in. A software component that integrates with a primary application by utilizing an API.

POTS. Plain old telephone service; basic telephone service (placing and receiving calls) using loop start signaling.

power cycle. To reset a device by interrupting and restoring power to the device.

primitives. Small application building blocks that can be combined to build a complex application.

PSTN. Public switched telephone network; the international phone system.

Publisher. The master database for CallManager.

Pull. The action of a client requesting information from a server. An HTTP GET is an example of a technology that pulls content from a server.

Push. The action of a client submitting a request to the phone to invoke client behavior. An HTTP POST to a phone's Web server is an example of pushing a request at a phone.

R

reorder tone. A fast, cyclical tone that CallManager uses to indicate some sort of problem during call establishment. Commonly referred to as fast busy.

RGB. red, green, blue.

RTP. Real-Time Transport Protocol; Internet-standard protocol for the transport of real-time data, including audio and video.

RTPRx. Real-Time Transport Protocol receive.

RTPTx. Real-Time Transport Protocol transmit.

S

SCCP. Skinny Client Control Protocol; a protocol used by devices to communicate with CallManager. Commonly referred to as Skinny.

scraping. Pulling content from other Web pages, manipulating that content, repackaging it, and sending it down to IP phones.

SDK. Software Development Kit; a set of programming interfaces and documentation provided to programmers seeking to interface to a given operating system, application, or other product.

secondary line. Any line appearance on a station other than the primary.

service parameters. Settings for Cisco AVVID IP Telephony services that take effect on a service-wide basis.

session cookie. A mechanism to track a unique identifier for state management; the client returns the cookie with each request and the server can then keep information about the current session indexed by a session identifier. The session management layer of most Web servers use session cookies.

SGML. Standard Generalized Markup Language; a universal language for creating device-independent documents with useful formatting and content.

soft key. Context-sensitive digital display buttons on the bottom row of the display on Cisco IP Phones 7940 and 7960.

SQL. Structured Query Language; a standard language defined to permit reading from and writing to databases.

station. Any device that provides a user with a direct interface to a voice network.

stream. A one-way, active media session connected through a simplex logical channel from one device to another.

stream control. The ability to start and stop RTP streams on channel 1 (to and from the phone) using G.711 μ-law.

Subscriber. One or more duplicate databases serving the CallManager system. Subscriber databases are updated with information from the Publisher database.

subscriber. A user of a (usually public) telephone network.

switchback. The process whereby devices unregister with one CallManager node and reregister with a higher-priority CallManager node.

switchover. A process whereby a secondary call agent assumes control of the call signaling and media control for a call that was earlier controlled by a different call agent.

T-U-V

tag. A simple text phrase enclosed in angle brackets.

TCP. Transmission Control Protocol; a connection-oriented protocol that provides for the reliable end-to-end, ordered delivery of IP packets.

TCP/IP stack. An interface used by the low-level firmware in the Cisco IP Phone for network communications.

TDM. Time Division Multiplexing; a method of transporting information for multiple endpoints across a single interface that relies on assigning each endpoint a specific window of time when it has exclusive access to the interface.

TFTP. Trivial File Transfer Protocol; a User Datagram Protocol-based (UDP) protocol that permits the transmission of files between network devices.

TSV. Tab separated values; a file format in which individual data fields of a record are separated by a tab character and records are separated by new lines.

URI. Uniform resource identifier.

URL. Uniform resource locator.

User Options Web page. *See* Cisco CallManager User Options/Cisco IP Phone User Options.

Validator. A program on the CD-ROM provided with this book that checks Cisco IP Phone XML objects for validity. It does this by parsing the objects and comparing the syntactic elements against the XML schema.

VAT. Voice anomaly tracking; a service provided for your use on the book's CD-ROM. VAT enables users to log call information for a system administrator.

VoIP. Voice over IP; the process of routing voice communications over a network running Internet Protocol.

W-X-Y-Z

W3C. World Wide Web Consortium (www.w3.org); W3C is comprised of researchers and engineers from around the world who develop interoperable technologies (specifications, guidelines, software, and tools) to lead the Web to its full potential as a forum for information, commerce, communication, and collective understanding.

WAN. Wide area network.

XML. Extensible markup language; a simple dialect of SGML that enables generic SGML to be served, received, and processed on the Web. Also, the universal format for structured documents and data on the Web.

XML schema. Same as DTD except it is written in XML. XML schemas provide the same functionality as DTD, plus the ability to define acceptable content. XML schema seems to be replacing DTD as a way to define documents.

XSL Transformations. A language that is used to process and reformat XML documents. You can find additional information at `http://w3.org`.

INDEX

Symbols

A

B

Learning is serious business. **Invest wis**

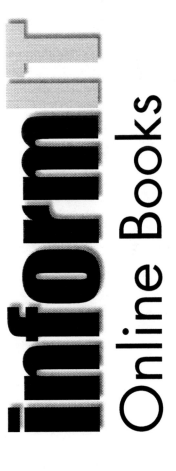

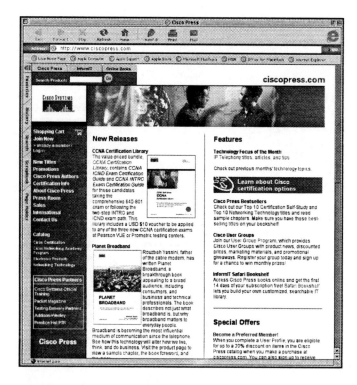
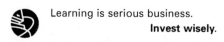

ISCUSS

TWORKING PRODUCTS AND CHNOLOGIES WITH CISCO PERTS AND NETWORKING OFESSIONALS WORLDWIDE

T NETWORKING PROFESSIONALS
SCO ONLINE COMMUNITY
/W.CISCO.COM/GO/DISCUSS

THIS IS THE POWER OF THE NETWORK. now.

CISCO SYSTEMS